BRIDGING THE ATLANTIC

SUNY series in Latin American and Iberian Thought and Culture,
Jorge J. E. Gracia, editor

BRIDGING THE ATLANTIC

Toward a Reassessment of
Iberian and Latin American Cultural Ties

Marina Pérez de Mendiola

STATE UNIVERSITY OF NEW YORK PRESS

F
1416
.S7
B75
1996

Published by
State University of New York Press, Albany

©1996 State University of New York

All rights reserved

Printed in the United States of America

For information, address State University of New York Press,
State University Plaza, Albany, NY 12246

Production by Kay Bolton
Marketing by Nancy Farrell

Library of Congress Cataloging-in-Publication Data

Bridging the Atlantic : toward a reassessment of Iberian and Latin
    American cultural ties / [edited by] Marina Pérez de Mendiola.
        p.   cm. — (SUNY series in Latin American and Iberian thought
    and culture)
        "This collection of essays grew out of an international conference
    ... organized and hosted by the University of Wisconsin–Milwaukee
    and the Center for Latin America in March 1991"—Prelim. p. 1.
        Includes bibliographical references and index.
        Contents: The Battle of Roncesvalles as nationalist polemic / John
    Tolan — America is in Spain : a reading of Clarín's Boroña / James
    D. Fernández — Valle-Inclán's Bradomín and Montenegro, and the
    problem of Hispanic caciquismo / Virginia Gibbs — [etc.] —
        ISBN 0–7914–2917–2 (alk. paper). — ISBN 0–7914–2918–0 (pbk. :
    alk. paper))
        1. Latin America—Relations—Spain—Congresses. 2. Spain-
    -Relations—Latin America—Congresses. 3. Latin America-
    -Civilization—Philosophy—Congresses. 4. Spain—Civilization-
    -Philosophy—Congresses. I. Pérez de Mendiola, Marina, 1960– .
    II. University of Wisconsin–Milwaukee. Center for Latin America.
    III. Series.
    F1416.S7B75 1996
    303.48'24608—dc20   95-47527
                                                                          CIP

10 9 8 7 6 5 4 3 2 1

CONTENTS

ACKNOWLEDGMENTS

This collection of essays grew out of an international conference that gathered a group of distinguished humanists and social scientists to evaluate the impact of Peninsular Spanish thought on Latin American culture from the colonial period to current times. This conference was organized and hosted by the University of Wisconsin–Milwaukee and the Center for Latin America in March 1991. The National Endowment for the Humanities, the Society for Iberian and Latin American Thought, the U.S. Department of Education, and Spain's Ministry of Culture provided financial support for this event. The organization and concerns of this book differ from those of the conference, and many of the works presented at the conference could not be accomodated in the volume. I would like, however, to extend my thanks to all the participants for their outstanding contribution to this event.

I am greatly indebted to Iván Jaksic, former director of the Center for Latin America at the University of Wisconsin–Milwaukee, for entrusting the edition of this collection of essays to me. His continuous support and encouragement were essential for the completion of a project whose future seemed, at times, uncertain. My thanks and appreciation also go to the College of Letters and Science at the University of Wisconsin–Milwaukee for providing me with seed money; to Carmen Cavallo and Robin Pickering-Iazzi for their valuable editorial insights and criticisms; to the contributors for reworking their original papers and for their patience and cooperation. Finally, I would like to express my personal gratitude to Panivong Norindr for being a constant source of comfort, intellectual support, and for playing a vital role in every project I undertake.

INTRODUCTION

The concept of 'bridging' evokes several different images. The one that first comes to mind is a materially visual and tactile structure that links spaces: the bridge. This structural construction prompts, in turn, mental representations commonly associated with the bridge: a pathway or roadway over a depression or a body of water, a device used to connect, allowing for transit between spaces. The sight of a bridge linking different places is always a comforting one since it implies conciliation, collaboration, contact, and communication. In times of conflict, the bridge is usually the first strategic "location"[1] coveted by the warring factors and, therefore, secured and guarded against occupation or destruction.

The constructional metaphor of the title of this collection first points to the bridge the Iberians threw across the Atlantic in 1492, a roadway open only to the conqueror to carry back to the Peninsula the gold extracted from the "New World." However, it also calls attention to the steady yet varied intellectual and historical relations between Spain and Latin America over the centuries. Heidegger reminds us that

> a bridge does not just connect banks that are already there. The banks emerge as banks only as the bridge crosses the stream. . . . One side is set off against the other by the bridge. With the banks, the bridge brings to the stream the one and the other expanse of the landscape lying behind them. It brings stream and bank and land into each other's neighborhood. (Heidegger, 152)

The essays in this anthology problematize the "setting off against each other" of two banks, namely Spain and Latin America. The collection delves into the terrain "lying behind" both banks and yet accessible only through multiple bridgings. One of the aims of the anthology is to sustain the critical interest in Iberian and Latin American cultures beyond the quincentennial celebrations. After the publication of numerous anthologies commemorating the quincentennial on both sides of the Atlantic,[2] we want to situate these essays as part of a post-1992 reflection. This calls for a reassessment of Latin America's and Spain's past and present cultural ties, which is necessary to enhance our understanding of the future of intellectual production and artistic expression encompassing the Iberian and American world. Bringing together a diversity of scholarly views, this collection of essays will try to show that the bridging over an ocean of history and history of ideas is a complex and intricate process that elicits a plurality of viewpoints. Each chapter brings a different disciplinary perspective and invites a diversified theoretical outlook on what Remiche and Scheier have defined as "the double tie of consanguinity and estrangement which has united for over half a millenium the two continents" (7). Accordingly, these studies on the interaction of the Iberian Peninsula and the Americas in the area of intellectual and cultural production over the centuries not only seek to provide a valuable insight into the history of ideas but also examine literary, sociopolitical, and philosophical issues. Moreover, the essays cover an extensive geography and take heed of a wide range of historical periods. The texts challenge, as Fernández put is in chapter 2, "the boundaries set up between Peninsular and Latin American studies and eschew the conventional categories and attitudes that too often circumscribe the discourse around those disciplines" (29).

In our attempt to bridge fields of study, continents, countries, critical approaches, and historical moments, we hope to "gather" in the Heideggerian sense but do not seek a circumscribing unity. This anthology is distinctive for its hybridity and collaborative tensions. By "collaborative tensions" we are referring to the divergent positions the contributors take in their respective studies—a divergency that suggests new questions, inviting the reader to engage in further examinations and discussions beyond those in this book. The essays in this collection shed light on some of the most complex questions that have been set off by the relationship between the Americas and Spain: the effects of Hispanic liberalism in the nineteenth century and at the beginning of the twentieth century on the development of Latin American postcolonial thought; nationalism versus universalism in Latin America; Iberian idealism and American *nostalgias,* or Hispanism versus Panamericanism; the problem of *caciquismo* and its presence on both sides of the Atlantic; and the elaboration of national and cultural identities as a result of the interaction of Spain and Latin America. Although Hispanism does not constitute the main theme of the book, it operates, nonetheless, as the common thread running through the chapters. They all address, by different means, the multiple figurations of the concept and outline some of its cultural and philosophical implications on both sides of the Atlantic.

The history of the initial and uneven bridging between Spain and Latin America is a dark and violent one. In chapter 1, John Tolan's reading of the writings produced by Spanish-born author Bernardo de Balbuena while in Puerto Rico in 1624 takes the reader back in an unusual way to the period of the conquest. In his analysis, Tolan shows how Balbuena manipulated history to vindicate the rights of empire and to justify Castilian rule in the Americas. He argues that Balbuena revived and romanticized the Iberian victory over the French in the Battle of Ronçeveaux, placing it at the root of the Spanish Empire and therefore justifying the conquest and subsequent Christianization of the natives. While Doris Sommer in her provocative study of the nineteenth-century Latin American romance novel reminds us of the "inextricability of politics from fiction in the history of nation-building" (Sommer, 75), Tolan's analysis calls attention to the fact that "foundational myths" such as the one Balbuena elaborated were also used in the early periods to legitimize Spanish presence and the colonization of Latin America. Balbuena's epic poem shows that the dissemination of Spain's legitimate "membership" in the world of empire builders was not only made possible through the use of arms and violence but through a vehicle that would have long-lasting and insidiously persuasive effects—language.

The linguistic planning process and the evangelizing mission implemented by the Spaniards in Latin America begining in 1492, made language and religion the kernel of the colonial mold. It is precisely, as A. Remiche-Martynow and G. Schneier-Madanes have argued, this colonial mold that, thus far, has denied Latin America's plurality (Remiche-Martynow and Schneier-Madanes, 7). By doing so, it has also kept alive the idea of a "Latin American unitary expression" in the Spanish mind. Indeed, this idea is widely shared by Spaniards. José Prat, for example (the lawyer and politician who is affiliated with the Spanish socialist party and who spent thirty seven years in Colombia), recently made reference to "the natural communication between Spain and Latin America born from the language identity, a spiritual identity signified by the Spanish language" (González Gómez, 316–17). Another recent declaration by Nicolás Sánchez Albornoz emphasizes this position. He writes: "Demographic and political reasons, as well as reasons of communication secure the *supremacy* of the Spanish language. This *ascendancy*, achieved throughout the centuries, *put an end to the desire* of those who wish to see the Spanish language broken off into national idioms" (*El País*, 11

December 1992, 11; my emphasis). However, the Argentinian writer Alicia Duvojne Ortiz in her article "Spanish a Fan-Shaped Language," adopts a more radical stance. She attests to the difference in the Spanish language spoken in different regions of Latin America. She provides examples of semantic differences and predicts that in a century we will no longer refer to the language as Spanish but, rather, as Puerto Rican, Argentinian, Mexican, and so on.

The pride Spaniards take in this colonial legacy was clearly indicated in the fourth room of the Spanish Pavillion at the 1992 Seville Exposition dedicated to the Spanish language. Its aim was to remind the visitor that Spanish is the second language spoken in the world of global communication. Accordingly, the audio-visual display of this room was there to prove that technology *also* speaks Spanish. Moreover, we should point out that The Plan Quinto Centenario supported the creation of The Cervantes Institute, which would "*oversee* the proper usage" of the Spanish language. Spain's emphasis on the unifying force of the Spanish language corroborates the significance of language as an assimilative force in the Iberian neocolonial dream.

In chapter 2, James Fernández addresses the issue of the "human" imports during colonial times. He studies another kind of bridging through the literary construction of the figure of the *Indiano*—the Spaniard who emigrates to the New World and later returns to Spain—during the nineteenth century. Fernández's reading of Clarin's "Boroña" sheds light on the ambivalence with which nineteenth-century Spain perceives the Indiano. He argues that the Indiano embodies the destabilization of Spain's insularity and social immobility. Fernández also discusses how the Indiano allows for the examination of Spain's problematic relationship, first to "modernity" and "desire" as signifiers of the "New World," and second to the notions of "identity" and "autochthony," considered specific to Spain.

Virginia Gibbs goes on to emphasize in chapter 3 the difficulties that arose from what she defines as "Spain's public and intellectual crisis in the concept of authority" during the second half of the nineteenth century. She is mainly concerned with the problem of *caciquismo* as a reflection and consequence of this crisis. In her exploration of Valle-Inclán's work, Gibbs contends that the writer's interest in the Hispanic tyrant did not originate with Valle-Inclán's sojourn in Latin America as other critics have argued. Rather, she sees it as an inspiration that grew out of his study of *caciquismo* as a power structure first present in the Iberian Peninsula and not as an exclusive Latin American phenomenon.

On the other side of the Atlantic the nineteenth century was also a period of great political turmoil. Many Latin American intellectuals of that time would have agreed with Gibbs, since they considered the *cacique* to be the product of Spanish colonization and in great part responsible for Latin American political, social, and economical "unrefinement" and backwardness.

Katra, in chapter 4, further develops this issue by examining the different beliefs of key thinkers of the 1837 generation in Argentina—Sarmiento, Gutiérrez, Alberdi—regarding the necessity for Latin America to turn away from the Spanish colonial legacy and to break all ties with *a* Spain that occupied a peripheral position within Europe at the time.

Yet, toward the end of the nineteenth century not all Latin American intellectuals sought the same solution—a "revisionism" inspired by France and England—to satisfy their desire for regeneration. In contrast to Sarmiento's generation, other intellectuals refused to see Spain in a negative light.

Jeane Delaney documents the shifts that took place in the way Argentina viewed Spain during that period. In her study on Manuel Gálvez's *hispanismo* in chapter 5, she explains that the revival of Spanish values and traditions—cultural as well as religious—sprung from Gálvez's fear of modernization in Argentina and, likewise, of the ensuing destabilization of the hierarchical social order. However, Delaney also argues that the renewal of ties with Spain allowed Galvez to posit himself and his fellow intellectuals as the ideal promoters of *hispanización;* they succeeded at the same time to redefine their precarious role and identity as "intellectuals."

Writing about Spanish *Krausismo* in chapter 6, O. Carlos Stoetzer focuses on a different type of Spanish influence in Argentina. He suggests that Spanish Krausismo had a positive influence on the development of political liberalism first in Spain and later in Argentina and Guatemala. He describes how a number of recently established social democratic governments in Latin America were founded on the basis of Kraussean philosophy.

Examining *Ariel* (by Uruguayan writer José Enrique Rodó) in chapter 7, Jaime Concha points to another issue that preoccupied many intellectuals near the end of the nineteenth century in Latin America: the proximity of North America and the threat its materialism posed to Latin America's emerging identity. This study of *Ariel* explains how Rodó's concern sprung less from a facile and primitive "anti-Yanquism" than from a genuine intellectual preoccupation about Latin American cultural identity. Concha is committed to elucidate what he calls Rodó's "physics of ideas," a synthesis of scientific materialist positivism and Spanish philosophical idealism. He also asks, "How is it possible that such a spiritual text as *Ariel* gives rise to a "Newtonian" conception of physics?" Through a shrewd deconstruction of *Ariel,* Concha redefines Rodó as someone who hoped for a reconciliation between the fulfillment of the European humanistic reasoning and the North American utilitarian values.

The Southern Cone and Central America were manifestly not the only Latin American regions to waver back and forth between the desire for restoration of Spanish values and traditions and, at the same time, their repudiation during a period that saw new cultural and political expressions emerging.

Taking the Island of Puerto Rico in the 1930s as a case study, Anthony M. Stevens-Arroyo demonstrates in chapter 8 how Pedro Albizu Campos, while struggling for independence from the United States, adopts concepts of nation and culture developed by the Catalán cleric and Catholic apologist Jaime Balmes. Stevens-Arroyo raises essential questions about the process of decolonization, nation building, autonomy and independence. He studies the links between Albizu's nationalist party (inspired by Balmesian conservative philosophy) and what he calls "The Mother Country"; namely Spain and the "*nacionalismo hispanizante*"[3] resulting from it. In her recent study *Colonialism and Culture,* Iris Zavala shows how part of the modernist project was "to activate productively the Christian and Latin part to reveal the material interest of North America" (Zavala, 98). Of particular interest in Stevens-Arroyo's contribution is his analysis of Albizu's return to the implementation of Catholicism in the thirties in the building of national identity—the means par excellence of Spanish colonization—in order to oppose North American imperialism and Protestantism. One could indeed see this "return" as "imperial nativism" (Deane, 9). By relying on the Spanish colonial legacy and cultural continuity to resist a neocolonial situation, Puerto Rico found itself caught in a vicious circle that would amplify and deepen the problems intrinsic to its quest for emancipation.

By the end of the 1930s a new type of bridging took place between Spain and Latin America. With the Republicans fleeing from Francisco Franco's dictatorship to settle in the Americas, the increasing presence of a growing Spanish intellectual diaspora exiled in Latin American countries such as Mexico, Argentina, and Venezuela greatly contributed to the creation of new links in the area of Iberian and Latin American thought.

Several studies have shown that Spanish intellectuals exiled in the Americas considerably changed their views of Latin America; they also came to question and reassess their own culture and country, Spain.

In chapter 9, Santiago Daydí-Tolson's analysis of Luis Cernuda's writings about Latin America illustrates how, in spite of his genuine interest and attraction for Latin American culture and life, the Spanish poet ultimately viewed the "New World" as a mere object of desire, which paradoxically could constitute a reality only if seen as an extension of Spain. Daydí-Tolson's study undermines the romantic idea that the Republican in exile was first and foremost Republican, and secondarily a Spaniard. He calls attention to the fact that even Republicans could be overcome by neocolonialist sentiments.

Ironically, Cernuda's view of Latin America as an intrinsic part of Spain is not that different from the myth of *Hispanidad* disseminated by Franco's regime. Escudero's chapter complements Daydí-Tolson's analysis in that it deconstructs the rhetorical framework through which Franco's regime articulated its idea of Hispanidad.

Studying, in chapter 10, the evolution of Hispanist thought from the Franco era until today, María Escudero takes the journal *Cuadernos Hispanoamericanos*—the vehicle for articulating the ideology of the Franco regime regarding Latin America—as her point of departure. She draws a parallel between the ideology underlying *Cuadernos Hispanoamericanos* and the one patent in speeches of eminent Iberian political figures in the last twenty-five years, constructing a juxtaposition that leads her to a disquieting conclusion. She contends that under the cover of a "democratic gloss" the post-Franco regimes have perpetuated the idea of a "Hispanic community of Nations" as it was first conceived during the Franco era. Escudero imputes this situation to Spain's unswerving attempt to be granted full membership in the exclusive Western European unity and North American clubs.[4] Furthermore, she adds that by accepting the role of mediator between Europe, North America, and Latin America, Spain abandoned the search for less corrupted "rapports" with Latin America.

In the same vein, Marina Pérez de Mendiola's work may be seen as paradigmatic of Escudero's theories, providing, in chapter 11, a critical analysis of the representation of Latin American countries at the 1992 Seville Universal Exposition. In her essay, Pérez de Mendiola explores the logic underwriting Spain's articulation of the Latin American presence at the exposition and shows that Spain required the "presence" of Latin

America as its *former colonies* in order to reaffirm herself, as physical evidence of her past accomplishments and glory.

Ofelia Schutte rounds out this collection in chapter 12 by offering a reflection on the state of Latin American cultural identity. She asks, "how could a discourse on Latin American cultural identity position itself five hundred years after the conquest?" Building on Nietzsche's, Sarmiento's, and Marti's analyses of culture, she denounces "technological determinism" as a force that plunges historically underdeveloped regions into a deeper state of dependency. She urges the Western hemisphere to go beyond the traditional and orchestrated showcase of technical know-how, as exemplified by the Universal Exposition, and argues for the creation of new criteria to define people and civilization, Spain and the Americas.

Bridging the Atlantic cannot exhaustively cover each aspect defining the long-lasting and problematic relationship between Spain and Latin America since 1492, and it is not concerned with conclusiveness. Rather, it invites others to challenge this work, to generate alternative positionings while pursuing the many questions that have been raised and merit further reflection. Heidegger in his essay "Building, Dwelling, Thinking" asserts that to think of a bridge from where we are

> belongs to the nature of our thinking *of* that bridge that in *itself* thinking gets through, persists through, the distance to that location. . . . From right here we [with these essays] may even be much nearer to that bridge and to what it makes room for than someone who uses it daily as an indifferent river crossing. (Heidegger, 156)

This selection of historical, philosophical, sociopolitical, and literary essays aims to alter broader debates, and to intrigue a wider audience. The last ten years have been marked by an increasing interest in colonial and postcolonial studies. However, one could question the dearth of anthologies in English chronicling the complex relationship between Spain, Latin America, and its colonial legacy. *Bridging the Atlantic* intends to stimulate new "dialectical encounters" and more comparative research on postcolonial questions.

Notes

1. According to Heidegger a bridge is a location, and a location "proves to be a location *because of the bridge* . . . a location comes into existence only by

virtue of the bridge" (*Poetry, Language, Thought*. Trans. by Albert Hofstadter [New York: Harper & Row, 1975], p. 155).

2. The body of work published around the quincentenary is too extensive to be fully represented here. I have, nevertheless, compiled a select list of magazines, journals, and newsletters published between 1986 and 1992. This should provide a good source of biographical information for scholars interested in analyzing different commentaries and opinions voiced on the quincentennial of the European arrival in the Americas. See the addendum following the works cited.

3. See Emilia de Zuleta's article "El hispanismo de Hispanoamerica". *Hispania* 75, 4 (October 1992): 950–65.

4. The creation of new journals such as *Encounters* and the proliferation of Spanish foundations in the U.S. as a result of the bilateral treaties of cooperation signed in 1989 between Spain and the United States is indicative of Spain's need to disseminate its new (?) message. In his presidential greeting to the readers of *Encounters*, H. E. Felipe González of Spain writes, "Spain has a long history of relations with the United States, from the Spanish pioneers of the sixteenth century to the crucial moments of American independence. We understand that the new bilateral treaties of cooperation signed in 1989 mark the beginning of an era rich in cultural and economic exchange. *Spain '92 Foundation* and *Encounters* are clear examples of this new spirit"(González, 5).

Works Cited

Deane, Seamus. Introduction to *Nationalism, Colonialism, and Literature*. Essays by Terry Eagleton, Fredric Jameson, Edward W. Said. Minneapolis: University of Minnesota Press, 1990.

Duvojne Ortiz, Alicia. "L'espagnol, une langue en éventail". *Notre Amérique métisse: Cinq cents ans après les Latino-Américains parlent aux Européens*. Paris: Editions de la Découverte, 1992, pp. 215–25.

González Gómez, Pilar. "José Prat: Recuerdos de Colombia". In José Luis Abellán and Antonio Monclús *El pensamiento español contemporáneo y la idea de América. El pensamiento en el exilio*. Barcelona: Anthropos, 1989, pp. 277–383.

González, Felipe. "Presidential Greetings from H. E. Felipe González of Spain." *Encounters: A Quincentenary Review* 2 (Spring 1992): 5.

Heidegger, Martin. *Poetry, Language, Thought*. Trans. Albert Hofstadter. New York: Harper and Row, 1975.

Remiche-Martynow, A. and Schneier-Madanes, G. *Notre Amérique métisse. Cinq cents ans après les Latino-Américains parlent aux Européens.* Paris: La Découverte, 1992.

Sommer, Doris. "Irresistible Romance: The Foundational Fictions of Latin America." In Homi Bhabha *Nation and Narration.* London: Routledge, 1990, pp. 71–99.

Zavala, Iris. *Colonialism and Culture: Hispanic Modernism and the Social Imaginary.* Bloomington and Indianapolis: University of Indiana Press, 1992.

Zuleta, Emilia de. "El hispanismo de Hispanoamerica". *Hispania* 75, 4 (October 1992): 950–65.

Addendum

Quinto Centenario, published by the Department of History of America at the Universidad Complutense in Madrid. It covers all aspects and periods of Ibero-American history.

The journal of the *Asociación de historiadores latinoamericanos europeos* published two issues respectively entitled "History of Latin America in European Research and Teaching" and "America in the Material Civilization of Europe, Sixteenth–Twentieth Centuries." Both issues were edited by Dr. Horst Pietschmann.

Encounter '92, newsletter of the quincentennial of Columbus's landfall in the Bahamas, Star Publishers, Nassau.

Latin American Archivist Association (ALA, published in Mexico City).

Columbus 92, monthly magazine published in Italian (1987–1992) in New York and Genoa.

Ideas '92, biyearly academic journal created to clarify the historical, cultural, and diplomatic perceptions that Spain, Latin America, and the U.S. have held of one another. Published at the University of Miami, Coral Gables.

Nueva sociedad, published in Caracas, Venezuela, this magazine published eight essays between 1989 and 1992 under the general title of "Lo propio y lo ajeno, 500 años después".

Latin American Population History Newsletter (LAPH), published by the Department of History at the University of Minnesota in Minneapolis.

The Courier, monthly magazine published by the UNESCO in thirty-five languages. See in particular the April 1989 issue "Portuguese Voyages of Discovery."

Sevilla Universal, magazine on the preparations for Expo '92.

Place, special 1992 issue from Partners for Livable Places, published in Washington D.C.

América indígena, journal published by the Instituto Panamericano de Geografía e Historia in Mexico City.

Five Hundred, quarterly magazine published by the Christopher Columbus Quincentenary Jubilee Commission, Washington D.C.

The New World, the Smithsonian Institution trilingual quarterly newsletter on the Smithsonian's quincentennial program, planning, and research.

Quinto Centenario, bimonthly newsletter published in Santo Domingo, Dominican Republic.

América Latina, a journal published by the Russian Academy of Sciences. See in particular issue 5, published in 1988.

Océanos, triannual magazine published by the National Commission of Portugal (Lisboa).

1992 Columbus Newsletter, biannually published by the John Carter Brown Library.

The Journal of the Society for Renaissance Studies produced a special quincentennial number in 1992. Published at the University of Glasgow, Scotland.

Rábida, semiannual publication produced by the Provincial Foundation for the Quincentennial of the Discovery of America. Published in Huelva, Spain.

Archeology Magazine published several issues around the quincentennial. See issues of September/October 1990, May/June 1991, September/October 1991, January/February 1992, May/June 1992. Journal published at the University of Boulder, Colorado.

América '92, published a special supplement entitled "IV Centenario del Descubrimiento de América", which describes the celebrations of 1892. Published by Sociedad Estatal Quinto Centenario in Madrid.

Aurora, newsletter published by the National Conference of Catholic Bishops V Centenary Committee.

Borinquen 500, newsletter published by the Puerto Rican Commission for the Celebration of the Quincentennial.

North American Congress on Latin America 1991–1992, published a special issue "Reports on the Americas."

Encuentro, biannual academic review published by the Association of Spanish Professors in Puerto Rico (San Juan).

La Española, newsletter published by the Dominican National Commission for the Celebration of the Quincentennial.

Encuentro de dos Mundos, magazine published by the Honduran Department of Culture and Tourism (Tegucigalpa).

Revista Texto y Contexto, published by the History Department at the University of the Andes. Several issues were published over a three-year period (1989–1992) under the title "Discovery and American Identity" (Bogota, Colombia).

Notas Mesoamericanas, a journal of Meso-American anthropology. See special issue on the quincentennial in 1990 (Universidad de las Américas, Puebla, Mexico).

Ecos del V Centenario, published by the Honduran National Commission for the Celebration of the Quincentennial.

Daybreak, published by the Indigenous Press Network, Highland, Maryland.

Boletín del V Centenario, published by the Peruvian National Commission for the Celebration of the Quincentennial.

Cuadernos Americanos, devoted a special issue in September/October 1988 on the quincentennial. Published by La Universidad Nacional Autónoma de México, Mexico.

Encuentro: A Columbian Quincentenary Quarterly, published until 1988 by the University of New Mexico and replaced in 1988 by *Encounters: A Quincentenary Review,* published by the Latin American Institute, Albuquerque, New Mexico.

500 Magazine, official magazine of the U.S. Commission, Miami, Florida.

Native Nations, magazine published in New York City. Reported primarily on Native American's preparations for the quincentennial.

Sephardic Highlights, monthly newsletter of the American Sephardic Federation. Provided worldwide coverage of the 1992 commemorative activities of Sephardic Jews. Published in New York City.

Amate, newsletter publication created in a related effort to conserve the vast quantity of documentation in archives throughout the Americas. Published by the Archivo General de la Nación, Mexico City.

Indigenous Thought, magazine created to serve as a principal source of information for individuals and groups interested in objecting to the celebrations of the quincentennial.

For more details on these publications and other sources see *Quincentennial of the Discovery of America: Encounter of Two Worlds,* a newsletter produced by the General Secretariat of the Organization of the American States, Washington, D.C.

1

The Battle of Roncesvalles
as Nationalist Polemic

JOHN TOLAN

*The Spanish people is like the Hebrew, in that
it is the chosen people of God.*

—Fray Juan Salazar (1619)[1]

Castilians of the sixteenth and seventeenth centuries saw themselves as occupying a unique privileged position: political center of the most powerful and far-flung empire in the world and bearers of the word of God to the ends of the earth. Spaniards looked back on their history as a glorious progression of conquest and Christianization: first of the Iberian Peninsula, then on the wider empire in America. As with any imperial power, history is used to vindicate the rights of empire; to glorify and justify Castilian rule.

Various Spanish authors had provided justification for Cortes' conquest of Mexico. For some, the missionary imperative was enough to justify it; for others, the barbarity of the Aztecs' practice of human sacrifice, a clear infringement of natural law, made the conquest legitimate. Yet again, the Aztec subjection of the Tlaxcala, who allied themselves with Cortes, justified the conquest.[2]

If history could be used to justify Spain's overseas conquest, it also could provide an explanation for the hostility of Spain's European rivals. Spanish might—both in Europe and overseas—was increasingly

15

threatened by rising powers: the rebellious Netherlands, England, Protestant princes in Germany, and restive vassal states in Italy. In many of these places, Spain found itself opposed—overtly or covertly—by its most formidable adversary: France.

For Frenchmen and Spaniards of the sixteenth and seventeenth centuries, this strife had a long history. It had begun with the battle of Roncesvalles (Roncevaux, in French), which each side saw as the embodiment of its own heroism and of the perfidy and military ineptitude of its adversary. For the French, Roncevaux was a sweeping victory of Christian knights over a hoard of infidels from Spain and beyond; for the Spaniards, Roncesvalles was the decisive repulsion of an invading French army, firmly establishing Spanish independence and resolutely chastising a power-hungry Charlemagne for his *hubris*.

Bernardo de Balbuena in 1624 weaves these various traditions together in his *Bernardo, o victoria de Roncesvalles*. Writing in Puerto Rico as the Spanish Antilles are under increasing threat from the French, Dutch and English, having lived most of his life in New Spain (Mexico), he saw Spain's Christianizing and imperial missions in the new world inextricably linked with its rivalry with France. The story of Roncesvalles, for Balbuena, is the first act in the long drama that culminates in Spanish world dominance: the Spanish hero of Roncesvalles, Bernardo del Carpio, is the founder of a great Christian empire.

The historical battle of Roncesvalles (as reconstructed from the scant mention in ninth-century documents) is a far cry from these later nationalistic renditions. In 776 or 777, Sulayman ibn Yaqzan, ruler of Zaragoza, appealed to Charlemagne for help against a threatened invasion by the Ummayad Caliph of Cordoba; in return, he promised Charlemagne overlordship of Zaragoza. Charlemagne, answering this call for help, marched across the Pyrenees, received the homage of Pamplona and Huesca, and, upon reaching Zaragoza, found that the citizens had closed its gates and were determined to refuse him entrance. He established a siege, which he soon had to abandon when news reached him of a revolt in Saxony. On his way back across the Pyrenees—on August 15, 778—his rear guard was ambushed by a band of Christian Basques; in the fray, several of Charlemagne's men were killed, including a certain Roland, duke of the marches of Brittany.

From these bare bones of fact the great epic of medieval France, the *Chanson de Roland*,[3] was brought to life, first written down sometime in the second half of the eleventh century. Charlemagne, says the *Chanson*, has conquered all of Spain except Zaragoza. Roland and his rear guard are surprised in the pass of Roncesvalles because the French traitor Ganelon, envious of Roland, has helped Marsile (the Muslim king of Zaragoza) plan an ambush. The entire French rear guard—including the twelve peers, the flower of French chivalry—dies in the fighting, though Roland and the archbishop Turpin manage to drive away the remnants of the Muslim force before dying of their wounds. Charlemagne, realizing what has happened, arrives on the scene too late, and sets out after the Muslims for vengeance. Muslim troops from abroad arrive to support Zaragoza, and the subsequent battle pits all of Christendom against all of Islam. Charlemagne's military victory is followed by the capture of Zaragoza, whose citizens are given the choice between baptism and the sword. The Christian knights purify the city by destroying idols in its mosques and synagogues. The *Chanson de Roland*, then, tells of a crusade between Christian Frenchmen and Spanish infidels; Spanish Christians are not mentioned.

The implications of this are made all the more explicit in the twelfth-century *Chronicle*[4] falsely attributed to Turpin, Charlemagne's archbishop in the *Chanson de Roland*. The Pseudo-Turpin comprises part of the *Codex Calixtinus* (an important pilgrimage manuscript in Santiago) and was translated into French several times during the middle ages.[5] This chronicle is an apology for the immigrant French community in Christian Spain, a community that owed its existence, in part, to the pilgrimage to Santiago de Compostela. In the *Chronicle*, St. James appears to Charlemagne in a dream, tells him that his body lies in Galicia, whither Charlemagne must make a pilgrimage. St. James also tells Charlemagne that he must reconquer Spain for the Christians. The *Chronicle* then describes a series of battles in which Charlemagne routs his Muslim enemies (often with divine aid). In the process, he founds the monastery of Sahagun and the cathedral of Santiago de Compostela (to whose bishop he grants authority over the Spanish church). All the states and religious institutions of twelfth-century Christian Spain, it seems, owe their existence in one way or another to the intervention of Charlemagne. The *Chronicle* lists over a hundred towns and castles in Spain: "All of these cities," it proclaims, "Charlemagne took, some without fighting and some through long war and great cleverness. . . . Charlemagne subjugated all of Spain in his time."[6] The inept Christian Spaniards have lost Spain to the Muslims twice (once before Charlemagne and once since), clearly showing both their military inferiority to the French and their lack of crusading zeal.

A Spanish reaction to this French polemic was not long in coming: it was embodied in the legend of Bernardo del Carpio. Bernardo's legend had evolved by the late twelfth century into one or more epic poems (now lost); these, in turn were used by three thirteenth-century chronicles: the *Chronicon mundi* of Lucas de Tuy (1236), the *Historia gothica* of Rodrigo Jiménez de Rada, archbishop of Toledo (1243), and the *Primera crónica general de España* of Alfonso X el Sabio (c. 1289, based to a certain extent on the earlier two chronicles).[7] The Battle of Roncesvalles, in these three slightly varying chronicles, is quite different from either that of the *Chanson de Roland* or that of the Pseudo-Turpin. Here Roncesvalles is connected with the reign of King Alfonso II el Casto of Asturias (which in fact began thirteen years *after* the battle, in 791). Alfonso, we are told, is without heir; he offers to leave Asturias to Charlemagne if the latter will help him fight the Moors. When Alfonso's knights, in particular his nephew, Bernardo del Carpio, hear of their king's plans, they are outraged, and threaten to expel him from his own kingdom if he should try to subject it to French rule. Under this pressure Alfonso revokes his offer to Charlemagne; this in turn rouses Charlemagne's ire and provokes his invasion of Spain.

At this point the three chronicles differ. Lucas de Tuy says that Bernardo, realizing that the Asturian forces will be outnumbered by those of Charlemagne, goes to the Saracens for help; the *Primera crónica general* specifies that he goes to king Marsil of Zaragoza. Rodrigo Jiménez de Rada passes over this in silence, clearly not wishing to give Muslims credit for defending the Asturian homeland. Lucas then mentions how, when Charlemagne crosses the Pyrenees, various Basque and Navarrese towns surrender to him; the nationalistic Rodrigo (and the *Primera crónica general* after him) here inserts florid prose describing the sufferings of these Spaniards, who have escaped the oppressive yoke of the Muslims only to fall under that of the Gauls. Rodrigo (and, again, the *Primera crónica general*) says that the people of Navarre, Alava, Vizcaya, Gascony, and Aragon all beg Alfonso el Casto for deliverance. In the thirteenth century, when the kings of León and Castile (the heirs to the Asturian kingdom) claimed theoretical hegemony over the whole Iberian peninsula, the political message of this is clear: the subjects of the various Pyrenean kingdoms owe their allegiance to the kings of León-Castile.

The three chroniclers then describe how the united forces of Spain, under Alfonso's and Bernardo's heroic leadership, destroy Charlemagne's rear guard at Roncesvalles, killing Roland and the other peers.

Charlemagne goes back to Aachen, vowing to return and get his revenge. Lucas de Tuy says that Charlemagne does indeed return, fights against the Moors, makes peace with Alfonso el Casto, goes as a pilgrim to Santiago de Compostela, and convinces Bernardo to return to France with him. Bernardo fights heroically for Charlemagne in numerous battles against various enemies of the Emperor. The nationalist Rodrigo will have nothing of all this:

> And some people say in their epics and their fables that Charlemagne conquered many cities and castles in Spain, and that he had many fights with Moors there, and that he cleared and opened the route from Germany to Santiago. But in truth this cannot be, except that in Catalonia he conquered Barcelona, Gerona, Ausona, Urgel, and their environs, and that these peoples' claim is not to be believed. . . . A man should rather believe what seems to be true and reasonable among those things that he finds written and recorded and not the fables of those who do not know what they are talking about. (Heinermann, 12–13)

Rodrigo, on the contrary, says that Charlemagne died soon after his return to Aachen.

> He was buried in a glorious sepulchre, which was circumscribed with epitaphs of his ancient victories, with one part remaining blank, on the side facing the valley where Charles, threatening vengeance, returned inglorious and unavenged.[8]

Here we already see two phases of the Spanish reaction to the French tradition of Roncesvalles. Both contain the same central episode: the Asturians decisively defeat Charlemagne's rear guard at Roncesvalles. But there are important differences as well: Lucas, incorporating a good deal of the French tradition, makes a joint Muslim-Christian Spanish force responsible for the victory and has Charlemagne and Alfonso el Casto (in the end) reconciled allies. Rodrigo is much more nationalistic: the Muslim troops of Zaragoza play no role in the battle. Moreover, Rodrigo clearly does not wish to give any undue credit to Charlemagne; all this nonsense about battles against Moors is dismissed as "fables." The Spanish epic traditions of Roncesvalles are history; the French epic traditions of Roncevaux are "fables of those who do not know what they are talking about."

Over the next three centuries, the only written sources that mention Bernardo are historical chronicles, most of them based on the *Primera crónica general.* Then, between 1550 and 1700, Bernardo flourishes: he figures in a number of lyric poems (*romances*), nine plays, and several novels. The authors who wrote on Bernardo included Juan de la Cueva, Cervantes, and Lope de Vega.[9]

The earliest of these works may be the *Romance del Rey Alfonso el Casto,* published in 1551 (Menéndez Pidal, 216–17). This brief poem narrates the events that lead up to the battle of Roncesvalles, carefully skipping over any mention of Charlemagne's subjection of the Pyrenean kingdoms. This is a battle for freedom, and for freedom of Castile (rather than Asturias): "The Castilians do not want to be subjects of the French." The battle is not against the rear guard (since both kings are directly involved), but it appears that Charlemagne is *advancing,* not withdrawing (and hence has not set foot in Spain). The victory is hence won over the full French force, and Bernardo fights and kills Roldan in single combat.

Five romances published between 1587 and 1604 narrate Bernardo's speech to Alfonso, in which he urges him not to abandon his kingdom to Charlemagne (Menéndez Pidal, 226–32). The message is always the same: *Castilla,* or *España* (the more appropriate *Asturias* or *León,* significantly, are almost never used), should not enslave itself to *franceses.* This is the theme, as well, of nine *Romances de la Batalla de Roncesvalles* from roughly the same period (1578–1605; Menéndez Pidal, 226–32). In none of these poems is the alliance between Alfonso and Muslim Zaragoza mentioned; one poem does mention the ally king Marsil, but makes him king of *Aragón* (Menéndez Pidal, 239).

These various poems indicate an even sharper nationalistic bent than that of Rodrigo Jiménez de Rada. For Rodrigo, Charlemagne's occupation of Navarre was an opportunity to deride his cruel oppression of a Spanish people and to paint the Asturian king as savior of the whole Iberian nation. These later poets are too full of Spanish pride even to let Charlemagne set foot on their side of the Pyrenees. Moreover, a sweeping military defeat of Charlemagne's full force is much more satisfying to national pride than is a mere ambush of his rear guard. Alfonso becomes king of Castile, Spanish political unity is assumed, and Muslims are brushed out of the way.

Along these same lines is Juan de la Cueva's play *La libertad de España por Bernardo del Carpio,* produced in 1579.[10] The battle, again, is for Castilla or España, words that are used interchangeably. Alfonso is foolhardy for "submitting indomitable Spain to the yoke of a foreign people" (lines 1033–34). Charlemagne, moreover, is *hubris* personified. When he hears that Alfonso is rescinding his offer of his kingdom, Charlemagne in ire warns of his coming invasion, threatening "I plan to leave no one alive in your land" (lines 1433–34) We learn that Marsil of Zaragoza is to send help. A messenger then comes from Navarre, saying to Alfonso: "Great lord of the Iberian kingdom, Navarre, sends you words that the enemy standards are on Celtiberian soil (lines 1467–70). Navarre wants help; Alfonso, as lord of Iberia, is its only possible savior.[11] Bernardo's reaction to the French invasion is righteous indignation: "Tame the arrogance and the rage of the enemy, so that they see that Spain is Spain; Spain is not France (lines 1487–90). A messenger now comes from Vizcaya, also asking for help. Cueva's culminating scene presents Bernardo raging on the battlefield, seeking out the French peers (*paladines*) and defeating them in single combat. In the final battle with Roldan he loses his sword and kills Roldan with his bare hands. Charlemagne comes on stage, bewailing his folly; Bernardo returns, to be greeted by Mars who puts a crown of laurel on his head, proclaiming "I crown you as second Mars" (lines 1872).

For these various Castilian authors, then, the theme of Roncesvalles is one of French *hubris* and Spanish military prowess. The battle is to take on larger proportions when seen from the other side of the Atlantic, by a poet living in Spain's American empire: Bernardo de Balbuena. Balbuena was born in Spain, lived most of his life in New Spain and Jamaica, and spent his final years as bishop of Puerto Rico. Part of a creole literary renaissance that looked back both to medieval Castile and to the Amerindian empires as its predesessors, Balbuena is best known for an elaborate panegyric of Mexico City, his *Grandeza mexicana*.[12] In 1624 he published *El Bernardo, o victoria de Roncesvalles*, a long epic poem comprised of 40,000 verses—5,000 *octavas reales*.[13] Balbuena took his inspiration from Homer and Virgil, and even more so from Ariosto's *Orlando furioso* and Boiardo's *Orlando innamorato* (the latter two, of course, both based on the adventures of Roland, whom Balbuena will refer to both by the Castilian *Roldan* and the Italian *Orlando*).

In Balbuena's huge and rambling poem, it is at times hard to keep track of Bernardo himself (much less the battle of Roncesvalles) amidst the flurry of digressions and distractions: Balbuena tells us of Morgana and other fairies, of the giant Ferraguto[14] and his adventures with various nymphs and satyrs, of the intrigues of Charlemagne's court magicians, of a struggle between a demon and the guardian angel of Spain (who recites a catalogue of Spain's holy martyrs), of countless knights, duels, noble *doncellas*, and figures from classical mythology.

When Balbuena does get to Bernardo, we hear of many new adventures: a trip to Persia on a magical ship to duel with the king of Persia and liberate the queen of China, whom the king has carried away in a flying chariot of fire; Bernardo goes to Greece to acquire the armor of Achilles (made by Vulcan); Bernardo liberates Angelica from the clutches of a dragon, liberates a *doncella* from a lion, and defeats numerous knights in duels. All of this, of course, should sound familiar to any reader of *Don Quixote*; here, however, there is nothing tongue in cheek about Balbuena's narration.

In view of the scale of the epic and of Balbuena's penchant for baroque effusion, any attempt to boil his poem down to some political message should be taken with several grains of salt. Nevertheless, the central theme is clear: the battle of Roncesvalles is a chastisement of the *hubris* of the French—and of Charlemagne in particular; it is also the reward granted to the virtue of Bernardo and his Spain. The epic opens with a discussion between the fairies Alcina and Morgana, who wish to punish the pride and impudence of Charlemagne and his twelve *paladines*; after a long discussion of Bernardo and his virtues, they choose him as the instrument for this punishment.

But this is more than a nationalistic battle of chastisement. Balbuena's description of Roncesvalles (and, perhaps more importantly, of the events leading up to it), shows that the battle has taken on even greater dimensions than in the Romances and in Juan de la Cueva. For Balbuena, residing in Spain's American colonies, Spanish nationalism is not enough; for him, Roncesvalles represents the birth of a great Spanish empire, the new Rome, which is destined to expel the Muslims from Iberian soil and to bring Christianity to new shores.

This is perhaps seen most clearly in an episode apparently unrelated to Bernardo and Roncesvalles. Before the battle, the magician Malgesí takes a journey on a flying ship with several of the French knights. They fly over much of Europe (in particular the Iberian peninsula), then cross the Atlantic to tour Spain's future American Empire. When they enter Spain from France (flying over, appropriately enough, Roncesvalles), Malgesí prophesies Spain's future imperial greatness, asking:

> In what region of the world will its banners not cast shadows, overawing the world? In Persia, Africa, Arabia, and in the distant islands girded and washed by the sea: O fortunate Spain, if you had a second

Virgil for your Aeneas, or a second Homer for your Achilles, how little envy men would have of the first! Your truths exceed their fictions.
(de Balbuena, 16: 72–73)

Spain is to exceed even the legendary achievements of the ancients;
the antique epics will be surpassed when Spain finds its own Homer
(who is meant, of course, to be Balbuena himself). Malgesí goes on to
compare Spain to Rome, so proud of its former status of imperial capital; it was Spain, he says, that gave Rome its greatest soldiers and states-
men.

Spain's future greatness is also the theme of Malgesí's description of
Madrid—or, rather, his prophecy of how it is to become seat of "the
monarchy of the world in golden reins" (de Balbuena, 16: 136) and
hence "de la Romana Iglesia la coluna" (16: 137). Spain's empire will
surpass Rome's:

Then [the Spaniards'] victorious banners, waving, rising up to the
sun as a brilliant guide, shall cast colorful shadows where the day is
beginning and there where it is ending. They [the Spaniards] will see
monstrous peoples and races. Discovering all that the sea hid, they
will be able to say that they found and conquered more of the world
than others had ever heard of. (de Balbuena, 16: 204)

When they cross the Atlantic, Malgesí shows his passengers the
lands that Spain will conquer and bring to Christendom: Brazil (since
Portugal and its empire had been taken over by Spain in 1580), Peru,
Central America, Mexico. They then enter the enchanted cave of the
Mexican magician Tlascala. Tlascala explains that his land is being bru-
tally subjected by a ferocious people, the Aztecs. He says, however, that
in future centuries the Aztecs will pay for their bloody conquest: he
enthusiastically foretells Cortes' conquests and the subsequent Christianization of Mexico. Here Balbuena provides a twin justification for
Spain's conquest of Mexico: Cortes not only brings Christianity to Mexico, he also is the unwitting agent of the divine punishment for the
Aztecs' bloodthirsty subjugation of other peoples.[15]

The scene shifts back to France, as Charlemagne leads his troops out
from Paris (*not* Aachen) and approaches the Pyrenees. He has dreamt
that a Lion devoured his twelve *Paladines*. Shortly before the battle,
twelve swans fly over from France; they are met by a ferocious eagle who
swoops over from above the Spanish camp and kills them all. Charle-

magne ignores these portents of defeat, further showing his hubris. This is a battle between Christians only. Marsilio, king of Zaragoza, is hostile to both the French and the Asturians; he is far from the battlefield.[16] The one-on-one duels of the battle are described in detail; Spain and Bernardo gradually win the upper hand. Charlemagne flees the battlefield, and Bernardo allows the archbishop Turpin to escape alive as a witness to the French humiliation:

> he alone Spain left as a witness and chronicler of its victory, though he with his pen was to act not at all as a friend; he knew how to obscure Spain's glory. (de Balbuena, 24: 194)[17]

Balbuena is telling the truth; any variant (i.e., French) version of the battle is a malicious lie, which can be traced back to Charlemagne's archbishop. The epic ends with a fight to the death between Bernardo and Roldan.

The past is an ever-changing picture: a historical event (in this case, a small ambush in a narrow mountain valley) becomes the inspiration for an epic poem (the *Chanson de Roland*), which is in turn was paraphrased into a prose history (the *Pseudo-Turpin*). The implications of this legend provoke a Spanish response, found in various early chronicles; these chronicles in turn inspire romances, plays, and an epic poem. The legend explains the implacable hostility of the French. When Balbuena weaves it together with traditional justification of Spanish conquest of the Americas, the legend becomes a foundation myth for a great Christian Empire.

It is striking how much the past described in each of these works resembles the author's present (or, perhaps, an idealized present). The warriors are patriotic, they are fighting for Spain (or France); the fact that in 778 France did not exist and Hispania was no more than a vague geographical term is resolutely overlooked. This tendency increases in the later texts: Charlemagne's capital moves from Aachen to Paris; Asturias becomes León, then Castilla or España. In the Spanish legend, Muslims and Charlemagne's French are given less and less of a positive role in the later texts; nationalism crowds out any recognition of the virtues of the adversary. Throughout the centuries, the moral virtues and military prowess of Spaniards (or Frenchmen) are seen to be constant; so are the hubris and perfidy of the enemy. Perhaps any powerful nation needs voices to convince it that the sway it holds over subjected peoples (e.g., the Aztecs) is justified, and that continued hostility towards its enemies (the Muslims or the French) is necessary.[18]

Notes

1. Fray Juan de Salazar, *Política española,* ed. Miguel Herrero García (Madrid: Instituto de Estudios Políticos, 1945), p. 88; quoted from J. H. Elliot, *Spain and Its World: 1500–1700* (New Haven, CT: Yale University Press, 1989), p. 115.

2. The latter justification is used by Fray Toribio de Motolinía, a Franciscan missionary to the Tlaxcala. Cf. his *Historia de los indios de la Nueva España* (1541; ed. Mexico City: 1941), pp. 50–51, 76–77. (Thanks to Anthony Stevens-Arroyo for bringing Motolinía's text to my attention.) It also appears in a mid-sixteenth-century Tlaxcalan account edited by Miguel Leon Portilla in his *Visión de los vencidos* (translated by Lisander Kemp as *The Broken Spears: The Aztec Account of the Conquest of Mexico,* Boston: Beacon Press, 1966). Francisco de Vitoria provides a mix of these various justifications of the conquest. (See Francisco de Vitoria in *Political Writings,* Anthony Pagden and Jeremy Lawrance, eds. and trans., Cambridge: Cambridge University Press, 1991.) The validity of these various claims is the subject of the 1550 Valladolid debate between Juan Gines de Sepúlveda and Bartolome de las Casas (see Stafford Poole's annotated translation of Las Casas' *In Defense of the Indians,* DeKalb: Northern Illinois University Press, 1974 and 1992). See also David A. Brading's *The First America: The Spanish Monarchy, Creole Patriots, and the Liberal States, 1492–1867,* (Cambridge: Cambridge University Press, 1991).

3. Pierre Le Gentil, ed. *La Chanson de Roland* (Paris: Hatier, 1967). G. Moignet, ed. *La Chanson de Roland* (Paris: Bordas, 1969).

4. Hans-Wilhelm Klein, ed. *Die Chronik von Karl dem Grossen und Roland: Der lateinische Pseudo-Turpin in den Handschriften aus Aachen und Andernach* (Munich: Wilhelm Fink, 1986).

5. Ronald N. Walpole, ed. *An Anonymous Old French Translation of the Pseudo-Turpin Chronicle: A Critical Edition of the Text Contained in Bibliothèque Nationale MSS fr. 2137 and 17203 and Incorporated by Philippe Mouskés in his Chronique rimée* (Cambridge: Harvard University Press, 1979); Ian Short, ed., *The Anglo-Norman Pseudo-Turpin of William de Briane* (Oxford: Blackwell, 1973); Claude Buridant, ed., La traduction du Pseudo-Turpin du manuscrit Vatican Regina 624 (Geneva: Droz, 1976).

6. "Omnes prefatas urbes quasdam sine pugna, quasdam cum magno bello et maxima arte Karolus tunc aquisivit, . . . hic Karolus magnus totam

Hispaniam suis temporibus sibi subiugavit" (Klein, 42). The list of citations is at pp. 40–43.

7. The parts of these three chronicles that deal with Bernardo's legend are edited in a synoptic text (with parallel columns) by Theodor Heinermann, *Untersuchungen zur Entstehung der Sage von Bernardo del Carpio, Habilitationsschrift der philosophischen und naturwissenschaftlichen* (Halle [Saale]: Fakultät der Universität Münster, 1927), pp. 3–27. Heinermann (p. 77) has a diagram tracing these three versions back to putative earlier sources. One earlier chronicle (which Heinermann does not discuss) makes brief mention of Bernardo: the (apparently unedited) *Liber chronicorum* of Pelayo, Abp. of Oviedo (d. 1129); Lucas de Tuy takes his narration, in part, from there, according to Ramón Menéndez Pidal, *Romanceros del Rey Rodrigo y de Bernardo del Carpio* (Madrid: Gredos, 1957), pp. 143–44. It should be noted that Roncesvalles and the events leading up to it comprise but one episode in the long and various epic traditions about Bernardo.

8. "In glorioso tumulo sepelitur, qui erat priscarum victoriarum epitaphis circumscriptus, ea parte vacua remanente, qua valle Caroli vindictam minitans inglorius rediit and inultus"(Heinermann, 12). The translation of the *Primera crónica general* is more colorful: "Et fue y enterrado mucho onrradamient en un sepulcro mucho onrrado et bien fecho en que estauan pintadas todas las batallas que el vençiera; mas en aquella parte del sepulcro que estaua contra los montes Pireneos de Rônçasualles o el fuera desbaratado et vençido de los espannoles, non auie y pintura ninguna. Et esto fezieron por que tornara el sin prez et sin venganza ninguna" (Heinermann, 12). The *Crónica* mentions both Lucas' and Rodrigo's versions (citing them both by name), notes that they are contradictory, but makes no judgment between them.

9. See Heinermann, chap. 3, "Weitere Bearbeitungen der Sage (Überblick)," pp. 28–30. On the plays, cf. Lillian Frona Wester, *The Cycle of Bernardo del Carpio Plays* (Master's Thesis, University of Chicago, 1923). Lope de Vega wrote three plays dealing with Bernardo del Carpio, but Roncesvalles is treated only in *El Casamiento en la Muerte* (and even there only in the first half of the play). *El casamiento en la muerte, Obras completas* de Lope de Vega, *publicadas por la Real Acedemia Española*, v. 7 (Madrid, 1897). Cervantes' *La Casa de los celos y selvas de Ardenia* (1615; cf. Wester, pp. 1, 5), does not deal at all with the battle of Roncesvalles. On the romances, cf. Ramón Menéndez Pidal, ed., *Romanceros del Rey Rodrigo y de Bernardo del Carpio* (Madrid: Gredos, 1957).

10. Juan de la Cueva, *La Libertad de España por Bernardo del Carpio*, ed. Anthony Watson (Exeter: Exeter University Press, 1974). For a summary and analysis of this play, see David G. Burton, *The Legend of Bernardo del Carpio from Chronicle to Drama* (Potomac, MD: 1988).

11. Since Iberia includes Portugal, this appelation would seem to imply Castilian sovereignty over Portugal. This would run counter to Anthony Watson's interpretation of the play, which was written in the midst of the succession crisis that was to give the Portuguese throne over to Felipe II of Spain. Watson argues that Cueva was against Philip's claims, and meant Charlemagne's hubris to be a historical lesson to him (cf. Watson, *Juan de la Cueva and the Portuguese Succession* [London: Tamesis, 1971], pp. 81–99).

12. See Brading, *The First America*, 300.

13. Bernardo de Balbuena, *El Bernardo, o victoria de Roncesvalles*, Margaret Kidder, ed. Dissertation: University of Illinois, 1937. A good introduction to *El Bernardo*, and a very good guide to its contents, is John Van Horne, *El Bernardo of Bernardo de Balbuena: A Study of the Poem with Particular Attention to Its Relations to the Epics of Boiardo and Ariosto and to Its Significance in the Spanish Renaissance*. Illinois: University of Illinois Studies in Language and Literature 12.1 (1927).

14. Ferragut is a common figure in the French *chansons de geste*; he also appears in the Pseudo-Turpin, chap. 17 (Klein, 72–83).

15. This magician Tlascala seems to be Balbuena's invention. He is the eponymous representation of the Tlaxcala, who had (before the Spanish conquest) been in a constant state of warfare with the Aztecs, according to Fray Toribio de Motolinía, a Franciscan missionary to the Tlaxcala. Cf. his *Historia de los Indios de la Nueva España* (1541; ed. Mexico City, 1941), pp. 50–51, 76–77. Thanks to Anthony M. Stevens-Arroyo for bringing Motolinía's text to my attention.

16. The one brief mention of Marsilio is at 23: 19–21. Later, in further describing the battle, Balbuena says, "Dico, y contra Turpin, . . ." (24: 201). He also mentions Turpin as a source at 3: 190.

17. Bernardo de Balbuena is by no means the last author to rewrite the legend of Bernardo del Carpio; cf. Heinermann, chapter 3, "Weitere Bearbeitungen der Sage (Überblick)," pp. 28–30. The most recent work on Bernardo that I have found is a verse play by Obdulio Barrera Arango entitled *El Juramento: Poema de Bernardo*, published in the series *Poemas patrióticos* (Madrid, 1962). John Finnamore, an Australian playwright, wrote *Carpio: A Tragedy in Five Acts* (Melbourne, 1875), which, however, does not deal with Roncesvalles.

Works Cited

Barrera Arango, Obdulio. *El Juramento: poema de Bernardo*, published in the series *Poemas patrióticos*. Madrid, 1962.

Balbuena, Bernardo de. *El Bernardo, o victoria de Roncesvalles.* Ed. Margaret Kidder. Dissertation: University of Illinois, 1937.

———. *Grandeza mexicana.* Ed. Luis Adolfo Domínguez. Mexico City: Editorial Porrua, 1971.

Brading, David. *The First America: The Spanish Monarchy, Creole Patriots, and the Liberal State, 1492–1867.* Cambridge: Cambridge University Press, 1991.

Buridant, Claude, ed. *La traduction du Pseudo-Turpin du manuscrit Vatican Regina 624.* Geneva: Droz, 1976.

Burton, David G. *The Legend of Bernardo del Carpio from Chronicle to Drama.* Potomac, MD: Scripta Humanistice, 1988.

Elliot, J. H. *Spain and Its World: 1500–1700.* New Haven, CT: Yale University Press, 1989.

Finnamore, John. *Carpio: A Tragedy in Five Acts.* Melbourne, 1875.

Frona Wester, Liliana. *The Cycle of Bernardo del Carpio Plays* (Master's Thesis, University of Chicago, 1923).

Heinermann, Theodor. *Untersuchungen zur Entstehung der Sage von Bernardo del Carpio, Habilitationsschrift der philosophischen und naturwissenschaftlichen.* Halle (Saale): Fakultät der Universität Münster, 1927.

Kidder, Margaret, ed. *El Bernardo, o victoria de Roncesvalles.* Dissertation. University of Illinois, 1937.

Klein, Hans-Wilhelm , ed. *Die Chronik von Karl dem Grossen und Roland: Der lateinische Pseudo-Turpin in den Handschriften aus Aachen und Andernach.* Munich: Wilhelm Fink, 1986.

La Cueva, Juan de. *La Libertad de España por Bernardo del Carpio.* Ed. Anthony Watson. Exeter: Exeter University Press, 1974.

Le Gentil, Pierre, ed. *La Chanson de Roland.* Paris: Hatier, 1967.

Menéndez Pidal, Ramón. *Romanceros del Rey Rodrigo y de Bernardo del Carpio.* Madrid: Gredos, 1957.

Moignet, George, ed. *La Chanson de Roland.* Paris: Bordas, 1969.

Motolinía, Fray Toribio de. *Historia de los indios de la Nueva España.* 1541; ed. Mexico City, 1941.

Salazar, Fray Juan de. *Política española.* Ed. Miguel Herrero García. Madrid: Instituto de Estudios Políticos, 1945.

Short, Ian, ed. *The Anglo-Norman Pseudo-Turpin of William de Briane.* Oxford: Blackwell, 1973.

Van Horne, John. *El Bernardo of Bernardo de Balbuena: A Study of the Poem with Particular Attention to Its Relations to the Epics of Boiardo and Ariosto and to Its Significance in the Spanish Renaissance.* University of Illinois Studies in Language and Literature 12.1 (1927).

Vega, Lope Félix de. *El Casamiento en la Muerte. Obras completas* v. 7. Madrid: La Real Acedemia Española, 1897.

Walpole, Ronald N., ed. *An Anonymous Old French Translation of the Pseudo-Turpin Chronicle: A Critical Edition of the Text Contained in Bibliothèque Nationale MSS fr. 2137 and 17203 and Incorporated by Philippe Mouskés in his Chronique rimée.* Cambridge, MA: Harvard University Press, 1979.

Watson, Anthony. *Juan de la Cueva and the Portuguese Succession.* London: Tamesis, 1971.

2

America Is in Spain:
A Reading of Clarín's "Boroña"

JAMES D. FERNÁNDEZ

I

The contemporary Spanish novelist, Juan Goytisolo, begins his two-volume autobiography, published in 1985 and 1986, with a juxtaposition of two stories of origins, or beginnings: two genealogies. We see his father busily tracing, framing, and proudly displaying an invented coat of arms—irrefutable proof of the noble ancestry of this exemplary stock of the Catalonian bourgeoisie. But in these opening pages we also witness the adolescent Juan, the future novelist and autobiographer, stumbling across a bundle of crumbling family papers: letters from and about his paternal great-grandfather who had immigrated to Cuba and become a wealthy slave-holding businessman in the sugar-cane industry. The effect of this discovery on the youth is immediate and profound: "the family myth, carefully nourished by my father, vanished forever after the naked revelations of a world of abuse and robbery, outrages masked by pious phrases, unspeakable excesses and violence" (Goytisolo, 11).

I present this anecdote as an emblem, for it seems that time after time, if we look beyond the flashy pedigree and do honest work in the archive, we find America in Spain. I mean not only the blood and sweat, the money and products of the Americas—though they, of course, abound in Spain in its monuments, its banks, its diet, and in its very culture and infrastructure. But we can also find America, or competing conceptions of America, in virtually every reflection on the Spanish nation. The elaboration of a national identity is, I would argue, one of the principal tasks modern Spanish writers and intellectuals have set for themselves, and any such elaboration must inevitably come to terms with Spain's relationship to the New World.

Unfortunately, these ties are often ignored, and when studies of this relationship are undertaken in Spain, they are often hindered by buying into what we might call a bitter master narrative of "Imperio/Desastre." I might add that on the Latin American side, an equally impoverishing and facile *grand récit* of "Dominación/Independencia" has at times been an obstacle to the serious study of the complex relationship between the Americas and Spain. My current long-term project focuses on a series of issues and texts from late nineteenth- and early twentieth-century letters that explore America as a presence in Spain. The project aims to challenge the boundaries set up between Peninsular and Latin American studies, as well as to eschew the conventional categories and attitudes that too often circumscribe the discourses of those disciplines. A central section of this project will be dedicated to a corpus of texts from Spain and Latin America centered on the figure of the *indiano,* the Spaniard who emigrates to the New World and later returns to Spain.[1] In this chapter, I offer a reading of one of the texts of that corpus, Clarín's short story, "Boroña," from *Moral Tales* (see Leopoldo Alas). But first I would like to preface that reading with a brief exploration of some other possible meanings of my title.

II

"America Is in Spain": the phrase, or one more or less identical to it, comes up frequently in Modern Spain. In the 1740s, for instance, Benito Jerómino Feijoo, a Benedictine monk and the outstanding figure of Spain's halfhearted Enlightenment, would write, "We Spaniards are the Indians of the rest of Europe" (in Stiffoni, 103). He was referring, in part, to the results of the *leyenda negra,* and the infamy Spain had earned as the bloodiest and cruelest of nations. But he was also probably alluding to a paradox that has haunted Spaniards to this day. The American experience was what made the nation into the empire it had become in its Golden Age; but it is also true that Spain's dependence on the shipments of precious metals from the Americas had irreversibly stunted the country's development and modernization. Spain's past grandeur could be attributed to Columbus and his followers, but so could its present "backwardness" and its uncertain future; this much was abundantly clear to an enlightened thinker like Feijoo.[2] "The gold from the Indies," he writes, "has made us poor" (Stiffoni, 103). In another text, in a typically enlightened fashion, he opposes productivity to accumulation, dynamic modern wealth to stagnant mercantilism: "the glory of inventors is incomparably greater than the glory of conquistadores" (108).

A second, not unrelated, example: the phrase, in its identical form, "América está en España", appears towards the end of a popular book published in 1874 with a far from ambiguous title: "No vengáis a América". "Don't come to America," the book advises, "because here you will hear nothing but insults to your homeland and your person. Every day they will remind you that the sun, the air and the land do not belong to you here" (Llanos, 419). The book accumulates newspaper clippings and personal anecdotes related to the alleged lack of hospitality and opportunity for Spaniards in the New World. The project behind the book is as explicit as its title: to stem the flow of immigrants to the Americas. "Spain needs to regather her forces that have been too far-flung" (422). The solution proposed by the book is also quite straightforward: "If you are children of the south, and you feel like emigrating, emigrate to the north; if you are from the north, emigrate to the south" (423). After all, the author of this tract concludes, "America is in Spain" (423).

An almost identical point is made in "A las Indias", an early short story by José María de Pereda. The tale, which recounts the painful separation of a young emigrant from his mother and father, begins and ends with a brutal little song: "A las Indias van los hombres/a las Indias por ganar/las Indias aquí las tienen/si quisieran trabajar" (The men go off to the Indies; they go off to the Indies to get rich; the Indies, they have them right here/if they just wanted to work) (Pereda, 175, 184).

This kind of domestic, isolationist critique of the discovery, conquest, and resulting emigration—a critique that, significantly, does not depend on any defense of indigenous populations—was not peculiar to Spain. The essayist who won the French Academy's competition of 1792, on the topic of the influence of America on Europe, would remark, "If those Europeans who devoted their lives to developing the resources of America had instead been employed in Europe in clearing forests, and building roads, bridges and canals, would not Europe have found in its own bosom the most important objects that it derives from the other world?" (in Elliot 1970, 2). The repudiation of the American experience was not peculiar to Spain, though it apparently was felt there with exceptional force. It seems to reach peak intensity there in the second half of the nineteenth century: the very moment when Spain was losing its grip on its last overseas colonies, the remnants of empire, and when the brutal injustices of oligarchy and *caciquismo* were forcing hundreds of thousands of Spaniards to seek a better life in the former colonies.

III

In the countless little towns and villages that dot the green hills and valleys of Spain's northern coastal regions, two buildings often compete for the visitor's attention: the once stately mansion of the local noble family and the ostentatious *palacio* of the successful indiano, the local youth who emigrated, accumulated wealth in the New World, and returned to his native village. Indianos made their appearance as a social category almost as soon as Columbus returned from his first voyage. In the works of Lope de Vega, we can already see stereotypes of indianos, displaying their taste for the exotic and the grandiose and trying consciously to rival—architectonically and otherwise—the local aristocracy. The prominence of the indiano's house does in fact reflect the prominence that he himself earned in the social imagination of rural Spain. Late nineteenth-century critics of emigration might even compare the indiano's palace to some kind of malevolent lighthouse that steers local youth away from the home shores and toward that fickle land of promise, las Indias. If, during Spain's uneven, hesitant entry into the modern world of the nineteenth century, the aristocratic mansion was a sign of an unchanging, hierarchical social organization, the indiano's palace, and the indiano himself, came to be one of Spain's few images of social mobility.[3]

This prominence is reflected in Spanish fiction of the second half of the nineteenth century as well. Many of Spain's most important authors portrayed indianos in their novels and short stories, and often in key roles. The character also figures in a good deal of minor texts, such as *costumbrista* vignettes and forgotten works of theater. I would like to argue, however, that far from being just another stock figure in that *galería de tipos* available to the nineteenth-century novelist or playwright, the indiano is often an extraordinarily charged figure, through which

Spain's problematic relationship to the New World, or to modernity, for that matter, may be explored. The situation most frequently represented in the corpus of texts I have gathered is the return of the indiano to Spain, and his virtually always unsuccessful attempt to reinsert himself into life on the peninsula.

This process of reinsertion is almost invariably portrayed as a kind of transaction in a real and/or symbolic economy of prestige, desire and capital; in countless texts, marriage is the deal that will condition or characterize the indiano's reinsertion. One of the most frequent plots goes like this: the indiano, who returns with wealth but without lineage, seeks an alliance—literally a marriage—with a proud but impoverished aristocracy, which has lineage but, alas, no wealth. This portrayal is particularly common following the Bourbon restoration of 1874; after the peasant and proletarian uprisings of 1873 precipitated the crushing of the first Republic, Spain's ruling classes attempted to set up a kind of ersatz *ancien régime*. Wealthy returnees often sought a stable, comfortable place within that social hierarchy. Clarín, in his novel *La Regenta*, a masterly portrayal of a provincial city in Asturias during the first years of the Restoration, represents a whole cast of indianos in this context. During their years in the Americas, we learn from the narrator, these characters led laborious, libertine, irreligious lives; but upon returning to Spain with considerable wealth, they quickly and cynically sought alliances with the principal institutions of the Restoration: the aristocracy and the church. Religion is the only hope against socialism, they claim.

The collusions or alliances between aristocrats and indianos were probably more common in the underdeveloped regions of Galicia, Asturias, and Cantabria than they were in a more developed region like Cataluña. In the 1820s, for example, when most Latin American nations had gained their independence, *catalanes* returning to Spain with considerable American capital found a relatively thriving industrial economy already in place in which to safely invest their money. There, the American capital was a considerable force in modernization, particularly in the textile industry. But along the northern Cantabrian coast, where there was little or no industry to speak of, indianos returning with capital tended either to squander their money on their palatial homes or to use it to acquire more and more land. Some even bought titles of nobility and, like Goytisolo's father, fashioned coats-of-arms for themselves. Many of the returning indianos did become old-style philanthropists, founding or improving hospitals or schools, setting up orphanages or soup kitchens. Still, these enterprising men who had accumulated fortunes in the commercial and/or agricultural economies of the New World colonies or republics, generally returned to Spain in order to retire. Their money remained inactive as well.[4]

Claríns indiano tale "Boroña" first appeared in 1895 in a collection of short stories entitled *Cuentos morales* (*Moral Tales*).[5] Our indiano, like many indianos represented in the literature, indeed, like many protagonists of tales of innocence and experience, has two names. When he left his village he was Pepe Francisca, a name that bespeaks his extraordinary relationship to his mother, Pepa Francisca; when he returns to his hometown after thirty lucrative years in Mexico, he has become Don José Gómez y Suárez.

As the story opens, he descends from a coach and stands in a dusty road, which had been built during his absence, surrounded by four huge trunks (which hold don José's acquisitions) and an old, beat-up suitcase (a relic from Pepe's departure). He decides to pause and take in the sights before calling out to his sister and her family, so that they might come down to the road and help him with his luggage. During this hesitation, the narrator fills the reader in on the indiano's history: he left as a young boy, because he had to—it was either that or become a priest. He eventually became a successful businessman in Mexico but longed the whole time to return home, and, particularly, to return to his mother. His family urged him to stay in Mexico, though, and earn more money. Finally, his worst nightmare came true: his mother passed away while he was still in Mexico. Soon after, he himself fell ill.

He finally returns home, still sick, with nothing but disdain for the gold he carries in his trunks. He longs not for gold, but rather for "something else yellow" (Clarín, 32), *boroña*, the Asturian word for borona, a type of cornbread. The narrator tells us that during the indiano's years away from home and his travels through Mexico, France, England, and the United States, the memory and anticipation of eating boroña, "the bread of his infancy" (33), comes to symbolize the entire vague, complex, and ultimately ineffable object of the indiano's desire/nostalgia. The Spanish language has a cliché, much invoked throughout the nineteenth century, to refer to the emigrant's experience: "el amargo pan de la emigración" (the bitter bread of the emigrant). It is somehow fitting, then, that the indiano's hopes of returning home are focused on boroña, "el dulce pan del regreso" we might call it.[6] Don José, however, becomes even more ill after arriving home and is unable to partake of the boroña—he is even nauseated by its taste. Nonetheless, he asks for a piece of it each day, so that he might look at it. In a poignant juxtaposition, we watch the indiano drag himself around the house, literally sniffing out memories—"olfateando memorias"—among the barnyard animals, while his brother-in-law and nephews prowl around the locked trunks. The indiano finally gives up and hands the keys over to his relatives; he dies soon after, delirious, still unable to eat the boroña, crumbling a piece of it in his hands and calling out for his mother, while his relatives rummage through and fight over the contents of the trunks.

In a more or less contemporary text, Eusebio Blasco, a Spaniard who had been living in Paris, would describe his return to Madrid in the following terms:

> The strength of [Madrid's] local color is in a relation of inverse proportion to its progress. But does that really matter in the case of the patria? Was there ever a defective mother? . . . If in Spain people were to do what is done in other countries, this simply would not be Spain anymore. . . . Suppress the smell of olive-oil in the stairwells of a Madrid household . . . and there is no Madrid left. And sounds and smells, and music and scents constitute nationality, which emanates and penetrates in waves of smells, and that makes us shiver with pleasure upon returning to the maternal home. (Blasco, 113–14)

I cite this somewhat lengthy passage because in it, Blasco seems to be privileging the same elements as Clarín's indiano: for both, true (national, regional, and/or personal) identity is associated with the figure of the mother as well as with certain sensations—sounds and smells, in particular. What might these elements have in common?

The linking of the maternal figure, that goddess of the hearth and home, with authenticity or identity is an interesting by-product of the nineteenth century's rigid codification of gender roles: public man and private woman. As Bridget Aldaraca has written, "a perception of the public world as materialistic and threatening provokes in turn an idealization of the supposedly isolated sphere of female domesticity as a timeless, stable refuge, outside the turbulent flow of history" (Aldaraca, 62). In innumerable texts in the nineteenth century we will see the mother and the childhood home—very often the rural childhood home—erected as the space of authenticity. The father, by the way, is frequently the agent who provokes the child's expulsion from the domestic idyll; it is as if the father, a promotor of socialization, were to force the transformation of Pepe Francisca into don José Gómez y Suárez.

The sounds Eusebio Blasco invests with meaning—with the aura of identity—are the shouts and curses of Madrid's *aguadores*, the loud haggling and *pregones* of an urban economy not yet fully modernized. Sounds, that is, soon to be stifled thanks to indoor plumbing, enclosed markets, and silent price tags. In the case of Clarín's text, I would argue that the sound imbued with authenticity is the sound of the Asturian language, condensed into a few precious words, among them, of course, that talisman, *boroña*. The original text is careful to italicize these words, to set them off from the rest of the narration. A recent English version of this story is titled, sensibly enough, "Cornbread," but to paraphrase Robert Frost, identity is what gets lost in translation. The word *boroña* and the several other Asturian words are, I would argue, an essential part of that complex network of sensations the indiano hopes to recover upon returning home. During the process of centralization and modernization in nineteenth-century Spain, the peninsula's regional languages—particularly *el asturiano* (or *bable*) and *el gallego*—came increasingly to be seen as languages or dialects inextricably tied to an agrarian, premodern culture and, thus, destined to be obliterated by modernity's homogenizing force. *Gallego* and *asturiano* were often extolled for their "quaintness" and "musicality" but generally considered unfit for anything other than rural home talk, or, particularly in the case of gallego, nostalgic, sentimental lyric poetry. Even the most ardent *bablistas* and *galeguistas* were wont to conduct their "business"—to write their essays and to deliver their speeches—in Castilian.

The privileging of the senses of taste and smell is, in both Clarín and Blasco, undoubtedly related to the uncanny capacity of those senses to evoke striking memories. The protagonist of "Boroña", with his longing to inhale "el aire natal", and to recover childhood memories (or perhaps childhood itself) from household scents (and from the taste and aroma of boroña), clearly privileges olfaction in this way. Obviously, the appreciation of an aroma and that aroma's evocative power depend on difference; that is to say, one can be moved by a scent only after one has been distanced from the smell—spatially or temporally—and later reencounters it. The smell of a mother's lap, of a stable, the aroma and taste of boroña, or, for that matter, the "mellifluous" sounds and "gentle" inflections of a dialect are not—they cannot be—powerfully evocative for the people who live daily among them. Thus, the privileging of olfaction, like the privileging of maternity and of nostalgia-producing sounds, can also be inscribed within this tendency to constitute certain people and sensations as modernity's "others." As Alain Corbin has described in his book, *The Foul and the Fragrant: Odor and the French Social Imagination*, the elimination of odors in public spaces and in human dwellings was one of the primary aims of many eighteenth- and nineteenth-century hygienic reforms. It was precisely this deodorization, according to Corbin, that made possible the emergence of a "mystique" for the sense of smell. Eusebio Blasco seems to have these kinds of modernizing reforms in mind when he speaks of the suppression of odors as a threat to (national) identity.

In other words, in both Clarín and Blasco, not just any sensations or beings are constituted as the loci of authenticity but, rather, only those that can be perceived as holdouts or refuges from modernization; the "private" mother, isolated from the "turbulent flow" of business, socialization, and modernity, as well as sounds and smells that will eventually be suppressed by a more rationally planned and better ventilated architecture (Blasco), or by the abandonment of traditional ways of life based on dairy farming (Clarín). Both Blasco and Clarín's character are able to perceive Spain's (or Asturias's) characteristic *difference*—a difference founded on relative "backwardness"—and to invest it with the essence of identity, authenticity, only after they return home from their sojourns to the Modern.

IV

"Boroña" not only narrates a journey to the supposedly "premodern," it also mobilizes a series of images that cast the return of the indiano as a kind of arrival—an arrival to an apparently idyllic New World. The opening paragraphs describe what seems to be an untainted Nature, a "small, picturesque glade" of velvety green grass gently caressed by a "sweet breeze" (30). In an expression that immediately calls to mind the "encounter" between European explorers and native Americans, we are told that for the disillusioned indiano, the gold he carries back from the Americas to Spain is worthless: "in his eyes, those riches were no more than glass beads" (como cuentas de vidrio) (33). The indiano hopes to use this bait in exchange for some care, affection, and boroña. His relatives, on the other side of the transaction, are described as "salvajes" (33ff.) on more than one occasion, and are more than willing to give up the "whole harvest of boroña in exchange for the treasures held in the trunks" (34). However, the most important element in this geographical inversion (return to Spain = arrival to a New World of sorts), is the fact that the product, which for the indiano comes to encode absolute authenticity, autochthony, or identity, is made from corn—an American crop. I will return to this kernel shortly.

When, in the eighteenth century, Feijoo wished to defend the intellectual capacity of native Americans, he brought up the issue of the indians trading gold for glass beads. According to Feijoo, far from being evidence of the natives' stupidity, this kind of transaction simply demonstrates a difference in supply and demand between the European and the American economies. In America, gold abounded and glass did not exist; ergo, the kinds of trades made by the native Americans.[7] Two separate economies, which had developed independently, now entered into contact for the first time. It seems then, that this model is not altogether appropriate to describe the encounter between Clarín's indiano and the villagers, since here the two economies, rather than being independent, are locked in a kind of tragic, mirror relationship of difference. The indiano values, indeed he founds identity, precisely on those things either unappreciated or totally disdained by the relatives in the village, who long for another kind of life. The origin of this longing, ironically enough, can be traced to the phenomenon of the indiano, his prestige as traveler, self-made man, a problematic figure of mobility, of modernity.

In other words, Clarín's indiano is doomed to fail for two reasons. First, his travels have made it impossible for him to reexperience innocent identity; they have made him aware of difference. This dilemma is quite similar to what Carlos Alonso, in another context, has described as the "exoticism of the autochthonous": "The very *desire* for an autochthonous expression [or, in this case, for a return to "simple village life"] becomes the guarantee that that desire will never be fulfilled, since the nature of the concept [autochthony, or the simple village life] precludes the possibility of its ever becoming an object of desire" (Alonso, 3; my emphasis).

But more importantly, it is the very presence of the indiano as a prominent figure of social mobility in the minds of the peasants that has irrevocably transformed the small village don José once nostalgically invested with the aura of identity. In a certain sense, Clarín's indiano repeats, albeit in a different mode, the same error lamented by Feijoo and Pereda, the error that made emigration necessary to begin with; that is to say, the indiano would like to keep America, conceived of as a place of work and ambition, Modernity and Desire, separate from Spain, conceived of as a place of identity, autochthony, Presence. But America, alas, has come to form part of the national fabric, part of the collective imagination of these far-from-innocent villagers. In fact, the story demonstrates that America has "always" been there, despite the tricks that nostalgia plays on the indiano. "America," we must remember, is what expelled the indiano from the village in the first place. America, like corn, like the phenomenon of emigration itself and the figure of the indiano, has worked its way into autochthony.

The indiano's inability to eat boroña comes to seem like a kind of curse. We might think of it as a peculiar version of the curse of Midas. Everyone he touches, or everyone who is touched by the vision of his trunks—or, in other cases, the vision of his palace—is awakened to desire. Desire is what is conventionally banned from the pastoral, and yet "el aire natal" of the village has become an inaccessible object of desire for the indiano; and what is worse, the villagers have become subjects of desire, yearning for "something else." America is in Spain. This is what don José, literally and figuratively, cannot stomach.

Notes

1. The article written by Guadalupe Gómez-Ferrer Morant (see the works cited) has been very helpful for the constitution of the corpus.

2. This kind of repudiation of the Discovery and Conquest would become a commonplace of Spanish liberal historiography throughout the nineteenth and twentieth centuries. Curiously, similar opinions were being voiced as early as 1600. As J. H. Elliot pointed out:

> This growing realization of the burdens of empire was sharpened by the intense awareness of the misery of Castile. The Castile of Philip III and Philip IV went through a period of deep soul searching, accompanied by many anxious attempts to identify and analyze the causes of distress. It seemed an extraordinary paradox that Castile, the head of a great empire, should be poverty stricken, that it should be so rich and yet so poor. González de Cellorigo, analyzing in 1600 the troubles of Castile, traced at least some of them back to the psychological effects of the discovery of the Indies. In his view, the effect of an apparently endless flow of American silver into Seville had created a false sense of wealth as consisting of gold and silver, whereas true wealth lay in productive investment and the development of industry, agriculture, and trade. If this was so, the discovery of America could even be considered as prejudicial to Spain, because it had diverted the country's attention away from the real sources of prosperity and dazzled it with the mirage of false riches. . . . The Flemish scholar Justus Lipsius wrote to a Spanish friend in 1603: "Conquered by you, the New World has conquered you in turn, and has weakened and exhausted your ancient vigour." (Elliot 1989, 25)

3. George Mariscal, speaking of the sixteenth century, has noted how "the emergence of new groups of people—indios, indianos, mestizos, criollos, and others who were made visible through the contact with America—sufficiently problematized the idea of the social body so that the frontiers marking cultural inclusion or exclusion had to be radically realigned" (Mariscal, 94). The "mystique" of the indiano and his frequent association with the uncontrollable forces of anarchy or barbarity demonstrate, I think, that the "otherness" Mariscal describes lasted for several centuries.

4. For more detailed information on these and other aspects of the indiano, see *Indianos* (listed in the works cited).

5. The collection has recently been translated into English by K. Stackhouse. I quote from this translation, making minor revisions when necessary, and adding the original Spanish as needed.

6. See, for example, "Un cacho de vida privada y un mendrugo del pan de la emigración" in Flores, p. 148.

7. "Es discurrir groseramente hacer bajo concepto de la capacidad de los indios, porque al principio daban pedazos de oro por cuentas de vidrio. Más rudo es que ellos, quien por esto los juzga rudos. Si se mira con prevención, más hermoso es el vidrio que el oro; y en lo que se busca para ostentación y adorno, en igualdad de hermosura siempre se prefiere lo más raro. No hacían, pues, en esto los americanos otra cosa, que lo que hace todo el mundo. Tenían oro y no vidrio; por esto, era entre ellos, y con razón, más digna alhaja de una princesa un pequeño collar de cuentas de vidrio, que una gran cadena de oro" (Feijoo, 188).

Works Cited

Alas, Leopoldo ("Clarín"). *Moral Tales*. Trans. K. Stackhouse. Fairfax, VA: George Mason University Press, [1895] 1988.

Aldaraca, Bridget. "El ángel del hogar: The Cult of Domesticity in Nineteenth-Century Spain." In *Theory and Practice of Feminist Literary Criticism*, ed. G. Mora and K. S. Van Hooft, pp. 62–87. Ypsilanti, MI: Bilingual Press, 1982.

Alonso, Carlos. *The Spanish American Regional Novel: Modernity and Autochthony*. Cambridge: Cambridge University Press, 1990.

Blasco, Eusebio. *Recuerdos: notas íntimas de Francia y España*. Madrid: Fernando Fé, 1894.

Corbin, Alain. *The Foul and the Fragrant: Odor and the French Social Imagination*. Cambridge: Harvard University Press, 1986.

Elliot, J. H. *The Old World and the New: 1492–1650*. Cambridge: Cambridge University Press, 1970.

———. *Spain and Its World: 1500–1700*. New Haven, CT: Yale University Press, 1989.

Feijoo, B. J. *Teatro crítico universal*. Madrid: Castalia, 1986.

Flores, Antonio. *La sociedad de 1850*. Madrid: Alianza, 1968.

Gómez-Ferrer Morant, G. "El indiano en la novela realista". *Nueva Revista de Filología Hispánica* 466 (1989): 25–49.

Goytisolo, Juan. *Coto vedado*. Barcelona: Seix Barral, 1985.

Indianos. Cuadernos del Norte. Número Monográfico. No. 2. (no date) Oviedo: Caja de Ahorros.

Llanos y Alcaraz, A. *No vengáis a América*. Santander: J. Martínez, [1874] 1916.

Mariscal, George. "Persiles and the Remaking of Spanish Culture." *Cervantes* X 1 (1990): 93–102.

Pereda, José María de. "A las indias". In *Obras completas*, vol. 1. Madrid: Aguilar, 1990, pp. 175–85.

Stifonni, Giovanni. "Il tema americano como momento della politica culturale del *Teatro Crítico* di Feijoo". *Studi di Letteratura Ispano-Americana* 15–16 (1983): 89–108.

3

Valle-Inclán's Bradomín and Montenegro and the Problem of Hispanic Caciquismo

VIRGINIA GIBBS

Ramón del Valle-Inclán was one of those Hispanic authors who moved throughout the entire Spanish-speaking world, both physically and intellectually. All but his very earliest of works were written after he had travelled from his native Galicia to live both in Mexico and Madrid, and in his languages and images the influence of both Spain and America can be perceived. One of his later and most well-known works, *Tirano Banderas* (1925), provides us with the grotesque portrayal of a Latin American *cacique*, and it has been assumed that Valle's inspiration for this tale came from his experiences in Mexico. There is no doubt that this is largely true, but Latin America was by no means the only source of his concern with the figure of his Hispanic tyrant. Critics have often overlooked that the Restoration period in Spain, which saw the beginning of Don Ramón's maturation as a writer, was itself characterized by widespread caciquismo. Indeed, a rereading of the *Sonatas* (1902–1905) and the *Comedias bárbaras* (1907–1908, 1922) will show us that the power structure of caciquismo arises in a wide range of contexts throughout Valle's work from the beginning and that he viewed the problem of caciquismo as transhispanic or, in other words, inherent to both Peninsular Spain and Latin America.

Xavier, Marqués de Bradomín, the aristocratic seducer who protagonizes Ramón del Valle-Inclán's *Sonatas*, and his fictional uncle, Don Manuel Montenegro, the despotic Galician hidalgo of the *Comedias bárbaras*, represent two figures from Spain's feudal past. At face value, they seem to have little to do with Spanish society of the early 1900s, when they were created by Valle and first appeared in published works. Because of his interest in such figures from bygone days, it has generally been assumed that Don Ramón was, at least in the early years of his writing career, turning his back on the realities of Restoration Spain. And, because of his seeming glorification of Bradomín and Montenegro, it is also widely believed that his work prior to the *esperpentos* represents both a nostalgia for the closed hierarchy of the *ancien régime* and an aristocratic detachment from mundane reality and the problems of common folk.[1] It is my contention, however, that these two figures as well as others, their situation, and their actions, have a great deal to do with a major problem in Spanish *fin-de-siglo* society, a problem that proceeds from the nation's sociopolitical reality and is of widespread concern among the politicians and intellectuals who deal with Spain's difficult material and social situation. The name for this problem is *caciquismo*,[2] which is, in a sense, a rekindling of just those autocratic social relations that gave birth to Spain's Bradomíns and Montenegros.[3]

In order to explore, then, the connections that exist between Don Ramón's aristocratic Xavier Bradomín and his tyrannical Montenegro, and Restoration politics, we must first describe the nature of the Restoration cacique. The *sistema de turno*—a coordinated and institutionalized sharing of power among several sectors of the oligarchy—afforded the nation a period of relative stability for those decades just prior to and following the beginning of the twentieth century. This system was based fundamentally on a methodical and rigid control of political institutions and events. Cánovas del Castillo was the prime architect of this power structure, which Robert Kern describes in detail in his *Liberals, Reformers and Caciques in Restoration Spain 1875–1907*. Kern explains how Cánovas's early efforts to consolidate power following the Constitution of 1876 involved the placing at all levels of government of officials loyal to his cabinet (50). He thus developed close ties with these local officials who were, in turn, controlled by the central administration. By the year 1882, this caciquismo had become a national phenomenon, succinctly described by Kern in the following terms: "It was a sociopolitical system, dependent on the extreme forms of patronage dispensed by a diffuse local oligarchy, and useful as a means of reducing intraclass friction through the use of the cabinet apparatus as a control device" (Kern, 17).

As has usually if not always been the case in regimes based on influence peddling and favor seeking, this patronage system of government was rife with corruption and abuses: "No previous period had ever experienced the amount of boss rule, systematic corruption, and destruction of local government produced by the Restoration" (26). There were several types of individuals who played key roles in the edifice of caciquismo. At the top were, of course, the members of the central oligarchy. These were the supreme bosses of the *partidos turnantes*, that is, the conservative and the liberal parties who, through election fraud, handed power back and forth in an outward display of democratic pluralism. These men of the central oligarchy were the wealthy, the well-educated Cánovas, Mauro, Silva, Castelar, and others. Below them were the provincial party leaders and the network of local caciques from villages all over the nation. Kern dramatically summarizes the wide-ranging effect these caciques had on society in general:

> Civil governors, provincial assemblymen, municipal judges, or council members who refused to sanction the demands of the caciques would be unceremoniously removed. Worst of all, the electoral process lost all meaning as a test of public opinion, and, victories were dictated so frequently that corruption became a matter of course. In this way, caciquismo escaped from the confines of political affairs into other aspect of society. "Railways are constructed wherever the cacique desires. Excise officers wait upon the 'boss' daily for his commands. Honest men are condemned and criminals are acquitted. In examinations, the lowest pass may win the post, and even assistants to university professors sometimes owe their appointment to the caciques." Nothing was left untouched. (51)[4]

These negative aspects of caciquismo, far from being a problem of which we are only now and in retrospect aware, were a major concern to the era's intellectuals. The cacique system effectively removed most political control from the middle class to which belonged the majority of writers, journalists, professors, and other producers of discourses critical of the regime. These individuals were loud and long in their condemnation of the cacique system. Baroja, for example, speaks of the Restoration as "an oligarchy of politicians who view the state as little more than their own private property" (Comellas, 541), and he describes it in some detail in his *Arbol de ciencia*:

Alcolea had become used to the Mochuelos [conservatives] and the ratones [liberals], and he considered them a necessary evil. Those bandits were the pillars of society; they distributed the booty; they each felt for the other a special taboo, like the one that exists among the Polinesians. (169)

Historians have been quick to recognize that the figure of the cacique was not an isolated, new phenomenon, but was closely tied to Spain's past social and political structures. Juan Antonio Hormigón tells us that "the reactionary wave of the Restoration, by imposing the cacique, to a certain measure resurrected the nearly extinct figure of the noble *señor*, now lacking in his mythical charisma and solely dependent upon money and violence as the bases of his power" (Hormigón, 57–58). Luís Granjel, in a similar vein, describes the cacique as "reincarnation in caricature, but no less efficient a figure, of the feudal lord" (Granjel, 74).

Here, then, we begin to see a clear relationship between Valle's early aristocratic protagonists and the deep concern of his contemporaries with boss rule. As a result of the publicly recognized and rampant corruption of the cacique system, most sectors of society had lost confidence in the oligarchy as ruling body. In the eyes of the Spanish people, the widespread ill repute of a Restoration hierarchy with roots in the historical aristocracy cast long shadows of doubt over this traditional elite as well. Turn-of-the-century Spain thus suffers a public and intellectual crisis in the concept of authority. Both the historical and current moral legitimacy of the old aristocracy and the old-new oligarchy became suspect. Interestingly enough, it was precisely at this time that Nietzsche, with his ideas of the superior man and a consciousness beyond good and evil (and what this represents as a justification or explanation of power) became widely read in Spain, as Gonzalo Sobejano has so well documented in his *Nietzsche en España*. I believe that Valle's works enjoy an intimate relation with this concern, generational as it were, with the figures of existing oligarchic or aristocratic control. But Valle, instead of directly questioning or exploring the turn-of-the-century cacique, looks to analogous figures from a seemingly mythical past whose actions and character shed light on the Restoration power structure.

The Latin American Tirano Banderas is, therefore, not only the tyrant on Don Ramón's pages who reflects an Hispanic reality we can consider contemporary to Valle's own life. Years before his portrayal of the archetypal Mexican despot, his *Sonatas* and *Comedias bárbaras* present us with the prime examples as perceived by Don Ramón. I also contend that he fully explores two contrasting figures, the first of which is Bradomín, a wandering and aristocratic but landless Don Juan. Almost simultaneously he delves into the life and soul of the despotic *vinculero* or local autocrat Montenegro, bound to the earth of Galicia and governed by earthy passions.[5] In Valle's fictional microcosm both are, in fact, related figures—nephew and uncle.

We may begin then with the nephew Bradomín and review his escapades as presented in the four *Sonatas*. As the four novels pass from spring to winter, so the Marqués passes from youth to old age. At each stage his major concern is the seduction of a woman, and the dénouement of each Sonata involves tragedy for the woman. In *Primavera*, María Rosario, soon-to-be-novice, finally succumbs to Bradomín's amorous advances with an attack of nerves that causes the accidental death of her infant sister and her own resulting insanity. In *Verano*, the Niña Chole, already sexually degraded by paternal incest and violence, is used by our Marqués to fulfill his own conquest fantasies. *Otoño*'s Concha, trapped in the decaying world of an ancient aristocracy, herself dies in the act of adulterous love with her blasphemous cousin. And, finally, in *Invierno*, the white-haired Marqués' sensual approach to his own daughter ends in her apparent suicide. When all is said and done, these are not happy tales.

We can describe ways in which the character Bradomín contrasts with the real figure of the cacique. For example Marqués has little interest in the political wheeling and dealing that gives the cacique his very identity. In addition, he is essentially rootless since the Bradomín lands, which once were the heart of this landed aristocracy, are now either gone or undergoing legal disputes. He is a wanderer, but it is in fact this wandering that allows the figure of Bradomín to transverse symbolically key periods in Spanish history: the Renaissance with its extended empire, including Italy (*Primavera*); the discovery and conquest of America (*Estío*); the rural-feudal past (*Otoño*); civil strife and war, particularly the nineteenth-century Carlist crusades (*Invierno*). The four *Sonatas* spread before us vast panoramas of Spain's past through which the aristocratic Bradomín, ancestor of the modern Peninsular or Latin American cacique, moves and acts. At bottom, he shares with the cacique and the Restoration oligarchy key similarities—the destructive use of power, and the victimization of the weak.

In the moral and domestic realm of Valle's fiction (he is related to all his victims except Niña Chole who is already a victim of incest), he acts out the ethical abuses perpetrated nationally under the cacique system of the Restoration. In this manner, Valle-Inclán indirectly but effectively communicates both historical roots and present realities. Furthermore, in *Sonata de Estío* the same character simply takes these abuses to Mexico where Valle portrays Spanish colonization as fertile ground for his autocratic exploitation of the indigenous Niña Chole under the guise of the conquest fantasies. Bradomín's seduction and destruction of women proves to be transcontinental, that is, his aristocratic Don Juanism travels easily from Spain to Mexico.

The classic figure of Don Juan as a seducer is well adapted to this critical task. Don Juan is first so widespread in literature and popular culture as to be archetypical. He is easily recognized by all Spaniards and considered representative of key Spanish traits. Because of this, Valle is by no means the only intellectual of his generation, from Azorín to Unamuno, to revive and examine Don Juan. Since the figure of the seducer is that of the exploiter, that is, that of user and abuser, it is again a figure that matches that lack of productive commitment of the human actors within the cacique system.

Don Juan, the seducer, is also exemplary of the infertility or even demise of his own class, since his corruption (and even destruction) of young women removes them from the normal cycle of reproduction. Bradomín is the barren end of the line of a dynasty and plays an active role in its extinction. Again, as mythic representative of the nation's oligarchy, the Marqués effectively illustrates both the historical roots and present realities of what Don Ramón clearly sees a dissolute national ruling class whose actions are undermining the "national family."[6]

Concomitant in Valle's work with the Don Juan figure of Xavier Bradomín is the more earthy and violent character of Manuel Montenegro, protagonist of the *Comedias bárbaras*, who begin their appearance in 1907 with *Aguila de blasón*. Don Manuel is "a womanizing and despotic *hidalgo*, hospitable and violent, true Swabian king of his estate in Lontañón" (Valle-Inclán 1980, 22). While the *Sonatas* depict Bradomín from youth to old age, Montenegro is never anything but old, being, as he is, a more specific symbol of the nearly extinct rural Galician feudal lord and master. His total control and exercise of physical as well as charismatic power are the driving forces of his portrayal in the *Comedias*. In *Cara de Plata* the plot revolves around his abuse of *fuero* or hereditary privileges granted to peasants by the early Spanish Crown in exchange for their loyalty. Montenegro abuses his power by denying access rights, secured through a fuero, to several groups who need to cross his land, including shepherds, beggars, peddlers, and even a churchman on a mission of mercy. In this manner, Valle vividly highlights Montenegro's abuse of power on the legal and community level. But the misuse of authority is also dramatically portrayed in the domestic and moral realms, again, as we have seen with Bradomín, focusing on the mistreatment of women. In *Cara de Plata*, Montenegro confesses:

> I am the worst of men. No other has ever been so drawn to gambling, wine and women. Satan has always been my master. I cannot cast off my vices. I am consumed by them. I have never responded to other than my own laws for my actions. As a youngster, I killed a man in a card game dispute. I forced a sister to become a nun against her wishes. I have betrayed my wife with a hundred women. This is what I have always been. I do not expect to change! (1980, 137)

While Bradomín, as befits Don Juan, has no offspring other than Maximin whom he destroys, the tyrant Montenegro has six sons, thus allowing Valle to give a new narrative twist to the theme of aristocratic decadence. In the *Comedias*, we are able to see a process in which two generations of despots interact and are compared. Montenegro's sons present us with characters and acts in which the terrible but magnificent power of the *pater familias* has deteriorated. This has, of course, been well documented by a series of critics.[7] In *Aguila de blasón*, Montenegro's passion leads him to force his own *ahijada*, or adopted daughter, into concubinage. The resulting confrontation with an almost mythically drawn saintly wife is larger that life and full of tragic nuances. Valle portrays this same sexual passion in Montenegro's degenerate progeny with an ugly scene in which Don Pedrito turns his dogs on and then rapes the wife of a cuckolded miller.

Montenegro's sons are presented in two different lights. First there is Cara de Plata, the only offspring who seems to share Don Manuel's sense of noblesse oblige. When the patriarch carries off Sabelita, to whom his son, Cara de Plata, has declared his love, he thus produces the closure of the pairing and reproduction of his lineage. Cara de Plata breaks with his father at the end of the *comedia* that bears his name, and in *Aguila de blasón* he opts for the only choice available to an "aristocratic" being such as himself at that juncture in history—he goes to join the Carlist cause. Interestingly enough, it is the Marqués de Bradomín, protagonist of the *Sonatas*, who enters this fictional world and is given credit for Cara de Plata's decision:

> Xavier Bradomín has convinced me that for men like me this is the only possible road in life. The day we cannot take up arms for a king, we will take them up for ourselves and turn to ambushing and robbing in the forest. That will be my brother's end. (1980, 103)

Cara de Plata seems to be headed toward the adventuresome but ultimately rootless existence of his cousin Xavier, as portrayed in the *Sonatas*. His prophetic words concerning the fact of his other brothers represent the second avenue of the terminal generation of Montenegros.

Don Pedrito and his four remaining siblings indeed dedicate themselves to a life of thievery and extortion. All thought of noble obligation gone from their consciences, these Montenegro's descendants look simply to exploit any opportunity for profit or pleasure. Don Pedrito's visit to the mill to collect through hooligan violence the rent that was his father's tradition, signals the decadence and pettiness of this fallen aristocracy. This is a pattern not unlike the development of the cacique system, a veritable extension to petty levels of the self-profit and abuse power of the traditional landed aristocracy. And, lest one think that Montenegro's rejection of his sons signals Valle's belief that the widespread corruption of the Restoration period is due to forces exterior to the traditional oligarchy, we can quote *Aguila de blasón*'s Señor Ginero: "Race of savages, race of despots, race of madmen, you will soon see the end that awaits you, Montenegros!" (1976, 80). This and other similar quotes demonstrate that Don Pedrito and his brothers are not portrayed as the contemporary exceptions to a glorious past—they are the products of this past, "the offshoots of this [evil] blood" (Valle-Inclán 1976, 41).

Finally, I believe a case can be made that Valle was, at the writing particularly of the *Comedias*, aware of some of the ideas of Nietzsche that formed a part of the generational discourse on the character of authority.[8] The Bradomín of the *Sonatas* is indeed an individual who acts as though he believes that moral and social laws were meant for other, more mediocre beings. Montenegro and his offspring directly enunciate such ideas. While Don Manuel affirms "I am the king! . . . I am the lion" (1976, 68), Don Mauro much less magnificently says, "I say whatever I deem best, and if hearing it displeases anyone, they can go some place else" (1976, 75). The results of this living "beyond good and evil" in Valle's works are hardly exemplary, as we have seen, since they lead to the destruction of most female characters and the resulting extinction of families and finally meaningful society. Manuel Montenegro ultimately delivers himself up to the society of the poor in a messianic gesture of sacrifice and rejection of aristocratic privilege in *Romance de lobos,* the last of the *Comedias.* This suggests that Don Ramón felt that the self-absorption of the aristocratic spirit was certainly not the solution to the crisis of political as well as moral leadership in the nation. Therefore, while he superficially may seem to glorify the "superior" individual who makes his own laws,[9] above the world of common society, the results in his works of such actions seem to submit to ironize rather than legitimize Nietzschean thought.

In the end, then, we can affirm that Valle-Inclán's Bradomín and Montenegro are fictional recreations of several aspects of *fin-de-siglo* Spanish dialogue or discourse on the nature of the cacique system. Don Ramón examines the phenomenon in a series of quite different aesthetic options that rarely directly confront or even acknowledge caciquismo but almost constantly allude to it through the portrayal of a wide-ranging network of abusive power extending from the family to the nation. It is necessary to reiterate that while *Tirano Banderas* is considered an exploration of the Latin American cacique, we must also keep in mind that for Valle, caciquismo was hardly a foreign structure but rather one that had permeated the political, social, and economic life of his own region and country during his formative years. Xavier Bradomín, Manuel Montenegro, and Tirano Banderas are just three of the characters created over the years who display facets of what Valle-Inclán seems to have considered a broadly spread and deeply rooted Hispanic idiosyncrasy or attribute. Each male protagonist is connected to history in a unique way, each one represents a different geographical placement, but all share the destructive powers of the autocrat.

The Latin American tyrant, Tirano Banderas, is not, then, simply a unique product of Valle's travels to Mexico. The particularly manipulative and greedy system of hierarchy called "caciquismo" is a concern that surfaces in many different ways throughout Valle-Inclán's prolific career. This was an issue born of the destructive powers of the cacique structure of Spain's Restoration as Valle was able to observe even before commencing his travels. Experiences in Mexico and Madrid only provided more grist for the mill of Don Ramón's interest in portraying the twisted figure of the political or aristocratic despot on both sides of the

Atlantic. As we have seen, critics have been adamant in viewing particularly the early *Sonatas* in sharp contrast to such latter works as *Tirano Banderas*, in which Valle explicitly witnesses to deep political concerns for Spain and the American nations. I believe the opposite to be true. The *Sonatas'* Bradomín and the *Comedias bárbaras'* Montenegro display the peninsular origins of *Tirano Banderas*, one of the Hispanic world's most brilliantly drawn portraits of the tyrant.

Notes

1. A few examples of this widespread viewpoint will suffice. José F. Montesinos writes, in accordance with Ortega y Gasset's earlier 1904 judgment of *Sonatas de estío*, "By fleeing from all reality, totally delivering himself up to dreams, and turning his back on the anguish of daily life, the novelist sets about to 'disnovel' the novel" (Montesinos, 153). Although José Antonio Maravall's sociohistoric approach is in many ways quite the opposite of Montesinos' findings, he says in reference to *La lámpara maravillosa*, "His aesthetic, his philosophy, his politics, are all related to the statci vision of anarchaic society" (233). And concerning Valle's aestheticism, José Gómez Marín affirms that "the aristocrat distances himself from the world and criticizes society from the refuge of his aesthetics. . . . Valle's aristocratic tendencies lead him to the cult of *tradition*, desitory of nobility, a spiritual quality" (Gómez-Marín, 181).

2. The term *cacique* was originally a Taino Arawak word used in Hispaniola to mean *leader* or *chief*. It has spread throughout Latin America and to Spain, to mean a type of local political boss or oligarch (Schwerin, 5). Valle could not be unaware of the term and its significance but, if proof is needed, we can cite his own words in *Cara de Dios* (1899), when he describes one of the guests at a rural inn as "un famoso cacique electoral" (1972, 125).

3. José Carlos Mainer already pointed to this connection when he spoke of the feudalism that appears in the *Sonatas* and the *Comedias bárbaras* as "metaphorically normative" of "the grotesque vision of contemporary reality: caciquismo" (Mainer, 83).

4. Kern quotes here from part of a speech given by Francisco Romero Robledo (8 July 1876) and reported in the preceedings of the Congreso de Diputados.

5. I want to make it perfectly clear that I do not consider this relation with caciquismo to be the only or even the major goal of the *Sonatas* and the *Comedias bárbaras*. Don Ramón's works are multifaceted as they interact and intersect with the aesthetic, social, philosophic, political, religious, and personal

discourses of Valle's complex era. No one single "key" exists to his narrative, but to ignore his mediated commentaries on the Restoration and its oligarchy is to deny him his rootedness in Spanish reality and the concern for his nation and its people that made him a great artist.

6. In my book *Las Sonatas de Valle de Inclán* (Gibbs, 1991) I deal in some depth with the role of seduction, sexual deviation, and violence as used ironically in the Sonatas to indicate the decadence of Spain's aristocracy, as well as the hollowness of certain myths of past glories to which Restoration politicians gave lip service.

7. Clara Luisa Barbeito, *Epica y tragedia en la obra de Valle-Inclán*, José Antonio Gómez Marín, *La idea de la sociedad en Valle-Inclán*, and Lourdes Ramos-Kuethe, *Valle-Inclán: las Comedias bárbaras*, all deal in detail with the figure of Montenegro and his son.

8. This does not mean that Valle had in-depth knowledge of Nietzsche's complex and often contradictory philosophy, but rather that he was conversant in several general, and at times misunderstood, concepts such as 'God is dead', the 'superman', and 'beyond good and evil'," and that he reacted, in writing, to these trends, in very broad terms.

9. I purposefully use *his* in this context since neither Nietzsche nor any member of the Generation of '98, including Valle, conceived of women in this light.

Works Cited

Barbeito, Clara Luisa. *Epica y tragedia en la obra de Valle-Inclán*. Madrid: Fundamentos, 1985.

Baroja, Pío. *El árbol de la ciencia*. Ed. Gerard C. Flynn. New York: Appleton-Century-Crofts, 1970.

Comellas, José Luís. *Historia de España moderna y contemporánea*. Segunda Edición. Madrid: Rialp, 1968.

Gibbs, Virginia G. *Las Sonatas de Valle-Inclán: kitsch, sexualidad, satanismo e historia*. Madrid: Pliegos, 1991.

Gómez-Marín, José Antonio. *La idea de la sociedad en Valle-Inclán*. Madrid: Taurus, 1967.

———. "Valle: estética y compromiso". *Cuadernos Hispanoamericanos* 199–200: 175–203.

Granjel, Luís. *La generación literaria del noventa y ocho*. Salamanca: Anaya, 1966.

Hormigón, Juan Antonio. *Ramón del Valle-Inclán: la política, la cultura, el realismo y el pueblo.* Madrid: Alberto Corazón, 1972.

Kern, Robert W. *Liberals, Reformers and Caciques in Restoration Spain: 1875–1907.* Albuquerque: University of New Mexico Press, 1974.

———, ed. *The Caciques.* Albuquerque: University of New Mexico Press, 1973.

Mainer, José Carlos. *Literatura y pequeña burguesía en España.* Madrid: Cuadernos Para el Diálogo, 1972.

Maravall, José Antonio. "La imagen de la sociedad arcaica en Valle-Inclán". *Revista de Occidente* 44–45: 225–56.

Montesinos, José F. "Modernismo, esperpento o las dos evasiones". *Revista de Occidente* 44–45: 225–56.

Ortega y Gassett, José. "Sentido del preciosismo". Ramón del Valle-Inclán: An Appraisal of His Life and Works. Ed. Anthony N. Zahareas. New York: Las Américas, 1968.

Ramos-Kuethe, Lourdes. *Valle-Inclán: Las comedias bárbaras.* Madrid: Pliegos, 1985.

Schwerin, Karl H. "The Anthropological Antecedents: Caciques, Cacicazgos and Caciquismo." *The Caciques.* Ed. Robert Kern. Albuquerque: University of New Mexico Press, 1973.

Sobejano, Gonzalo. *Nietzsche en España.* Madrid: Gredos, 1976.

Valle-Inclán, Ramón del. *Aguila de blasón,* 4th ed. Madrid: Espasa-Calpe, 1976.

———. *Cara de Dios.* Madrid: Taurus, 1972.

———. *Cara de Plata.* 5th ed. Madrid: Espasa-Calpe, 1980.

———. *Romance de lobos.* 5th ed. Madrid: Espase-Calpe, 1980.

———. *Sonata de primavera. Sonata de estío.* 12th ed. Madrid: Espasa-Calpe, 1983.

———. *Sonata de otoño. Sonata de invierno.* 12th ed. Madrid: Espasa-Calpe, 1985.

4

Spain in the Thought of the Argentine Generation of 1837

WILLIAM KATRA

In *Facundo* (1845), by Domingo F. Sarmiento (*Obras completas*) and in *Bases* (1852, 1856, 1858), by Juan Bautista Alberdi, one finds the clearest and most coherent critiques of the role and status of the region's colonial Spanish culture for the new Argentina envisioned by the writer-activist and future statemen of Argentina's Generation of 1837.[1] Their ideas went beyond the treatment that had previously been offered by Juan María Gutiérrez, Esteban Echeverría, and even Sarmiento in some of his less inspiring passages, that is, works that circulated widely before the fall of Argentine dictator Juan Manuel de Rosas in 1852. An understanding of these earlier views will help to appreciate the later contributions of Sarmiento and Alberdi on this issue.

Gutiérrez had occasion to express his views on the issue of Spanish culture and its legacy for the Hispanic-American republics, in at least two different moments: first on the occasion of the 1837 inauguration of Marco Sastre's Salón Literario (Literary Salon) in Buenos Aires, he gave a speech entitled "Fisionomía del saber español: cual deba ser entre nosotros" (Outline of Spain's intellectual contribution: What it should be for us); and second, the series of letters published in 1876 under the title of *Cartas de un porteño (Letters from a Porteño, or Resident of Buenos Aires),* in which he justified his refusal to accept the invitation from Spain's prestigious *Real Academia Española* to become a corresponding member. At the risk of simplification, Gutiérrez's views on both of these occasions—separated in time by nearly a half century—can be summarized as a defense of cultural nationalism. His position arose from the romantic exhortation for Argentine leaders and writers to develop and celebrate those aspects that were particular to the country's culture and to leave aside the Spanish influences that, if dominant in the region during the colonial period, hardly served for its future development. In that first speech, he focused primarily on the issue of Spain's impoverished intellectual influence as manifested in the paltry number and inferior quality of books treating both cultural and scientific matters that emanated from Spain's foremost cultural centers. At that time, Gutiérrez characterized the Spanish literary and scientific cultures as totally lacking profundity and irrelevant to the social and material needs of the American republics. He fervently called for the cultural "emancipation" from Spain and the development of a national literature and culture that would speak to Argentina's and the Hispanic American republics' own customs and lived realities.[2] However appealing this view might have been for a rebellious youth, it did not take into account two important factors: first, however mediocre Spain's cultural and intellectual climates might have been, there are still individuals from Spain who rose above the norm and whose contributions set a high standard for the future leaders of the young American republics; and second, it was utopian to think that any individual or society could divorce itself from its own roots and historical past in the interest of forging a new identity.

Gutiérrez's romantic position was shared by other individuals of his generation. Generational cohort Florencio Varela, while seemingly criticizing him for these views, actually ended up embracing the same general enemy: Varela could not think of a single talented young man of the region who even remotely considered following Spanish influences in his own education or professional preparation. With this argument, Varela ironically confirmed precisely the point that Gutiérrez was arguing—that in the European theater Spain was the "most backward in all fields, but primarily with regard to intellectual life, whose development has been limited due to the fanatism of the country's leaders and its government's oppressive, centralized structures."[3]

That Gutiérrez's thinking on this same general denouncement of Spanish influences did not evolve significantly in the next half century, is evidenced by his letters of 1876, in which he rejected the *Spanish Royal Academy*'s attempt to honor a lifetime of cultural achievements by inviting him to become a corresponding member. In his published statement rejecting that offer, he criticized what for him was the Academy's retro-grade, if not ephemeral, goal of "freezing in time" the Spanish lan-guage's purity and elegance (Gutiérrez 1942, 6). Gutiérrez's justification for this stand harkened back to an argument used in the polemics between romantics and neoclassicists that had taken place in Montevideo and Santiago in the early 1840s. Then, as now, he argued that the American republics needed to reject the language of the Spanish colony because they required an ever-evolving language that would better serve them in their new role as participants in a world community undergoing continual innovation in all spheres of public and private life.[4] Again, there is a basic problem with this view. Gutiérrez correctly criticized the Academy's ephemeral defense of an atemporal, static language. However, he still erred by failing to accept that the Spanish-American language was inevitably formed and shaped by Spanish influences after centuries of colonial rule.

A similar variant of cultural nationalism flavored the early opinions of Echeverría, as expressed in the "Symbolic Words" of 1837, the short work that was later expanded and published under the definitive title, *Socialist Dogma* (1846). Echeverría's thesis was that his own generation's mission was to achieve a social emancipation in order to complement and fulfill the promise of the country's political emancipation won a generation earlier.[5] Although Echeverría spoke primarily of the need for a "social" emancipation, today's reader would interpret the examples he gives as speaking primarily to the country's need for a "moral" or ideo-logical transformation. According to Echeverría, Spain's most harmful legacy for the independent republics was the citizens' mental habits of "*la rutina*" (routine)—meaning their abnegation of the exercise of rea-son and examination; their blind respect for age and tradition; and their passive acceptance of social hierarchies, be they clerical, social, govern-mental, or professional. On the positive side, he admitted that the colo-nial experience under Spanish tutelage had been far more benign for Argentina than for the other recently independent American republics. Fortunately, Argentine society, upon emerging from its colonial slum-ber, was largely homogenous, and did not suffer from deep class divi-sions or hierarchies, nor did its people exhibit deeply ingrained social vices.[6] But the country's leaders, lacking intellectual "capacity," systemic ideas, a profound knowledge of the social sciences, and a high level of public spirit, had failed to build upon those advantages. Instead they had led the country into a destructive pattern of civil wars. On the basis of this largely "superstructural" analysis (this is, his emphasis on changing people's ideas), Echeverría derived what critics have largely called a "utopian" and "idealistic" program for societal change: according to Echeverría, the educated elite, through personal example and governmental action, would seek the means for educating the citizenry in the ways of progress and rewarding constructive work habits. Through these largely moral reforms, the educated elite would slowly be able to bring about a modification in the country's retrograde customs and beliefs that were holdovers from the region's Spanish colonial past.

While credit is due to Echeverría as an instigator of new ideas, Alberdi was the first of his generation to relate a cultural and historiographical practice in a determined theory or "philosophy." In *Fragmento preliminar al estudio de derecho (Preliminary Sketch for the Study of Law)* (1837) he argued that the "*grande hombre*" of a given society, or the pattern of laws and customs that existed at any given moment, were the result of "necessary nature of things that predictably derived from the conditions of existence in that given moment" (in Canal Feijóo, 129). Alberdi's convincing "materialist" argument was that whatever deficiencies existing in the country's culture and ideas resulted primarily from the region's underdeveloped economic structures that had remained largely unchanged since colonial days.

This materialist focus would account in part for the parting of the ways between Sarmiento and Alberdi after 1852. Whereas Sarmiento's dislike of the gaucho and caudillo-dominated society of the present would lead to a (not unambiguous) condemnation of the region's experience under the Spanish colonial order, Alberdi was more generously inclined:

> If the consequences have not been favorable, then the blame lies with those who established the premises, and the people have no other sin than that of having followed the most logical path. . . . Therefore, let's respect the poor majority population; they are our brothers and sisters; although they are inexperienced and uneducated, they are also vigorous and strong. (Canal Feijóo, 136)

In contrast to Sarmiento's outright condemnation of the past, Alberdi sought ways to temporarily accommodate those undesirable aspects of the region's cultural legacy, because he was confident that the latter would be modified and improved in the natural passage of time.

Sarmiento and Alberdi differed little with regard to objectives and basic values: no individual of their generation rivaled their commitment to transforming the country along liberal lines. The program of the one echoed that of the other: both came together in advocating free trade, republican institutions, development of agriculture and industry, and elevation of the masse's cultural level through schooling. More apropos to their views vis-à-vis Spain, both argued that Argentina needed to attract Northern European immigrants in order to supplant its inferior Spanish creole and mestizo populations with a people more biologically fit for civilization. Both advocated a massive immigration plan with the objective of populating the soils of their desired "Civilization," or the "Republic of the Future," with Anglo-Saxons and Northern Europeans, that is, "races" that had already demonstrated a capacity for progress and a centuries-long tradition of democracy and industry. While Sarmiento and Alberdi came together in supporting this plan for immigration, there was a basic difference in their advocacies. On the one hand, Sarmiento called for vigorous means to repress the country's backward elements if they rebelled against the modernizing fervor of the urban, liberal elites; during a later period of time (about 1852–1868) he even called for the outright extermination of those populations stubbornly embracing the retrograde practices associated with the Spanish colonial past. Alberdi, on the other, argued for a slower, less torturous path for the country's development. He urged society's new leaders to grant to those more backward population groups (which at that time comprised the majority) the respect that was due to any group of human beings while society's elites, at the same time, accelerated the pace of modernization.

Alberdi's *Bases y puntos de partida para la organización política de la República Argentina* (*Bases and Points of Departure for the Political Organization of the Argentine Republic*—1852, 1856, 1858) had the objective of providing a plan of organization for the country in order to guarantee not only social peace in the short run, but also a definitive transformation in the future. His evolutionary model argued for the need to accept for the time being certain institutions and practices inherited from the Spanish colonial past, irrespective of obvious defects. These would serve as a starting point, as a stable foundations upon which other changes would be enacted. Yet he also admitted Spain's positive contributions to the region's culture and institutions: in its first centuries of contact with the American continent, Spanish culture was "the highest expression of the Middle Ages, the beginnings of the Renaissance for European civilization."[7] It had served the positive function of planting on American soil the seedlings that would later bear the fruit of European civilization.

For that reason, Argentina was first and foremost a European society: "We are Europeans in race and culture, we are those who control America's destiny" (Alberdi, 56).

Regardless of this positive identification of Spain's role, Alberdi pointed out later problems. After the initial period of progress, the Spain of the Counterreformation denied that European identity for itself and its American colonies when it turned away from cultural and technological innovation and prohibited dialogue or commerce with other lands. Alberdi seemingly borrowed from Sarmiento the interesting idea of two radically different civilizations constituting the Argentina of his time. On the one hand, there was the medieval Spanish society of the interior provinces that had remained relatively unchanged for over three hundred years. On the other, there was the society of the Littoral that had enjoyed extensive transoceanic contact with other European centers over the past several decades and had consequently assimilated many progressive ideas; that region had a strong, undeniable North-European identity. In this analysis Alberdi went beyond the cultural nationalism inherent in the early view of Gutiérrez; he rejected the latter's desire to exclude one influence in favor of another (in this respect the liberal extremist Gutiérrez came together with his erstwhile foes, the scholastic extremists of the Spanish colony). In contrast to these cultural models based on the condemnation or exclusion of a part of the region's cultural past, Alberdi exhorted the unapologetic acceptance of the country's fusion of Spanish and North-European influences. But he also urged a new set of teachers: "initial Spanish influences have now been superceded by English and French initiatives" (55). In only a matter of years both Alberdi and Sarmiento would add another name to these two new influences: they would recognize the maximum model of development in the confident new democracy then taking root in the hemisphere to the north.

Alberdi projected that the most pressing need of the time was for the country's interior provinces to overcome their most backward aspects, in other words, their Spanish colonial heritage. He provided a catalogue of those institutional and psychological impediments to modernity: harmful individual habits such as "idleness, presumptuousness, and dissipation" (50); a religious practice centering around the worship of empty formulas, divorced from practical values such as industry and price in work (51); a legal system not providing protection for property and free enterprise (12, 88); and the related economic system based on monopoly interests and exclusion of competition (12, 84).

These, along with his racist preference for the North-European immigrants, reveal Alberdi's positivist orientation. According to him, any force or institution obstructing free trade and the economic potential of the individual had to be opposed. Also apparent was his now definitive materialist bias (in contrast to Echeverría's idealism), that guided his attacks against the vestiges of the Spanish colonial experience: he argued that the first step for overcoming the dead weight of the past was the development of agriculture and industry. Only with a developed and diversified productive base could a people progress in their moral, religious, and civic dimensions.

While Alberdi attacked many characteristics of the Spanish culture surviving from colonial times, he also indicated other aspects that had to be considered inherent to the experience of the new country. These were the realities that the country's leaders had to take into account and build upon in the formulation of new laws and institutions. "The constitution is to be found in the nature of things, in the Argentine Republic's mode of being. That law is the written expression of the constitution that resides in the reality of those elements that constitute the country" (Terán, 35). This was a more mature elaboration of the organic analysis that he had first expressed in *Fragmento*. What were some of those aspects (originating in the Spanish colony) that now constituted the essential characteristics of the country and its people? First, there was the colony's centralist, unitarian structure, which would not deny its deep-rooted practice of local autonomy and government. Second, was the region's culture, especially its shared language and history, and the catholic religion. Third, was a common legal tradition, with a shared legislation, that underlay all civil and commercial dealings. And lastly, there was the territorial unity that lent a name and defined the geographical extension of the country. According to Alberdi, all of these constituted the heritage of the Spanish colonial experience that had to be accepted as the sine qua non for reunifying Argentina in the present and upon which new laws and policies would be instituted to guide the country's development into the future.

Sarmiento, as suggested earlier, embraced many of the same liberal advocacies as Alberdi, but he differed with regard to important emphasis. He followed Echeverría with many idealistic projections and with his implicit opposition to the materialist stance of Alberdi. On this basis he proposed two fundamental measures for the country to achieve its desired progress. Yet Sarmiento was not consistent in arguing this view: he, who excelled more as a political activist and journalist than as a rigorous thinker. Indeed, his most reknown work, *Facundo*, presents a complex weave of perspectives, some of which coincided with the perspectives of Gutiérrez and Echeverría, and others that echoed the fertile analyses of Alberdi.[8]

As a point of departure, Sarmiento's widely diffused thesis about the contending forces of civilization and barbarism went beyond the largely culturalist or bookish emphasis of Gutiérrez and Echeverría, it also considered geographical, sociological, and historical factors. Critics have pointed to the probable influence of Vico and Herder, via the writings of the French historians Michelet and Guizot, but one must also not discount the impact that Alberdi's *Fragmento* must have had on ideas of the young writer-militant. In the untidy and contradictory—yet nevertheless brilliant—passages of *Facundo*, Sarmiento linked barbarism either explicitly or implicitly to a number of features inherited from the region's Spanish colonial past: Jesuit university education in Córdoba; feudalistic land tenure system, cattle-exporting economy; and sparse settlement across the pampa. He also linked to the region's Spanish past the traditional values of the gaucho who disdained manual labor and industry, worshipped equestrian life and violence, and hautily despised practices associated with family life, cultural elevation, communal association, and moral improvement. To his credit, Sarmiento ventured into a dimension of the region's underdevelopment about which Gutiérrez and Echeverría were glaringly silent, and about which Alberdi until then had only treated in passing: he highlighted the socioeconomic structures that had evolved from the region's colonial past that largely accounted for the retrograde rural society uniting despotic caudillos and brutish gauchos. In subsequent years these impressions first mentioned in the pages of *Facundo* would blossom into his generation's most radical critique of the latifundia cattle ranchers who had risen to prominence under Juan Manuel de Rosas, and who by 1880 would cement their position in the Spanish colonial pattern as the country's oligarchy with aristocratic claims.

In the 1840s none of his generational cohorts had positive words to say about the historical merits of *Facundo*: Gutiérrez saw in it a caricature, and Echeverría believed it highly deficient in systematic analysis. Alberdi's criticisms were even more poignant: it was a mystification of the highest order for Sarmiento to argue that the Spanish colonial influences still predominant in rural areas had produced only barbarism, and that the country's Europeanized cities were the only source of civilization. In truth, it is impossible to disagree with Alberdi's rigorous reading of both *Facundo* and Sarmiento's *Recuerdos de provincia* (*Provincial Remembrances*—1850). Alberdi pointed out that Sarmiento, in spite of his dualistic thesis, provided irrefutable documentation about the incivilization prevalent in the region's cities, and some positive contributions of Spain's late colonial institutions. Indeed, Sarmiento's early writings reveal that he harbored great respect for the type of society that had evolved in the small cities of Argentina's Andean region during the latter decades of the colonial period: here was his model par excellence for civilization, with an economy based on agricultural and commercial activity, a population committed to high standards in education and culture, and a society enjoying stable social and political systems under the enlightened direction of its respected cultural elite. Was it Sarmiento's comparison—whether correct or not—of that progressive colonial elite with the small group of powerful Porteño landowners and commercial agents wearing "the suit worn by the civilized world" (XV, 166) that accounts for the support he would offer in the 1850s and 1860s for that latter group's project of extending its hegemony throughout the nation?

While critics have continually registered their reservations about Sarmiento's simplistic opposition between civilization and barbarism, they have praised Sarmiento's then original sociological interpretation of the country's recent period of civil wars. In truth, Sarmiento was the first of his continent to take into account factors relevant to climate, geography, and demography, in addition to psychology and biography, in his interpretation of social life and historical events. In this respect, the highly dissimilar parts of *Facundo* ironically fuse into a tight conceptual unity. With the foremost objective of studying the caudillo, Sarmiento took into account aspects relative to culture and geography. Profound was his realization that "in *Facundo Quiroga* I see not only a caudillo, but also a manifestation of Argentine life such as it has been formed by [Spanish] colonial life and the nature of the terrain.... Facundo[is] the faithful expression of people's way of life" (VII, 12–13). The caudillo Facundo, he argued, was the personification of the most backward and harmless aspects of the life and culture still surviving from the region's dark colonial past.

In the last decade of his life Sarmiento suffered from the disillusionment that had accumulated from years of passionate and not altogether successful political action. This led him to cast into doubt upon some of the ideas he had formerly embraced. While governor of San Juan between 1861 and 1862, he had been unable to interest the new provincial elite in his ambitious plans for immigrant settlement and promotion of agriculture. Then, during his tenure as the country's president from 1866 to 1872, he met with obstacle after obstacle—some even emanating from his erstwhile generational colleagues—in implementing his plans for an activist state. This is because the new elites had by now resigned themselves (with a certain degree of self-interest) to the region's domination by the aggressive latifundia that monopolized the cattle-exporting industry. In the 1870s the legislative defeats of land or industrial programs aimed at benefiting an incipient middle class, and then the obscene success of the rich landowners in appropriating the greater part of the lucrative real estate made available after Julio A. Roca's "Desert Campaign," sealed his disillusionment. Thereafter, Sarmiento became a stalwart foe of the province's latifundia oligarchy, on whose behalf he had sacrificed the greater part of his vitality over the previous twenty years. But by now his talents as a writer and a thinker had largely faded; his fervent opposition to the country's oligarchy and the state it controlled under the stewardship of President Roca after 1880 deserved, but would not receive from his tired pen, the passionate inspiration of another *Facundo*. Unfortunately for Argentina and posterity, he could only offer the rough, inconsistent page of *Conflicto y harmonía de las razas en América*, in which he denounced the region's Spanish colonizers on account of their inferior racial stock and miscegenetic practices with the Amerindian race. He now placed major blame upon the Spanish for the region's unmovable, if not fatalistic attraction to retrograde practices: "In what way did the Spanish colonization process distinguish itself? First and foremost, it created a [social, cultural, and economic] monoply for its own race, that had no need to venture beyond the Middle Ages when it transferred itself to American shores and absorbed into its blood a servile and prehistoric race of beings"(37, 405). Critics are divided as to whether this effort by the disillusioned septagenarian should be considered an integral part of Sarmiento's lasting intellectual contributions.

Given the importance of Echeverría, Gutiérrez, Alberdi, and Sarmiento, it is understandable that their ideas have exercised an immense influence over the Argentine culture, both past and present. If one were to undertake a new x-ray of the pampa toward in the latter years of the present century, one would have to admit the lingering traces in the region's culture of all these thinkers. The country's impressive development over the past century is due to many factors, not the least of which is the implementation of many ideas of the 1837 generation of nation builders. Their positivist ideas have won out, and the country has benefited enormously from the liberal development that they advocated. Argentina, following their advocacies, became a nation of immigrants who quickly outnumbered the previously majority Spanish stock. The immigrants' new blend of influences and institutions relegated to a position of lessened importance the values and practices of the region's colonial past. In truth, Argentina survives today as perhaps the country in Spanish America with the least degree of Spanish influences. That being said, perhaps the judgement of Spanish intellectual Miguel de Unamuno holds as true today for the country as a whole as it did for Sarmiento's *Facundo*, which he pretended to criticize. Sarmiento's anti-Spanish views, Unamuno argued, were the strongest evidence possible of that writer's Spanish personality. In a similar vein, Argentina's rabid claims to a superior status vis-à-vis the rest of the continent perhaps confirms more than contradicts the longering presence of Spanish traits and culture.

Notes

1. The names most commonly linked with Argentina's 1837 generation are Juan Bautista Alberdi, Esteban Echeverría, Domingo F. Sarmiento, Juan María Gutiérrez, Vicente Fidel López, Bartolomé Mitre, Félix Frías, Miguel Cané, Luis Domínguez, and Florencio Varela. These individuals of Argentine nationality were also linked through friendship and shared ideological orientations with Chileans Manuel Montt, José Victorino Latarria, Manuel Bilbao; and Uruguayans Andrés Lamas and Juan Carlos Gómez.

2. Juan María Gutiérrez, "Fisionomía del saber español: cual deba ser nosotros", in Marcos Sastre et al., *El Salón Literario*, "Estudio preliminar" by Félix Weiberg (Buenos Aires: Hachette, 1958), pp. 135–52.

3. Letter from Florencio Varela to Juan María Gutiérrez, Montevideo (1 August 1837), reprinted in Sastre et al., *Salón Literario*, pp. 183–88.

4. Those articles by Sarmiento for the polemics on language and romanticism in Chile between 1841 and 1842 are undoubtedly the most interesting of this literature. See Domingo F. Sarmiento, *Obras completas*, vol. 1 (Buenos Aires: Luz del Día, 1948–1952), pp. 212–52. Other references to this edition will be indicated by volume and page numbers in the text of the paper.

5. Esteban Echeverría, *Obras completas de Esteban Echeverría*, compilation and biography by Juan María Gutiérrez (Buenos Aires: Antonio Zamora, 1972). Pages 55 to 294 reproduce *Dogma socialista*. The most important ideas

relative to Spain and Argentina's Spanish heritage are expressed under the eighth and ninth "palabras simbólicas", which bear the titles "Independencia de las tradiciones retrógradas que nos subordinan al antiguo régimen" (Independence from the Retrograde Traditions that Subordinate us to the Ancient Regime) and "Emancipación del espíritu americano" (Emancipation of the American Spirit).

6. Many of these ideas were expressed in Echeverría's "Discurso de introducción a una serie de lecturas pronunciadas en el 'Salón Literario' en setiembre de 1837", *Obras completas*, pp. 98–109.

7. Juan Bautista Alberdi, *Bases y puntos de partida para la organización política de la República Argentina*, prologue and notes by Raúl García Orza (Buenos Aires: Centro Editor de América Latina, 1979), p. 55. Further references to this edition will be indicated by page number in this chapter.

8. In *Domingo F. Sarmiento: Public Writer (Between 1839 and 1852)* (Tempe: Arizona State University, 1985). See chapter 4, "*Facundo* an Exercise in Bricoleur Historiography." I investigate the different ideological strains of Sarmiento's historical ideas, as expressed in *Facundo*.

Works Cited

Alberdi, Juan Bautista. *Bases y puntos de partida para la organización política de la República Argentina*. Prologue and notes by Raúl García Orza. Buenos Aires: Centro Editor de América Latina, 1979.

Canal Feijóo, Bernardo. *Constitución y revolución: Juan Bautista Alberdi*. Buenos Aires: Fondo de Cultura Económica, 1955.

Echeverría, Esteban. "Discurso de introducción a una serie de lecturas pronunciadas en el 'Salón literario' en septiembre de 1837". *Obras completas*. Compilation and biography by Juan María Gutiérrez. Buenos Aires: Antonio Zamora, 1972.

Gutiérrez, Juan María. *Cartas de un porteño: polémica en torno al idioma y la Real Academia Española, sostenida con Juan Martínez Vilergas, seguida de "Sarmenticido"*. Prologue and notes by Ernesto Morales. Buenos Aires: Americana, 1942.

———. "Fisionomía del saber español: cual deba ser nosotros". In Marcos Sastre et al., *El Salon literario*. "Estudio preliminar" by Félix Weiberg. Buenos Aires: Hachette, 1958.

Katra, William. *Domingo F.Sarmiento: Public Writer (Between 1839–1852)*. Tempe: Arizona State University Press, 1985.

Sarmiento, Domingo F. *Obras completas,* vol. 1. Buenos Aires: Luz del Día, 1948–1952.

Sastre, Marcos, et al., *El Salón Literario,* "Estudio preliminar" by Félix Weiberg (Buenos Aires: Hachette, 1958)

Terán, Oscar. "Alberdi póstumo". *Alberdi póstumo.* Buenos Aires: Puntosur, 1988.

5

Rediscovering Spain: The Hispanismo of Manuel Gálvez

JEANE DELANEY

During much of the nineteenth century, relations between Spanish and Latin American[1] intellectuals were fraught with tension and ill will. With few exceptions, elites in both regions regarded their trans-Atlantic counterparts with a mixture of suspicion and disdain. By the opening years of the twentieth century, however, this situation changed, as many intellectuals in both Spain and Latin America began to call for closer ties between the two regions. This paper examines the growing rapprochement between Spain and her former colonies, focusing on the new, pro-Spanish attitudes in Argentina. In doing so, I will look specifically at the ideas of Argentine novelist Manuel Gálvez (1882–1962). One of the nation's most prolific and widely read writers, Manuel Gálvez was also one of Argentina's most ardent proponents of hispanismo. The case of Gálvez, while in some ways extreme, provides important insight into the reasons behind this new shift and into the factors underlying the increasingly widespread attempts to define a common Hispanic culture and identity.

Evidence of the nineteenth-century hostility between Spain and Latin America is abundant. Many Spaniards believed that the former colonies had, since independence, slid into barbarism and were irredeemably backward and bereft of cultural achievement. Conservatives, of course, were appalled by the anticlericism exhibited by many of the republics, singling out Argentina and post-Reform Mexico for special

71

censure. Even Spanish liberals, despite their support for Latin American anticlerical measures, were often repulsed by the region's seemingly chronic instability and violence, which many suspected were due to the unfortunate taint of inferior races.

Latin American elites, with few exceptions, reciprocated this disdain and hostility in kind. The tardiness with which Spain recognized the region's independence, Spain's complicity in attempts to establish a monarchy in Ecuador in the 1840s, as well as Spanish occupation of the islands off the coast of Peru, provoked and intensified anti-Spanish sentiment throughout the continent. Besides the threat of military interventions, however, was the issue of the Spanish cultural legacy and its continuing impact on the American republics. Latin American liberals were especially critical in their assessment of Spain and the colonial heritage. Spain, they believed, was hopelessly mired in past. A captive of rigid traditionalism and religious fanaticism, it had proved unwilling to open up to the renovating currents of progressive Western thought. Indeed, much of the liberal program in Latin American—in theory at least—was an attempt to extirpate the remaining vestiges of the Hispanic legacy, which many progressives argued, prevented the new nations from achieving political stability and prosperity. Attacks on the church, the destruction of monopolies and privilege, and the drive to secularize education and to implement more "practical" school curricula, were all symptoms of a generalized contempt for Spain and its role in shaping the New World.

In Argentina, where liberal thought established an early if tenuous foothold, the rejection of Spanish culture and institutions was particularly marked. Bernardino Rivadavia, one of the most important leaders of the postindependence period, publicly described Spanish habits as "degrading," and argued that the Spanish legacy represented the new republic's most serious obstacle to equality, liberty, and prosperity. These sentiments were echoed by later leaders such as Domingo Faustino Sarmiento, who argued that Argentina's economic backwardness and political chaos could be traced, in large part, to its Spanish heritage. Throughout the century, liberal Argentines looked toward the industrializing nations of northern Europe as models for their own country to emulate. To progress, according to these individuals, Argentines must strive to adopt the civilized habits of thrift and industry that came naturally to Anglo-Saxon peoples. Where education and socialization failed, immigration from northern Europe should be encouraged. The influx of non-Hispanics, they believed, would help develop in the native population the virtues needed for civilization and economic progress.

The late nineteenth century, however, witnessed a lessening of hostilities between Spain and Latin America. One important example of new attitudes in Spain is the case of politician and journalist Emilio Castelar, who briefly served as president during the First Republic. Both an ardent pan-hispanist and a republican, he proclaimed as early as 1867 that Spain and Latin America were inextricably bound by spiritual and historical ties, forming a common family and *raza*. Granted, Castelar failed to win many converts on either side of the Atlantic to the cause of pan-hispanism. But as Charles Hales has noted, by the late nineteenth century, many Latin American intellectuals were becoming more receptive to such overtures (Hales, 371). The conservative nature of Castelar's liberalism had widespread appeal among Latin American elites who sought to reconcile their own inherited liberal ideology with the desire for a strong, authoritarian state.

Yet it was not until the very end of the century that Spanish-Latin American relations underwent a marked rapprochement. Closer ties between the two regions received a major impetus with the 1898 defeat of Spain in the Spanish American war. Stunned by their disastrous defeat, Spaniards of diverse ideological persuasions engaged in an orgy of introspection and mutual recrimination. Whatever their interpretation of Spain's weakness, many saw Latin America as the key to rebuilding their nation's future. Spanish liberals in particular believed Latin American could provide a model for a new, more viable state on the peninsula. Perhaps the most important advocate of this position was Miguel de Unamuno who argued that the Latin American republics had successfully married the requirements of modernity with the essence of Spanish culture, and that Spain herself would do well to imitate them (Pike, 60).

The war also altered Latin American attitudes toward Spain. In the words of Carlos Fuentes, the conflict served to "desatanize Spain and satanize the United States" in the eyes of Latin Americans. The near destruction of the Spanish navy eliminated the possibility of Spanish military aggression in the Western hemisphere. Thus, Spain was no longer perceived as a threat to Latin American autonomy. More importantly, the United States' intervention in the Cuban independence movement and its subsequent domination of Cuba and Puerto Rico, fueled fears of increasing U.S. activity in the region. José Martí's earlier warnings about U.S. imperial designs seemed, in the aftermath of war, grimly prescient. The specter of the U.S. aggression in the hemisphere was also raised by Argentine writer Manuel Ugarte, who like Martí, urged a union of Hispanic nations to serve as a bulwark against the North American threat.

Undoubtedly, the growing belief that a trans-Atlantic defense was needed to check U.S. power did much to shore up the idea of a Latin or Hispanic community based on shared ideas and a common historical experience. Yet I would argue that the new appreciation of Spain and the desire for closer ties to the *patria madre*, evinced by Manuel Gálvez and many of his Argentine contemporaries, had little to do with fears of U.S. imperialism. Manuel Ugarte notwithstanding—who, by the way, spent little of his adult life in Argentina—the new, pro-Spanish sentiments among Argentines and the attempts to define a common Hispanic community vis-à-vis the United States were in large part independent of U.S. activities in the international arena. Instead, it is essential to consider events and developments internal to Argentina, specifically, rapid modernization and the changing role of intellectuals in this new society.

I will argue two things. First, Gálvez's attraction to Spain and the Hispanic culture can be traced, in large part, to his dissatisfaction with many of the changes brought on by the great export boom Argentina enjoyed during the late nineteenth century. In a period of extraordinary economic growth, massive immigration,and increasing working-class militancy, Gálvez's hispanismo represented a nostalgic attempt to recuperate a past and a cultural/religious tradition that he believed was essential to the preservation of Argentina's hierarchical social order. As a member of the traditional elite, Gálvez was understandably hostile to what he saw as the new destabilizing forces brought on by rapid modernization.

A second argument, related to the first, is that Gálvez's call for a new appreciation of Spain must also be viewed in the context of his own self-proclaimed identity as a writer and intellectual, and the concrete interests that underlay this identity. Gálvez believed that the project of hispanización was one that must be guided by individuals of special talents and sensibilities. Only artists, intellectuals, and writers, he claimed, had the ability to diagnose the ills of Argentine society and to lead the nation back to spiritual well being. In an era when the traditional roles of writers and intellectuals were in flux, this project of hispanización can be seen as an effort to legitimate new roles for such individuals in Argentine society.[2]

Any analysis of Galvez's thought and motivations must begin with an understanding of his personal history. Born in 1882, Gálvez was the scion of a wealthy and politically powerful family from the province of Santa Fe. Like many young provincial elites, he came to Buenos Aires to study law at the National University, arriving in 1899. His real passion, however, was literature, and while at the university he developed a close circle of friends who shared similar interests. Included in this group were such individuals as Ricardo Rojas and Emilio Becher, both of whom would become distinguished writers. These two, plus Gálvez, formed the core group of young intellectuals who would collectively become known as the literary Generation of 1910.

This generation of writers and intellectuals, although not monolithic by any means, was united in its belief that Argentina suffered from a profound intellectual and spiritual crisis. Argentines, these individuals claimed, had become indifferent to "things of the spirit" and had become obsessed with luxury, money, and profits. According to one young writer of the period, Buenos Aires had developed an "opaque, factory-like atmosphere" hostile to any endeavor not directed toward material gain (Olivera, 3–10). Another author complained that the luxury had been corrupted by a "new ostentation, the love of luxury, and the pursuit of wealth, all leading to a disdain for ... art, letters and scholarship" (Rubianes, 643–52).

The source of this cultural impoverishment, according to Gálvez and many other members of his generation, was the excessive cosmopolitanism of Argentine society. It is important to note at this point that the term *cosmopolitanism* was not completely unproblematic and had different meanings during this period. Often it was used to describe the nation's liberal elite, which had slavishly imitated European customs, fashions, and trends. Many of the young intellectuals believed that the generation of their fathers, in its rush to acquire sophistication, had betrayed the nation and had judged *lo argentino* to be inferior. "Cosmopolitan" could also be meant as a criticism of the nation's growing immigrant population. Many Argentines of the period believed the massive influx of foreigners had undermined the nation's traditional culture and, thus, were a threat to Argentina's very identity.

In whatever sense it was used, "cosmopolitanism" was widely viewed as the source of Argentina's woes. The solution, many young Argentines believed, was to reject foreign influences and to defend and consolidate an authentically Argentine culture. During this period, we see an enormous preoccupation with the issue of Argentine national identity and the question of whether or not Argentina possessed a truly authentic national literature and art. This question, of course, raised another: Just what was and was not authentically Argentine? Was Argentina essentially a New World society, or was much of its identity rooted in the Old World? Should it reject cosmopolitan influences entirely, or was cosmopolitanism part of the Argentine character?

This is not the place to go into the complexities of the early twentieth-century debate over Argentine identity and its political implications. Let it suffice to say that for Gálvez, the answer was straight forward: Argentine identity was fundamentally Spanish. Spanish values and traditions, he believed, constituted the very bedrock of Argentine culture and identity. While not completely rejecting either continued immigration or cultural influences from other European nations, Gálvez believed that in order for Argentina to regain its true or authentic character, it had to return to its Hispanic roots. It was time, he argued, "for us to call ourselves Argentine . . . and ultimately Spanish, for this is the race to which we belong" (Gálvez 1936, 57). Only then could Argentines regain their special qualities of "*desinterés*" and spirituality.

This identification of Argentine and Hispanic culture with idealism drew, of course, from the widely held association of Latin peoples with spirituality and idealism, promoted most forcefully during this period by José Enrique Rodó and his concept of *arielismo*. In contrast to the francophile Rodó, however, Gálvez believed that only Spain had managed to preserve the special qualities of *latinidad*. Italy and France, although praiseworthy nations, had unfortunately been "bitten by the microbe of decadence"—their spirituality undermined by the intrusion of the modern world (1936, 26–27). Moreover, it was to Spain that Argentina was most tightly bound by history and by blood.

The key to Spain's unique resistance to the corrosive forces of modernity, Gálvez believed, was the continued strength of its mystical, Catholic atmosphere formed during the medieval period. Echoing Spanish conservative Marcelino Menéndez Pelayo, Gálvez believed that Catholicism was the essence of Spanish national existence. He argues—by extension—the same was true of Argentina. By returning to their Hispanic roots, Gálvez hoped that Argentines would also return to the true faith.

A fervent Catholic, Gálvez looked to Catholicism both as a means of restoring Argentina's lost spirituality and as a solution to the nation's growing social unrest. During this period, Argentina witnessed increasing worker militancy, culminating in the famous *semana trágica* of

1919, when scores of striking workers were killed or injured by the police. Construing the social question in essentially moral terms, Gálvez believed Argentina's social problems were rooted in the individualism and greed unleashed by rapid modernization. By returning to the Catholic faith, equilibrium and harmony between the social classes could be restored. Workers would accept its traditional responsibility for protecting the welfare of the poor.

Clearly, then, much of Gálvez's attraction to Spain can be traced to nostalgia and his fear of social upheaval. By returning to Spanish values and traditions, he hoped that Argentina could recuperate a lost way of life and rebuild, in a hierarchical fashion, a national community newly threatened by class strife.

Yet there is another way to interpret Gálvez's hispanismo, that goes beyond the issue of class interests and simple nostalgia and adds another dimension to our understanding of his call for a return to Spanish idealism. Earlier, I suggested that Gálvez's concern over Argentina's putative spiritual crisis and the threat of materialism to the national character cannot be separated from his self-proclaimed identity as a writer/intellectual. This identity, in addition to his upper-class background, helped shape his analysis of the Argentine situation and drew him toward Spain as a solution.

That Gálvez identified himself primarily as a writer/intellectual is unquestionable. Although at the beginning of his career, he enjoyed a public sinecure as a school inspector, Gálvez's professional life clearly revolved around both writing and publishing. An extraordinarily prolific writer, Gálvez published over sixty novels, essays, and works of nonfiction during his long and varied career. Besides writing, he was also extremely active in other areas of the literary field. In 1903, for example, he founded the literary magazine *Ideas*. Later, he organized an important publishing cooperative that published sixty-eight volumes in its first five years. Gálvez was also tireless in his efforts to promote the interests of professional writers, often referring to the "gremio" of writers. Toward that end, he founded the Argentine branch of the PEN club in Buenos Aires in 1924.[3]

In claiming a connection between Gálvez's identity as a writer and his call for closer ties with Spain, it is important to keep in mind the kind of relationship between the two nations he proposed. As noted earlier, Gálvez was attracted to Spain because, in his eyes, it had successfully resisted the lure of modernity and materialism. This is made very clear in his most important pro-Spanish book *El solar de la raza*. This long essay was essentially a meditation on and a eulogy for Spain's traditional provincial cities. About Salamanca, for example, Gálvez writes that the spirituality of that city was like a "well from which to drink the miraculous water that would immunize us from the germs of materialism we carry inside ourselves" (1936, 109).

Clearly, Gálvez was completely uninterested in establishing closer economic, political, or military links with contemporary Spain.[4] The renewal of ties with Spain was, in his formulation, of an extremely limited kind. What Argentina needed from Spain lay solely in the cultural realm: religious traditions, idealism, and spirituality. These were the qualities threatened by rapid modernization that Argentina must recover if the nation were to maintain its distinctive, Hispanic identity. Moreover, the special relationship between Spain and Argentina that Gálvez envisioned was one that could only be effected by individuals endowed with special sensibilities, that is, artists, writers, and intellectuals. Significantly, he notes in El Solar de la raza, that only poets and artists (and of course he included himself in this category) could feel or comprehend the real Spain. The task at hand, then, was not one to be undertaken by bankers, merchants, or diplomats but, rather, by people like himself.

This privileging of the writer/intellectual in this project of hispanización deserves further scrutiny, for it occurs at a moment when the role of writers and intellectuals in Argentine society was in flux. Before this period, the nation's writers and intellectuals were essentially one and the same with the political elite. Men such as D. F. Sarmiento and Juan Bautista Alberdi in the mid-nineteenth century, and later Miguel Cané and Eduardo Wilde—to name just two of the members of the Generation of 1880—all played important roles in the affairs of the nation.

By the early twentieth century, in contrast, a new type of writer/ intellectual, had emerged. For the first time, we see a generation of writers and scholars who were able to dedicate themselves almost entirely to a life of letters. Due to the expansion of the reading public and new opportunities in journalism, writing became for the first time a true profession, as individuals were finally able to live by the trade.[5] This professionalization of the world of letters had many implications, but the one that interests us is that for the first time, writers and intellectuals formed a semiautonomous group with a newly developing corporate identity and—this is key—one that, as a whole, enjoyed no formal political power.

Clearly then, the role of writers and intellectuals was in transition. No longer synonymous with the "politically powerful," this emerging group was forced to stake out a role with new responsibilities and new claims to status that would secure for its members a central place in Argentine society. With these changes in mind, Gálvez's call for a return to the idealism of Spain takes a new cast. By claiming that Argentina was in crisis and then arguing that the solution lay in the return to her Hispanic roots that only special individuals such as himself could effect, Gálvez elevates the writer/intellectual to the status of a national savior.

Key to Gálvez's privileging of the writer/intellectual is his conviction that such individuals were immune to the contamination of greed and materialism. Standing apart from the burgeoning system of capitalist production, they supposedly remained free from its allure. Thus untouched by the new climate of modern values, writers/intellectuals enjoyed a privileged position from which to see, to judge, and to prescribe for a society they deemed to be in crisis.

The special purity of the writer/intellectual is a common motif in Gálvez's novels and, indeed, is the central theme in his 1916 work, *El mal metafísico.* The novel, which Gálvez describes as the "history of his generation" (Gálvez 1961, 43) is the story of Carlos Riga, a young poet from the provinces. Like Gálvez, Riga is sent by his father to Buenos Aires to study but finds literature more appealing than academics. Bored by his studies, Riga spends time writing poetry and frequenting cafés, where he and other disaffected intellectuals sip endless cups of coffee while lamenting the gross materialism of porteño society. His provincial father is incensed by this behavior and cuts off the young man's living allowance. (Here is where Gálvez's and Riga's stories diverge.) Impoverished and alienated from the "great city of action and energy," Riga continues his lonely literary endeavors. Finally however, he succumbs to the hardship and dies alone and poor in a squalid boarding house. Thus, this "true sower of the spirit" (Gálvez 1916, 69), as Gálvez describes him, sacrifices himself for the ideals of beauty and art.

Martyrdom, alienation, marginality—such, according to Gálvez's formulation—is the fate of the artist in Argentine society. Significantly, in Gálvez's formulation, marginality is transformed into centrality. For it is only the writer/intellectual who enjoys the critical distance needed to diagnose the nation's ills, and the purity of heart, and "*desinterés*" to lead it back to spiritual health. Clearly then, Argentina needed her writers and intellectuals more than ever before, for only such special individuals were capable of defending Argentina's very essence from the corrupting forces of modernity. Only under their guidance could the nation regain its true identity.

What, in the end, are we to make of Gálvez's call for a return to Argentina's Hispanic roots? Given that his attraction to Spain can be traced to his own ambivalence toward modernity and to the concrete interests that underlay his identity as a writer, what impact, if any, did his ideas and exhortations have on his fellow Argentines? Although a definitive answer is impossible, the varying responses to his ideas allow for some tentative conclusions.

Among the reading public who eagerly purchased his most important pro-Spanish essay, *El solar de la raza*, it seems that Gálvez's hispanismo struck a responsive chord. The book's success was immediate and long lived. Several thousand copies were sold in the first few weeks, and it was reprinted eight times in thirty years. The work also enjoyed critical acclaim in the press and was favorably reviewed in many of Argentina's major newspapers and literary magazines. Such "best sellers," especially in the category of nonfiction, were a rarity during this period. Clearly then, Gálvez's ideas were enthusiastically received by a broad segment of the reading public. We can only assume, then, that many of the author's complaints about Argentina's spiritual and cultural crisis rang true to his compatriots.

Among fellow writers and intellectuals, reaction to Gálvez's hispanismo was mixed. Some prominent scholars, such as Ernesto Quesada and José Antonio Amuchasteguí agreed with his perception that Argentina was indeed in danger of losing its national character, and could only save itself by returning to its Hispanic roots. These individuals, moreover, shared many of Gálvez's fears of social upheaval and saw the renewal of traditional Spanish values as a partial solution. Some even took concrete steps on the level of social policy. In 1919, for example, Amuchasteguí, to stress the importance of Spanish influence in shaping Argentine culture, initiated a campaign to revise the teaching of history in public schools.[6]

Other intellectuals, in contrast, while accepting both the idea that Argentina's national character was threatened by materialism and the notion that the writer/intellectual should be at the forefront of the struggle of respiritualize Argentina, rejected Gálvez's hispanismo as excessively conservative. Accusing Gálvez of not being forward looking, prominent intellectuals such as Roberto Giusti and Eduardo Maglione viewed Argentina's culture as an amalgam of diverse influences of which

Spain was only one. The new Argentina, which they believed was still in formation, would have to accommodate and reflect this diversity.[7]

Thus, while it can be argued that attitudes toward Spain improved during the early twentieth century, it would be an overstatement to conclude that this period represented a definitive watershed in Argentine perceptions of Spain. Even though many Argentines began to cast a more generous eye on the former metropolis, few embraced the ideal of hispanismo with Gálvez's fervor. Indeed, many believed that Argentina was primarily a New World society and had little in common with the former metropolis.

Nor did Gálvez's celebration of *lo español* have any tangible consequences in terms of Argentine-Spanish relations. This is not surprising, given the type of rapprochement he envisioned. The cultural and spiritual links he sought were exceedingly ephemeral, and of course his desire for such links were contingent upon the survival of Spanish traditionalism. With the electoral victory of republican-socialist forces in 1931, Gálvez's interest in Spain predictably waned. Thus the importance of Gálvez's hispanismo, I believe, lies not in its lasting significance, but for what these more pro-Spanish attitudes reveal about the tensions and transformations of turn-of-the-century Argentina.

Notes

1. Throughout this chapter, I have adopted the commonly used term *Latin America*. It should be recognized, however, that the term, particularly during the period I am treating, was not uncontested. Spaniards in particular objected to its use, preferring *Spanish America* instead. For a discussion of the controversy over the two terms, see Frederick Pike, *Hispanismo, 1898–1936: Spanish Conservatives and Liberals and Their Relations with Spanish America* (South Bend, IN: University of Notre Dame Press, 1971), pp. 198–200.

2. This argument is similar to that made by Julio Ramos, in his analysis of turn-of-the-century Latin American intellectuals *Desencuentros de la modernidad en América Latina*. See pp. 209–14.

3. For Galvez's own discussion of these activities and his identity as a writer, see volume 1 of his memoirs, *Amigos y maestros de mi juventud* (Buenos Aires: Hachette, 1961).

4. This selective approach helps explain an apparent paradox in Gálvez's thought. While urging his countrymen to return to their Hispanic roots, he

expressed great ambivalence about continued immigration of Spaniards to Argentine shores. These immigrants, of primarily working-class origin, had no connection with the traditional Spanish culture and values he so admired. Indeed, these immigrants were very likely infected with modern values of individualism and materialism, and of course proved a threat to the social order.

5. For a discussion of this phenomenon and its impact, see Jorge B. Rivera, "La forja del escritor profesional (1900–1930)", *Historia de la literatura argentina*, vol. 3, pp. 337–84.

6. For a brief discussion, see Pike, p. 193.

7. See for example, Roberto Giusti, Review of Martiano Leguizamon's *De cepa criolla*, in *Nosotros* II, 3, 16–17 (Nov.–Dec. 1908). See also Eduardo Maglione, "Cosmopolitismo y espiritu nacional", in *Renacimiento* I, 2, 6 (Nov. 1909): 320–29.

Works Cited

Gálvez, Manuel. *El Solar de la raza*. Buenos Aires: Editorial Tor, 1936.

———. *El mal metafísico*. Buenos Aires: 1916.

———. *Amigos y maestros de mi juventud*. Buenos Aires: Hachette, 1961.

Giusti, Roberto. Review of Martiano Leguizamon's *De cepa criolla*, in *Nosotros* II, 3, 16–17 (Nov.–Dec. 1908).

Hales, Charles. "Political and Social Ideas in Latin America, 1870–1930." *Cambridge History of Latin America*, vol. 4. Edited by Leslie Bethell. Cambridge: Cambridge University Press, 1986, pp. 367–441.

Maglione, Eduardo. "Cosmopolitismo y espiritu nacional". In *Renacimiento* I, 2, 6 (Nov. 1909).

Olivera, Ricardo. "Sinceridades". *Ideas* 1, 1 (May 1909).

Pike, Frederick. *Hispanismo, 1898–1936: Spanish Conservatives and Liberals and Their Relations with Spanish America* (South Bend, IN: University of Notre Dame Press, 1971).

Ramos, Julio. *Desencuentros de la modernidad en América Latina*. México: Fondo de Cultura Económica, 1989.

Rivera, Jorge. "La forja del escritor profesional (1900–1930)". *Historia de la literatura argentina*, vol. 3. Buenos Aires: Centro Editor de América Latina, 1981, pp. 337–84.

Rubianes, Joaquín. "El retroceso moral de Buenos Aires". *Revista argentina de ciencias políticas* II, 4, 23 (August 1912).

6

Krausean Philosophy as a Major Political and Social Force in the Modern Argentina and Guatemala

O. CARLOS STOETZER

I

One of the major intellectual movements in modern Latin America was the Krausean philosophy that penetrated the Iberian world at a time when Positivism was also sweeping that part of the globe. However, while Positivism was a reaction to the earlier Romantic movement, the Krausean philosophy was part of German Idealism and, thus, in effect, an echo of Romanticism. Although it had arisen in the first half of the nineteenth century, its great influence in the Spanish and Portuguese world has actually been felt much later parallel to Positivism. In this sense the impact of the Krausean philosophy did not differ from other European cultural and intellectual movements that, firstly, had always arrived in the Iberian world somewhat later and also stayed in this world a much longer time, and secondly, went through a metamorphosis once they crossed the Pyrenees and the Atlantic; in other words, they became personalized, individualized, humanized, that is, Hispanicized.

I.I.

The Krausean philosophy and its Iberian derivation, *krausismo*, is derived from the Romantic impact of Karl Christian Friedrich Krause

(1781–1832). Krausismo also included those who followed the Krausean philosophy and applied it to a variety of scientific fields: Heinrich Ahrens and Carl August Röder in philosophy of law; Heinrich von Leonhardi in philosophy of history; Guillaume Tiberghien in philosophy of religion, and Paul Hohlfeld in the field of ethics. Although Krause belonged to the school of German Idealism, he pretended to be the only real successor of Kantian rationalism. Actually, despite his opposition to Fichte, Schelling, and Hegel, Krause's harmonious rationalism contained "the analytics of Kant, the reforming of humanitarian aspirations of Fichte, the pantheism of Schelling, and the system of universal categories of Hegel" (López Morillas, 31). In his harmonious rationalism Krause had come up with a new term, *panentheism*, the doctrine of everything-in-God, the relationship of God to the world. It was this doctrine that represented the synthesis in which the opposition of pantheism to Deism was dissolved. Panentheism was thus Krause's own version of the dialectic.

As a young boy, in the schools of Eisenberg, in eastern Thuringia, Krause excelled in the ancient classics and translated Homer's *Odyssey*. Later, as a student of philosophy in Jena, he became the pupil of both Fichte and Schelling. With his famous *Wesenslehre* (Doctrine of Being), published in his early career, Krause developed a new look on ontology. Already in his youth he speculated about an ideal for the harmonization of discordant humanity, and his vision imagined a future social organization that could attain the highest possible realization in Truth, Goodness, Beauty, and Peace (MacCauley, 9). As a student he pursued these goals further by setting forth principles of personal conduct and social regulation that led him to a close relationship with the masonic lodges. He saw in the Masonic Fraternity a means of achieving his cherished goal of a human brotherhood. His association with masonry and his publication of the *Three Oldest Art Documents of Free Masonry* got him into deep troubles since his enemies' hostility harmed him for the rest of his life. In 1811 he published his *Urbild der Menschheit*—the Ideal for Humanity: "a vision of a possible human future to which some of the most exalting panegyrics ever offered to an intellectual and spiritual social idealization have been given by capable judges" (MacCauley, 11).

Krause's life, which represented an extraordinary struggle for survival, was spent in Dresden, Berlin, and Göttingen. He and Hegel were both candidates for the chair of philosophy at the University of Berlin, but Hegel was preferred in view of his greater compliance with the authorities. Undeterred, he continued his career. The *Philosophy of Reli-*

gion and the *Philosophy of Right* were just a few of the many works he published in the 1820s. The tragic life of this true man of peace, accused of subversion, took a turn for the worse so that he had to find refuge in Munich where his former teacher Schelling refused to lend him a helping hand. It was there, in Bavaria, that in 1832 his harassment ended, and as Clay MacCauley said: "yet he died a real martyr to what he cherished as supreme truth for man's thought and as the best guidance for Humanity in the manifold round of life in this world"(15).

I.II.

The central point of Krause's philosophical analysis was his concept of right and law that is best illustrated in his *Urbild der Menschheit*, but more completely developed in his *Abriss des Systems der Philosophie des Rechtes oder des Naturrechts* and *Das System der Rechtsphilosophie*. Krause's concept of right was based on two columns, an analytical and a synthetic foundation; one was deduced from the rational consciousness of man, the other was drawn from his metaphysical presuppositions, that is, the all-embracing concept of God. The latter, based on his ontological evidence of God, led him to affirm that all conditions of the existence of rational beings must be anchored in God; thus, also law was the basic essence of God.

As Peter Landau stated, there were three basic currents of a pre-Kantian philosophical tradition in Krause's thought: "In the first place, the Platonic tradition, of which he considered himself to be the heir, and even felt that he was continuing this legacy in modern times. In the second place, St. Thomas Aquinas, who reflected the Christian echo of Aristotelianism, and finally, in the third place, the *iustitia universalis* of Leibniz" (Landau, 82; see also, Krause's *Das System*, 371, 118, 403ff.). Although he criticized Spinoza's concrete version of the concept of law, he admired him and even praised the metaphysical foundation of his legal philosophy. Thus, in sum, Krause's metaphysical foundation of law was linked to St. Thomas, Spinoza, and Leibniz but kept outside the Kantian tradition (Landau, 82).

The consequences of Krause's metaphysical deduction meant that neither enforcement nor recognition were criteria for the validity of legal norms, only their concordance with Divine Law (Landau, 82), which was obviously in accordance with traditional Natural Law. Thus, the concept of law could not be deduced from the common ground of the historic legal systems (Landau, 82; see Krause's *Das System*, 17ff.).

Krause believed that there existed a sufficiently strong consciousness in mankind that stood above unethical Positive Law.

Krause's definition of law was the sum of the conditions that were subordinated to the freedom of the rational life of many and human nature (Kodalle, 83). Moreover, in his legal system, legal duty was not based on ethics but on the reasonableness, the rationality of the legal order. In other words, legal enforcement could only be recognized if based on reason (Kodalle, 83, n. 13; see Krause's *Das System*, 77).

For Krause, almost all conditions of human existence were socially transmitted, and freedom meant social transmission as a contrary concept to pure natural conditions. In other words, law should guarantee to man an equality of opportunities in society. Thus, Krause went beyond Kant's legal philosophy. For Kant, law appeared only as a restriction of individual arbitrariness in accordance with the general ideas on liberty, whereas for Krause law should not only guarantee any free and ethical activity of the individual person but should establish all those conditions that would enable man to achieve his rational self-realization through the attainment of all ingredients necessary for life. However, despite the fact that Krause had emphasized the individual, he put society on a higher pedestal, since the individual must necessarily be subordinated to society (Kodalle, 84; see Krause's *Das System*, 166).

As a consequence of Krause's legal philosophy, men possessed basic natural rights, not in regard to any unjustified intervention by the state, since Krause always considered the state's power as limited in its role toward its citizens. These were more social rights, such as the right to food and shelter, and to protection. This also included the right to education, since an uneducated person could hardly have any chance of freedom (Kodalle, 84; see Krause's *Das System*, 481). Another such right was the development of one's capabilities; hence, for Krause society not only had the duty to establish a legal order based on freedom for all men but had to incorporate all possibilities for the harmonious development of all human capabilities (Kodalle, 85; see Krause's *Das System*, 55, 68).

In his legal philosophy, Krause went further than his contemporaries who recognized all men as persons. In contrast to them he made no distinction concerning age, sex, and race, and he thus defended the rights of children with parents accountable for their well being; he was a convinced defender of women and emphasized womens' equality in all careers of political life, the arts, and the sciences (Kodalle, 86; see Krause's *Das System*, 471). Krause was also well ahead of his time in regard to slave trade and slavery, and he considered fighting any kind of racism to be one of the main legal duties of man. What is most extraordinary, however, is the fact that Krause did not believe that nature must be subordinated to man's wishes. Thus, he proclaimed also that the world of animals and plants, of stones and crystals, had to be respected and that nature deserved as much respect as all other divine creations, in accordance with its essence and dignity. Thus, a right of nature, although he was well aware that human greed would make it difficult to protect nature from exploitation. Penal law, in Krause's view, could not be revenge and punishment but had to be based on education. Since he considered a criminal a sick man, society had to find ways to lead him back to his right path. He needed help and love, not the whip.

Finally, Krauses's theory of the state and society differed profoundly from that of his contemporaries Fichte, Hegel, and Schelling. The state of Krause is an association of a league of right (Kodalle, 88–89; see Krause's *Das System*, 82), and its end was to establish a framework within which man could develop his proper rational life. Within the state there existed many social groups, beginning with the family, associations, peoples. The state had no right to intervene and direct the lives of all these different groups. Hence, the role of the state, in contrast to Fichte, Hegel, and Schelling, was quite limited, and all groups within the state had to develop in full liberty. Thus, groups—like scientific organizations, universities, and labor unions—also had to have full autonomy, and the Church had to be separated from the state—coordination, not subordination, was the trademark in their relationship.

Since the state in Krause had no absolute rights, the source and origin of law was not exclusively the consequence of the state's will. In a formal way, law was created through the social expression of will in all human associations, and ranged from the family to the state, and finally ended in a future League of Nations, but from a substantial point of view, all these associations were determined by Divine order (Kodalle, 89–90; see Krause's *Das System*, 332ff.).

Krause's ideal State was based on his legal philosophy. Thus, a rationally established State could only be a representative democracy, a democratic republic. The Constitution of the United States came close to his ideal.

I.iii.

Krause's political thought makes sense only if one takes into account his ethical foundation. Since no human culture can live without law, no world State could function with a world legal order. Krause's world system was part of his natural-law theory and was based on the solidarity of all men since, in his view, the individual who had legal obligations should at the same time be interested, not only in his own achievements but in those of others, because both sides had claims against each other. Krause's ideas on solidarity were perhaps his most important contribution to any future philosophy of law, and although these concepts were imbedded in Christianity, it was Krause who developed them for the first time in a systematic manner.

Krause's idea of ethics were based on two elements: the idea of goodness—the highest good—and the idea of freedom; the one was linked to Plato, the other to Kant. In Plato he identified both the Good and the Divine. What was the Good? The Divine; What was Divine? The Good (Wettley, 51–52). Krause arrived at this construction essentially through the source of good in itself, through the view that there existed something absolutely good without any relation to a certain being for which there was a good. With this concept of the good, Krause was definitely basing himself above a Kantian foundation (52). Krause's ethics thus started from a Kantian Premise and contained numerous Kantian elements but went further and showed a great reliance on the deepest truths of Christianity.

Krause's ethics also had a psychological foundation, since Kant lacked any mystics, and Krause defined mystics as men with an intimacy with God (*Gottinnige Menschen*). For Krause the perception of good for a good action was of utmost importance and was linked to a most profound intellectualism, hence the high value given to science, and the perception of the good as a very special science, the highest truths. Thus, in Krausean ethics, the highest principles were always men's most inner religious convictions, expressions of character, and manifestations of will, and thus also the enormous importance of enthusiasm. Here again Krause gained another point over Kant, since enthusiasm was lacking in the ethical psychology of the categorical imperative. The highest feelings of religious enthusiasm were linked in Krause's ethics to the calm and unsuppressible actions of men's original drives that aimed, first of all, at self-exhibition and self-perfection of mind and body; thus Krause was able to determine the ethical importance of selfish drives (Wettley, 57–58).

The discussion of the egoistic and altruistic drives and dispositions in Krause's ethics led to significant and original consequences in the ethical relationship between individual and society. It also led, on the one side, to a remarkable opposition to Kant and the latter's ethical individualism, which made it impossible for Kant to see beyond it and thus fully understand the ethical importance of the objective structure of community life, and on the other hand, to a powerful rejection of Hegel's system, which while fully acknowledging the justice of the ethical significance of the community, lowered the importance of the individual, even if he did not contradict Platonic-Aristotelian ethics (Wettley, 59).

The relationship between the ethical components of the individual and the higher life of human society represented one of the most thoroughly examined parts of Krause's ethics, and finally, without neglecting the lower associations of tribes and people, he emphasized the highest human association: the existence of One Humanity to which he gave highest priority in his idealistic system. The highest goal of the individual person, as it was of all lower social or natural associations, was to lead this humanity to an ever greater perfection (Wettley, 60). In the final analysis, Krausean ethics led to a real cult of humanity, quite dissimilar from that visualized by Auguste Comte—the one was metaphysical and idealistic; the other realistic, materialistic, and antimetaphysical.

In his ethics, Krause went beyond the ten commandments and established twenty-one, which included definite duties toward God, reason, and nature, toward one's own person and toward others, toward marriage and family, toward higher organizations and humanity. Starting from the Kantian categorical imperative, Krause had affirmed that the ethical duty was based on the moral essence of man and independent from the behavior of others toward us as an orientation for our own actions (Wettley, 80). Thus, in conclusion, Krause's ethics contained both Kantian and Christian elements and both were not chosen in an artificial form only, but were joined together in an organic Whole to grow into a unique system that, as Emil Wettley stated, reflected the very special personality of Krause: on one side, his critical and courageous speculation, and on the other, his deeply religious soul (Wettley, 80).

II

II.1.

As in other parts of Western Europe, Krausean philosophy arrived first in Spain through Heinrich Ahrens and his natural law theories of Krau-

sean vintage, but the real impact came through the famous journey of
Julián Sanz del Río (1814–1869) to Germany in 1843. The latter had
been commissioned by the Spanish Government of Pedro Gómez de la
Serna to go to Germany and study philosophy in Heidelberg. Through
the acquaintance of von Leonhardi and Röder, he learned about the philosophy of Krause, which by that time was forgotten in Germany.

Sanz del Río returned to Spain and introduced the Krausean philosophy in a way Ahrens had not been able to do earlier through the
Spanish translations of his works. Actually Krause, Ahrens, and Röder
became the models for Spanish legal krausismo: it echoed an idealism
that in the view of Gil Cremades and in a theological sense reflected the
spirit of both Aristotle and St.Thomas Aquinas (Cremades, 356).

The reason the Spanish Government sent Sanz del Río to Germany
was because the Spanish universities found themselves in a deplorable
state of affairs, and in reality Sanz del Río's journey to Germany had
similar consequences in Spain as the famous discovery of German culture by Germaine de Staël for France half a century earlier, or the works
of Coleridge and Carlyle on England (López Morillas, 85). Spain had
suffered for too long the excessive French influence, and German
Romanticism had actually dug up the glories of the Spanish past that the
Spaniards themselves had forgotten during the period of the Enlightenment. Since the Germans fought this French cultural domination it
seemed logical for the Spaniards to look for solutions in Germany. Thus,
Sanz del Río's journey to Germany did not lead to the discovery of Krausean philosophy but quite generally to the discovery of Germany and its
culture, which in time would be strengthened in the twentieth century
with José Ortega y Gasset. It was also within this context that Friedrich
Carl von Savigny's Historical School reached the Iberian Peninsula.

In the nineteenth century, Spain followed three definite schools of
thought: (1) either a neo-Scholastic or neo-Thomist course (Jaime
Balmes), (2) a Traditionalist route (Juan Donoso Cortés), or was gradually caught up in the web of the neorationalism of Positivism, and (3)
in-between were the Liberals who, based on English and French models, were followers of the Doctrinaire Liberal movement of Pierre-Paul
Royer Collard and the Liberalism of Benjamin Constant de Rebecque as
expressed in the constitution of 1837 and 1845. However, the more
progressive Liberals soon realized that in order to combat the conservative and traditional elements, Spanish Liberalism had to have an idealistic basis. This explains the successful Krausean inroads since the new
Liberal breed saw in a Spanish adaptation of Krausean philosophy—

krausismo—an effective way to fight both the conservatives on one end of the political spectrum and the Positivists on the other. The earlier Liberalism of the first part of the nineteenth century had been unsuccessful—too materialistic and utilitarian, too atomistic and mechanistic—and what was needed was a totally different and new Liberalism with an idealistic face, or as Hennessy stated:

> In reacting against French influence intellectuals were echoing popular feeling, but in German thought suited the radical's purpose for a number of reasons. Strauss and Feuerbach fostered a rationalist criticism of Catholicism; Krausist moralism gave a criterion for judging "immoral" doctrinaire Liberal political thought, its pantheism provided a religious alternative to Catholicism, and its legal implications a criticism of the whole legal structure. But above all Krausism with its doctrine of *armonismo* provided an all-embracing ideology, making it a potent force for moral regeneration. Although the Krausists did not have any specific political affiliations, many of them saw republicanism as a vehicle for imposing reforms on the country. (Hennessy, 79–80)

Krausismo became the most important intellectual movement in Spain against Traditionalism and neo-Scholasticism and also affected the Positivists' inroads, turning many followers of the latter philosophy into Krauso-Positivists or idealistic Positivists. The Krausean impact in the middle of the century was such that krausismo attained a dominating position in the years 1854–1874 (López Morillas, 13; cf. Cremades). The September coup of 1868 (Prim, Serrano, Topete) was much influenced by krausismo and the First Spanish Republic of 1873–1874 was essentially a *krausista* endeavor. Even the Second Spanish Republic of 1931–1938 echoed a fading projection of nineteenth-century krausismo. It found fertile ground among the intellectuals and radiated a great influence in the fields of religion, philosophy, law, education, and government, which is hardly understandable unless one is familiar with the essence of Hispanic character and temperament.

In Spain krausismo became a quasi-religion, even a mystic movement, a religion of humanity with a new vision of man as the synthesis of the universe (Menéndez y Pelayo, 1082). It also represented a humanitarian movement that attempted to establish new laws in regard to the individual's own conduct in life and that wanted to reform the country's institutions within a liberal mold, endeavors that translated themselves into many cultural and political actions, especially of an educational nature (see Jobit). It also meant legal political liberalism: self-government, parliamentary rule, judicial autonomy.

Krause's entire moral outlook—his idealism, and the Krausean notion of the immediate vision of God's substance—corresponded very much to the traditions of the Spanish mystics of earlier centuries. As in Erasmus, earlier, Krause's system contained traits of the theological nature—in this case the idealistic evolution of humanity in a world ruled by God, or as Sanz del Río echoed it:

> The entire human being and the entire humanity will be elevated in God, will live more faithful toward its eternal destiny, more harmonious with the life of the world, in higher spheres both of nature and spirit. All men will know one another and will love one another as one family of the sons of God and destined to develop in the plentitude of divine life, and in this last hope they will remake once again their history as a new construction. (López Morillas, 277)

Krause's *Urbild der Menschheit* furnished the basis of Sanz del Río's *Ideal de la humanidad para la vida,* which was published in 1860 and soon became the standard text for an entire generation of Spanish and Spanish American krausistas: it represented a moral system based on a metaphysical foundation that in turn was linked to a philosophy of history (see Fernando Martín Buezas; López Morillas, 40–47; and Menéndez y Pelayo). Sanz del Río's krausismo thus envisioned a legal theory of a clear ethical substance and where a variety of problems, the law as ethical conditionality, and others, would be further developed by his disciples as variation on the same theme (Cremades, 59).

Spain produced several krausista generations and, as Jackson wrote in 1984 from Madrid, when he spoke of the *vigencia del krausismo,* the actuality of Krausean philosophy in today's Spain is a fact. The main krausista centers were Madrid, Oviedo in the north, and Seville and Granada in the south. Besides Sanz del Río, the first krausista generations included such personalities as Hermenegildo Giner, Francisco Giner de los Ríos, Francisco de Paula Canalejas, Manuel Fernández y González, Federico de Castro y Bravo and Urbano González Serrano in literature; Fernando de Castro in religion, and Emilio Castelar, Nicolás Salmerón and Gurmesindo de Azcárate in politics.

Francisco Giner de los Ríos (1839–1915) represented, after Sanz del Río, the greatest krausista exponent because he was especially identified with the ethical reform and a moral regeneration that found in Manuel

B. Cossíos (1855–1935) and Adolfo Posada their greatest continuity (Valdeavellano, 20). Giner de los Ríos was linked to the *Institución Libre de Enseñanza*, his brainchild, a kind of graduate school and a truly pedagogical institution. In his view, the *Institución* was the major instrument to execute the philosophical idea of Sanz del Río: science at the service of Man (Valdeavellano, 83). Cossíos was the favorite student of Giner de los Ríos who continued the work of his teacher. As director of the Museo Pedagógico Nacional, another krausista institution, he continued the great work initiated by his mentor and teacher.

II.ii.

In the context of Krausean philosophy Lorenzo Luzuriaga could well be considered to be the perfect bridge over the Atlantic. An important member of the "Generation of 1914," which also included Ortega y Gasset, Luzuriaga not only played a great role in Spain but also in Argentina and, indirectly, in Guatemala.

Born in Valdepeñas in 1889, Luzuriaga entered Madrid's Teaching College—the *Escuela Normal Central*—at the age of twenty and studied philosophy. Much influenced by Cossío, who also introduced him to Giner de los Ríos, his greatest impact at the time came from Ortega y Gasset. However, his link with the *Institución Libre de Enseñanza*, both as a pupil and teacher, strengthened his ties with krausismo. With a scholarship from the Institución, and where Natorp, Dilthey, and Wundt as well as others influenced him. Upon his return to Spain he published *Dirección actual de la pedagogía en Alemania*, and for some twenty years collaborated in the Publicaciones of the earlier mentioned *Museo Pedagógico Nacional*. In the years 1917–1921 he directed the section "Pedagogy and Public Education" of the newspaper *El Sol* of Madrid, whose mentor and director was no other than Ortega y Gasset (Pelosi and Dabusti, 188, 209–11).

The "Generation of 1914" believed very much in the urgent need to reform Spain's educational system in order to change Spanish society, and as member of this generation Luzuriaga contributed with great zeal and enthusiasm to this goal. It led to the establishment of yet another institution, the *Liga de Educación Política* with its *Revista*, which followed the line of thought of the teaching of such French educators of the Third Republic as Buisson, Lavisse, and Pacault (Pelosi and Dabusti, 211). Luzuriaga's social concern was included in his *Bases para un programa de institución pública*, which appeared in 1918, and in 1922 this led to the *Revista de Pedagogía* with which he launched educational theories. Actually his *Bases* were included into the political program of the Spanish Socialist Party (PSOE) in its 1918 Congress.

Luzuriaga's summit occurred with the second Spanish Republic when he became a member of the National Council of Public Education. However, the Civil War forced him into exile to Argentina where he succeeded in establishing a remarkable prestige in both Buenos Aires and Tucumán (Pelosi and Dabusti, 212). His arrival in Argentina brought yet another wave of krausismo to the Río de la Plata and actually extended krausismo to the interior far north of the country. It was through him that his pupil Juan José Arévalo Bermejo, later President of Guatemala (1945–1950), introduced krausismo into his country and shaped his "Human Socialism." Finally, Luzuriaga's career in Argentina produced a high point in 1956 when he obtained the chair of Education and Pedagogy at the University of Buenos Aires. Three years later, however, he died.

III

III.i.

To understand the connection of Spain-Argentina-Guatemala in this Krausean context we must now turn to the River Plate area. Argentine democracy is fundamentally rooted in Krausean philosophy. Even today's Argentine Constitution of 1853 is very much a krausista document (see Barraquero), a fact that for a long time was not recognized as such.

The first wave of Krausean philosophy arrived here in 1856 when Luis Cáceres, at the University of Córdoba, acquainted his students with Ahrens's philosophy of law. After 1860, at the same university, the legal theories of Heineccius, as well as Grotius and Pufendorff, were replaced with Ahrens's *Curso de Derecho Natural*. At the same time Ahrens's theories also became known at the University of Buenos Aires, and in the early 1880s the Faculty of Law inaugurated a chair of philosophy of law. Since 1884 this chair was held by Wenceslao Escalante (1852–1912) with whom for a quarter of a century the Krausean philosophy would become the greatest instrument against Positivism. Escalante had also been Minister of the Interior (1893), Minister of Finance (1897–1898), and Minister of Agriculture (1901–1904), which obviously gave him additional influence. The first wave also included Julián Barraquero who with his dissertation *Espíritu y práctica de la Constitución Argentina* interpreted the Argentine Constitution as a krausista document and analyzed its spirit and practice from a krausista point of view. On the surface the Constitution followed very much the model of the United States, but its substance was totally different in spirit and practice; it also was more generous, and the Preamble stated clearly that the Constitution would promote well being and secure freedom, not only for the citizens of the Republic but for all the people who wished to live on Argentine soil. Thus, the Constitution followed more the solidary Liberalism of Krausean impact, quite a unique case in constitutional law (Barraquero, 51–70, 139, 171).

A second wave of krausismo arrived at the beginning of the twentieth century, at a time when three fundamental philosophies became important and fought each other ideologically: Neo-Thomism, Positivism, and krausismo. So far, the Krausean philosophy had reached Argentina mainly through Ahrens, but as time went on, Tiberghien also had to be added to the list of intellectual vehicles for Krausean philosophy. However, the Spanish variety of Krausean philosophy became an increasingly important element in the first decades of the new century. The bridge of this new projection was the Spanish policy of cultural expansion under Francisco Gines de los Ríos that targeted especially the Spanish community in the River Plate as a natural recipient. The journeys of the krausistas Rafael Altamira y Crevea (1909) and Adolfo Posada (1910), at the time of the centennial festivities, had a particular strong impact since they coincided with the new University of La Plata, under its president Joaquín V. González, becoming the center of the cultural exchanges between Spain and Argentina.

This last wave of krausismo strengthened the concept of solidarity and applied Krausean philosophy to political action: the right of association and of labor unions as well as the right to strike as part of Natural Law within the general principles of the Constitution of 1853.

A further krausista influence of the Spanish variety came with the Spanish Civil War. It unleashed an impressive new wave of intellectuals who were all more or less connected with the *Institución Libre de Enseñanza*; men, like Claudio Sánchez Albornoz, Lorenzo Luzuriaga, Manuel García Morente, Pedro Corominas, Luis Jiménez de Asúa, and others. Obviously, they were not all krausistas, but still krausismo in Argentina received a new impulse, especially through Luzuriaga and García Morente. Luzuriaga introduced krausismo at the University of

Tucumán, thus bringing krausismo to the northern parts of the country. In 1939 Luzuriaga revived the *Revista de Pedagogía*, founded in 1922 but no longer published, which then became a powerful vehicle for the diffusion of further krausista philosophy in Argentina during World War II. Finally, when Luzuriaga came back to Buenos Aires in 1944, his return meant another revival of krausismo in the Argentine capital.

III.ii.

Perhaps the most remarkable and no doubt the most profound influence of Krause in the entire Ibero American continent concerned Hipólito Yrigoyen Argentine President (1916–1922, 1928–1930), with whom krausismo became a social and political force. His life and career coincided with the first two waves of krausismo.

Yrigoyen's entire life and behavior were molded in the Krausean spirit. His seriousness, dignity, gravity, lack of humor, and appearance resembled that of his Spanish colleagues of a generation earlier. When in 1896 he took over the Unión Civica Radical (UCR), he never compromised with the government—he preferred to wait two decades than to weaken his principles by cooperating with the governing elite. The Krausean philosophy also explained the fact that as president he refused to live in the presidential mansion but preferred to govern the country from his shack; he also refused to accept a presidential salary and instead gave it to the poor. Thus, no doubt, when the UCR came to power in 1916 it signaled not only something entirely new in Argentine politics, in the sense that the middle class had not arisen, but Yrigoyen gave his presidency a special mark, original and quite distinct, which was unique. From the very beginning his regime was linked to the social question and Yrigoyen became the idol of the masses. His concern for the poor was honest and in practice it led to the introduction of social legislation and to the protection of labor unions.

Yrigoyen's entire domestic and foreign policies only make sense if one understands his intellectual formulation and background. He obtained harmony with the mind imposed by self-education, and Krausean ethics perfected this moral outlook. He was a Quijote of democracy, of political liberties, of absolute justice (Gálvez, 226). This austere man hated all kinds of exhibitionism, led the life of a hermit, an apostle, a spiritualist, a moralist; in sum, of a krausista of strict asceticism and unbending idealism in the midst of rising materialism, sensualism, disbelief, and superficiality (Gálvez, 208). His writings show the echo of

Ahrens, Tiberghien, and Krause (Roig, 188ff.). Among those that are especially important for an analysis of Yrigoyen's personality are the manifestoes concerning the Revolution of 1905, the polemics against Pedro C. Molina of 1901, his annual messages to Congress, and the writings he addressed in 1931 to the Argentine Supreme Court for his defense (Roig, 189).

Yrigoyen called his administration "*La Reparación*"; in his view, to straighten things out after half a century of immoral government. La Reparación was to usher into a period of democratic renewal where ethics would be the guiding star and where all the wrong doings of past presidencies would be corrected. His letters, declarations, and manifestoes of those years, as well as those before 1916 and thereafter, all exude basically the same spirit: intransigence, revolutionary zeal, idealism, integrity. To give but one more example, in his First Letter to Dr. Pedro C. Molina, dated September 1909, he stated:

> Frugal and virtuous men and peoples make free peoples and centers of civilization, but men and societies dominated by licentiousness and wantonness of material pleasures will only achieve conglomerates exposed to all kinds of risks and decompositions. (Del Mazo, 78)

The UCR, which Yrigoyen led since 1896, fought a battle similar to the Spanish krausista liberals and adopted similar policies. The entrenched privileged classes, the oligarchy, professed Liberalism, even if it had constantly abused its powers; hence, the new middle-class party, the UCR, had to be different, although also liberal. Thus, the liberalism of the UCR had by necessity to wear different clothes; it had to be based on a different intellectual and spiritual foundation. In Argentina, the question arose, how could middle-class liberalism fight the so-called liberalism of the entrenched Conservatives? The answer in Argentina was identical to the Spanish situation: the new liberalism of the UCR had to be based on an idealistic philosophy, and this meant krausismo.

Krausean philosophy also became visible in the famous University Reform of 1918 (the Córdoba movement that influenced all Ibero America except Brazil and Mexico at that time), which attempted a total democratization of the universities with professors and students running their government. It was also the Argentine president who in the same spirit and with profound love for Spain and all Spanish Speaking countries proclaimed October 12 (Columbus Day) the *Día de la Raza*, the day of Hispanity, as a day for all Spanish- and Portuguese-speaking countries to celebrate and show solidarity. The Día de la Raza was then adopted by all members of the Iberian world in that same spirit Yrigoyen had given it. Finally, we should not forget the two famous slogans that Argentina proclaimed time and again: "La victoria no da derechos" (Victory does not give rights)—now incorporated as a guiding principle in the Charter of the Organization of American States—and "Argentina para la humanidad" (Argentine for Humanity).

Argentine foreign policy during Yrigoyen's presidency showed an identical Krausean impact. Yrigoyen continued the policy of neutrality of his predecessor Victorino de la Plaza—a pantheist idealist—and defended the independence of Argentina with a moral heroism that was again truly remarkable (Gálvez, 221). Even when the United States entered the war in 1917 and the economic situation deteriorated rapidly, Yrigoyen did not change course, not even when two Argentine ships were sunk by German U-boats and when the German Ambassador Count Luxburg had made some undiplomatic remark about Yrigoyen and his government, which the Allies only too gladly made known to the Argentine authorities. Even the increase of diplomatic pressure with the United States, even sending a fleet and demanding unconditional reception, did not deter Yrigoyen. Olympically he refused any different policy but the continuation of neutrality. For Yrigoyen participation in a war in which humanity was split into two hostile camps was out of the question.

Yrigoyen showed the same idealistic zeal when Woodrow Wilson launched his League of Nations in Geneva. Argentina became the first nation in Ibero America to join it (12 July 1919). However, when Wilson pressured for incorporation into the Convenant of the League of "such regional understandings as the Monroe Doctrine," which Argentina had not accepted and which it considered tantamount to the continuation of exclusively national policies, Yrigoyen felt deeply disappointed. Hence, Argentina attacked it as incompatible with true Pan Americanism and with an international organization such as the league (Peterson, 367).

But much worse was to come: as soon as Argentina joined the league, Yrigoyen proposed that the covenant be changed so that any sovereign State could join and that all members of the Council be elected by a majority vote of the league assembly, instead of allowing the victorious powers a permanent tenure of five places (Levene, 506–7; Spencer Bassett, 95–97). When the league showed no inclination to change the Covenant and to adhere to the Argentine proposals, Argentine withdrew from the league on 4 December 1920. It was the first country to be disillusioned with the postwar settlement. It showed Yrigoyen's personality, his remarkable courage, and extraordinary defense of true international morality. It also showed pride and dignity. No doubt, it represented a high point in Argentina's idealistic foreign policy. Like the previous policy of neutrality, the Argentine attitude was also interpreted as a tough "Argentina First" or pro-German stand, but in reality it was Yrigoyen's fundamental adherence to krausista philosophy. Germany also interpreted this attitude as pro-German and honored it when on Argentina's national holiday, 9 July 1920, all German warships remaining in German hands after Scapa Flow flew the Argentine flag. It had become apparent to Yrigoyen that the league was not the symbol of universal solidarity based on the metaphysical harmonious rationalism of Krause's dialectics, but simply a club of victors to use such an international body for their uniquely selfish designs.

IV

It was this Argentina where Krause and krausismo were an intellectual and political force between 1916–1922 and 1928–1930 that now influenced the future Guatemalan President Arévalo. Born in Taxisco, on the Pacific coast of Guatemala in 1904, young Arévalo followed a teacher's carrer. As such he graduated in 1922 at the *Escuela Normal Central*. At the same time that he was teaching on the primary and secondary levels he was also working as Inspector General of the Department Schools, and in 1924 became the chief of the Technical Section of the Guatemalan Ministry of Public Education. He graduated as a bachelor in Jalapa and in 1925 began legal studies in the capital. Here the text was León Duguit, and as Arévalo stated, his studies included the works of "Ahrens, Miraglia, Del Vecchio, Cathrein, the Argentine Carlos Octavio Bunge: these were the authors and the texts which he could read and reread" (Arévalo, 128). It was in that same year that Arévalo was appointed honorary director of the student magazine *Hebe*, which became the mouthpiece for a new idealism: social problems were to be aired and attacked, and pedagogy should be converted into political action. *Hebe* and the *Teacher's College* manifesto of 1925 already demonstrated the spiritual and intellectual path Arévalo had chosen and that clearly was shifting toward the Krausean ideals (Arévalo, 135). Then a scholarship took him to Europe and on his return to Guatemala he visited Mexico where he was profoundly influenced by José Vasconcelos and his Mexican educational revolution. This Mexican influence was the second encounter with krausismo, although the deepest and most important was shortly to come in Argentina. It should also be mentioned that at that time the two Latin American presidents who were acclaimed as worthy men of continental projection were Hipólito Yrigoyen and Plutarco Elías Calles (Arévalo, 201).

Back in Guatemala he received an Argentine scholarship with which he began his studies at the University of La Plata in 1928. He graduated in 1934 with a doctorate in philosophy and educational sciences. Between 1934 and 1936 he was back in Guatemala working in the Ministry of Education. He also gave several lectures at the University of San Carlos, on such topics as "The Argentine University Reform" and "Humanistic Studies in Argentina." Arévalo's lecture aimed at university reform in his country, taking as a model the Córdoba movement of 1918. He also wanted to establish a Department of Humanities at the University of San Carlos, again following Argentine examples. From that date two basic goals in Guatemalan higher education headed the list in the reformist movement: autonomy for the University of San Carlos and the establishment of a Faculty of the Humanities within it (Del Mazo, 242–43). However, soon after these lectures President Jorge Ubico closed the University and, in view of the repressive measures, Arévalo preferred to leave the country voluntarily, which he did in 1936.

Again he went to Europe from where he sailed to Argentina. Here in his second stay in Argentina he was to remain until 1944, waiting for the opportunity to return to Guatemala. In 1937 he joined the Faculty of Philosophy and Letters of the University of Tucumán. Thereafter he held the position of secretary of the Faculty of Humanities at the University of La Plata and simultaneously taught at the University of Buenos Aires. In 1941 he accepted an invitation of the National University of Cuyo where, in its branch in San Luis, he directed the Escuela Normal. A year later he founded the *Instituto pedagógico*. Soon afterwards he taught at the Mendoza branch's faculty of Philosophy and Letters and at the same time held the position of Inspector General of all the educational centers of the National University of Cuyo. For a short time he was also the Inspector General of Schools for the Province of Mendoza. Finally, in 1944, he returned to the University of Tucumán where he held three chairs in psychology and pedagogy. The fall of Ubico in that same year took him again to Guatemala, where in

December, 1944, he was elected that country's president for the term 1945–50 (Dion, 10–12).

It is obvious that any intellectual, and particularly an educator and political scientist who had spent some fourteen years in Argentina as Arévalo did, would at some point come into contact, approvingly or disapprovingly, with the krausista movement, which so effectively had influenced the UCR in that country. Arévalo saw krausismo first hand in his hero President Hipólito Yrigoyen, and furthermore, at the university of La Plata, which prior to World War I had developed a close link to Spanish krausismo. Finally, the third wave of krausismo, again from Spain, arrived with the many Spanish republican intellectuals. Among them, the most important krausistas were Luzuriaga and García Morente. Both settled in Tucumán, and Luzuriaga taught at the National University there between 1939 and 1944, at the same time Arévalo was also in Tucumán. It was in Tucumán that Luzuriaga, after June 1939, began publishing the *Revista de Pedagogía* of the Pedagogic Museum of Madrid. Not only did the University of Tucumán radiate now a belated krausista message, but the *Revista* strengthened this influence since it reached both Argentines and foreigners (and many more than just the students who listened to their respective teachers at the University) and was closely linked to the Spanish krausista movement and its attempt at educational renewal.

It should not come as a surprise, then, that Arévalo was highly attracted to the message that the Spanish krausista delivered from Tucumán and through the *Revista de Pedagogía*. It was an impact that came on top of the earlier krausista influence that Arévalo had received from UCR, and particularly from his hero Yrigoyen. It was this krausista philosophy, totally based on an ethical foundation, which Arévalo had already brought to Guatemala in the early 1930s but which he introduced with even greater depth after his return in 1944. These krausista ideals found a profound echo in his political program, his "spiritual socialism" of 1945–1950, that guided his administration in his goal of achieving a society based on social justice, liberty, freedom of the spirit, solidarity, and harmony. No doubt, Arévalo's "spiritual socialism" was something of a novelty in Central America. It had nothing to do with Marxism, or even with social democracy. Neither was it linked to Christian Democracy. Arévalo was a patriot, a great friend of Argentina, an admirer of Yrigoyen. Gabriel del Mazo, in his recollections, tells us that he had developed a great friendship with Arévalo at the University of La Plata and that when the Guatemalan left Argentina in 1944 he gave him as a gift his book *EL pensamiento escrito de Yrigoyen*. Emotionally, Arévalo told him: I assure you, Gabriel, that I shall govern with this book" (Del Mazo, 242–43). It was in that Argentine environment that Arévalo acquired the old Greek notion that politics could only be carried out within ethics, which had been the krausista message of Yrigoyen in particular and of the UCR in general.

The most important works of Arévalo were his doctoral thesis *La pedagogía de la personalidad*, published in 1937, which dealt with the German School of Personalistic Educators based on spiritualist philosophy of Rudolf Eucken, an admiror of Krause and initiator of a new idealist activism that attempted to overcome the decay of modern dehumanizing civilization; *La filosofía de los valores en la pedagogía* (1939); *La adolescencia como evasión y retorno* (1941); *Escritos pedagógicos y filosóficos* (1945), which dealt with Plato and Kant; *Estudios políticos* (1945) and *Fábula del tiburón y las sardinas* (1980). Besides these works, Arévalo's bibliography also includes the *Discursos presidenciales* and *Mensajes presidenciales*, compiled in 1953 (Dion, 12–13).

Besides Krause and krausismo, Arévalo was much influenced by German philosophy and psychology: he was the first to introduce Eucken to Latin America (Dion, 31), and tried to harmonize and overcome the antagonism and contradictions between an objectivist absolutism and a subjectivist relativism. He thus reached a pluralistic solution to the problem of values that came close to the theories of Max Scheler (29–30),

Arévalo's views of the states and of democracy were idealistic. Arevalism, in his own words, was "a romantic movement which believes in the excellence of the human person and the dignity of popular greatness" (Dion, 59). Thus, democracy for Arévalo, could not be the nineteenth-century version, individualistic and atomistic, materialistic and selfish. For him democracy meant the organization of all social classes of the country, harmonized by generous laws that gave to each his value and his place in the economic and cultural development (59). Social harmony was not based on absolute personal liberty but was conditioned "by the economic and social interest of the Nation" (62). Within his "spiritual socialism" the state did not have an omnipotent and repressive character—its goals were to establish a republic of free and worthy beings, and for that reason it would result in a free worthy Republic (96). Arévalo's "spiritual socialism" turned out to be the Central American version of Krausean philosophy and Spanish krausismo. And it goes without saying that his Krausean philosophy and his own experience meant solidarity and love for his Latin American fellow countrymen and their nations as well as for the *Madre Patria*, Spain. In sum, it is fascinating to point out how ideas move from one place to another and how they influence the environment. In this case Krausean philosophy renewed Spanish liberalism and Spanish culture, crossed the Atlantic, and had an impressive impact in Latin America. In some cases this influence was very strong, as in the River Plate area. In many cases it developed an interesting cross-fertilization, as in the case of the Guatemalan Arévalo, whose krausismo, to which he became especially attracted in Argentina—Buenos Aires, La Plata, and Tucumán—was reinforced by the Spanish republican intellectual, the krausista Luzuriaga, thus producing a bridging of the Atlantic.

Works Cited

Arévalo, Juan José. *La inquietud normalista. Estampas de adolescencia y juventud, 1921–1927.* San Salvador: Editorial Universitaria de El Salvador, 1970.

Barraquero, Julián. *Espíritu y práctica de la Constitución Argentina. Tésis presentada por Julián Barranquero a la Facultad de Derecho y Ciencias Sociales de Buenos Aires en 1878, para optar al grado de doctor en jurisprudencia,* 2d. ed. Buenos Aires: Tip. Lit. y Enc. del Colegio Pio IX de Artes y Oficios, 1889.

Cremades, Juan José Gil. *El reformismo español. Krausismo, escuela histórica, neotomismo.* Barcelona: Ediciones Ariel, 1969.

Del Mazo, Gabriel. *Yrigoyen. Su pensamiento escrito.* Compilation and preface by Gabriel del Mazo. Preliminary notes by Eduardo H. Passalacqua. Buenos Aires: Pequén Ediciones, 1984.

De Zan, Julio. "Der Krausismo in Argentinien". In Kodalle's *K. chr. F. Krause (1781–1832). Studien zu seiner Philosophie und zum Krausismo.* Hamburg: Felix Meiner Verlag, 1985.

Dion, Marie Berthe. *Las ideas sociales y políticas de Arévalo.* México: Editorial América Nueva, 1958.

Gálvez, Manuel. *Vida de Hipólito Yrigoyen. EL hombre del misterio.* Buenos Aires: Club de Lectores, 1983.

Guissani, Pablo. *¿Por qué, doctor Alfonsín?* Buenos Aires: Sudamericana Planeta, 1987.

Hennessy, C. A. M. *The Federal Republic in Spain*. Oxford: Clarendon Press, 1962.

Jackson, Gabriel. "Vigencia del krausismo". *El País* (26 February 1984): 9.

Jobit, Paul. *Les éducateurs de l'Espagne contemporaine*. Paris: Editions de Boccard, 1936.

Kodalle, Klaus M. *K. chr. F. Krause (1781–1832). Studien zu seiner Philosophie und zum Krausismo*. Hamburg: Felix Meiner Verlag, 1985.

Krause, Karl Christian Friedrich. *Das System der Rechtsphilosophie. Vorlesungen über Rechtsphilosophie*. Published by Karl David August Röder. Leipzig: F. A Brockhaus, 1874.

Landau, Peter. "Karl Christian Friedrich Krause Rechtsphilosophie". In Klaus M. Kodalle, *K. chr. F. Krause (1781–1832): Studien zu seiner Philosophie und zum Krausismo*. Hamburg: Felix Meiner Verlag, 1985.

Levene, Ricardo. *History of Argentina*. Translated and edited by William Spence Robertson. New York: Russell and Russell, 1963.

López Morillas, Juan. *El krausismo español. Perfil de una aventura intelectual.* México: Fondo de Cultura Económica, 1956.

Luna, Félix. *Yrigoyen*. Buenos Aires: Editorial Desarrollo, 1964.

MacCauley, Clay. *Karl Christian Friedrich Krause: Heroic Pioneer for Thought and Peace. A Memorial Record*. Berkeley: Gazette Press, 1925.

Martín Buezas, Fernando. *La teología de Sanz del Río y del krausismo español.* Madrid: Gredos, 1977.

Menéndez y Pelayo, Marcelino. *Historia de los heterodoxos*, vol. 2. Madrid: Biblioteca de Autores Cristianos, 1956.

Pelosi, Hebe C, and Teresa M. Dabusti. "Lorenzo Luzuriaga y la autonomía universitaria". *Cuadernos de Historia de España* (separata). Buenos Aires: Facultad de Filosofía y Letras, 1989

Peterson, Harold. F. *Argentina and the United States, 1810–1960*. Albany: State University of New York Press, 1964.

Roig, Arturo Andrés. *Los krausistas argentino*s. México: Gajica, 1969.

Spencer Bassett, John. *The League of Nations: A Chapter in World Politics*. New York: Longmans, Green, 1928.

Valdeavellano, Luis G. "Prólogo" in Adolfo Posado's *Breve historia del krausismo español*. Oviedo: Universidad de Oviedo Centro de Publicación, 1981.

Wettley, Emil. *Die Ethik Karl Christian Friedrich Krauses.* Inaugural Dissertation zur Erlangung der Doctorwürde bei der Philosophischen Fakultät der Universität Leipzig. Leipzig: Bär und Hermann, 1907.

7

Rodó's Ariel
or
Youth as Humano Tesoro

JAIME CONCHA

There are, I believe, two main reasons behind the writing of this chapter. The first is a wish to clarify a few aspects of Rodó's *Ariel* and the second stems from an old personal anecdote. This anecdote harkens back to my days of youth during a rainy night in Concepción. There, under a steady southern deluge, the door of a bar opened up and a group of students spilled out onto the street. To the amazement of everyone present, one of the revelers came out with this almost oracular pronouncement, "Youth is the discovery of life's immense horizon." Those of us present were a little surprised. The deserted street harbored neither traces of life nor youth, and its absence made the horizon all the more noticeable. However, the shock was even greater when we noticed that the ventriloquist in question was a member of the despised caste of petty lawyers, a group we always associated, in our exclusive and elitist humanism, with every form of ignorance. And it was we, the night owl littérateurs, who were the ignorant ones, unaware of Renan's[1] saying that, through the Uruguayan, *Ariel* had permeated the southern city. Renan maintained that youth's "human treasure" was a priceless privilege that one had to carefully invest in order to enjoy a comfortable return later on in life. This maxim, after being refined perhaps in the weekly and provincial liturgy of the Masonic temples,[2] was to be discovered and vigorously adopted by the middle class.

This memory comes to mind in connection with a more recent interest in Rodó's book as well as with his enigmatic notion of youth. The notion, anchored in Man's vital cycles that lack well-defined socio-logical contours, obviously lends itself to all of the twists and turns of Rodó's idealism. It is clear, on the other hand, that his idea has a definite, steadfast core and that it maintains a central position in his writing. Without a deep understanding of the meaning of youth and all of its nuances in *Ariel*, it is difficult to comprehend Rodó's ideological base and the particular circumstances that his message/program addresses. In short, it becomes difficult to understand his Americanism. His idea of youth, an intrinsically problematic concept, derives its power by rep-resenting a point of equilibrium between utopia and a new but real world.[3] In this light, in the pages that follow I take seriously what Rodó has to say about youth as I attempt to analyze both his conceptual mod-ulation and his use of metaphor. As we will see, these two do not always coincide. It is true, however, that this discrepancy—at times more of a collision—illustrates both its dynamism and its aporias. Therefore, this chapter is dedicated to the theme of youth, or to be more precise, to the quadripartite articulation of the terms linked to the notions of "ideal," "future," and "action." With these terms, the idea of youth establishes a series of correlations that form a highly flexible and extremely func-tional ideological network.

Dedicated to "America's youth," *Ariel* takes place between a portico presided over by Shakespearean inspiration and a final scene that mir-rors the first. Between these two brief poles, the work is composed of six sections, each treating a precise theme. The first section deals mainly with the theme of youth, although it also incorporates other elements. The second section discusses the defense of a human being's integral development, without mutilations and over and above vocational prep-aration. The third debates the cultural and social importance of an aes-thetic principle. The fourth undertakes the question of modern utilitar-ianism but turns primarily into a justification (against Renan) of the historic need for democracy as well as of democracy's legitimacy, con-ditioned on its recognition of hierarchies and of superior quality. The fifth section studies the United States of America as expounder of the "utilitarian spirit." On the one hand, it appraises the North American role in human progress, but on the other, it criticizes the elements of vulgarity and brutality that it has brought to civilization. Finally, the last section speaks of the metropolitan environment (especially Buenos

Aires) and explores the possibilities surrounding the spiritual creation of the future.

From Zum Felde to Real de Azúa, Uruguayan critics of Rodó have reached a precise conceptualization of *Ariel*. They have done so mainly by including it in the academic discourse of the eighties, a discourse whose framework is reciprocal academic back-patting and whose institutional features closely approximate a rectorial homily.[4] By placing Rodó's essay in this subgenre, one can clearly observe the time transpired between Sarmiento's militant stance in *Facundo* around the middle of the last century (1845), and this text published in 1900. In *Ariel*, the dominant, almost absorbing tone is one of terseness and serenity— emanations of a majestic voice that seem to descend from the heavens. In the work, one sees *Facundo*'s force and agony substituted by surface details and the value of the contours. Between the antidictatorial pamphlet that feverishly started appearing in exile and this well-thought-out and polished booklet, there exists a distance that not only reflects the historical change in the Rio de la Plata region but also reflects something related to the avatars of South American liberalism. Or, applying the witty observation of the learned Guatemalan writer, Cardoza y Aragón, who knew a great deal about the topic: while the Argentine found himself hounded by Rosa's goons, the Uruguayan seemed only to be persecuted by his own misprints.[5] Out of the militant and heroic liberalism that established civilization as the historical and philosophical principle from which to overcome the status quo, there surfaces a more lenient liberalism. This new tolerance, whose mannerist tone has long prevented the indispensable impartiality necessary to judge and evaluate it without *parti-pris*, would later try to break free from every form of Jacobism. If Sarmiento's strategy, the trajectory of his cannon shot, was, through the use of Quiroga's image, to wage war against Rosas by raising the specter of a regional caudillo, in *Ariel* the trajectory is part of an evangelical rhetoric whose curve traces the outline of intimacy by projecting itself *ad extra*.[6] If the Argentine's vision of the Orient was ideologically linked to his perception of American barbarity (the Bedouin hordes symbolize the gaucho guerilla fighters, etc.), Rodó's orientalism, in contrast, is diffuse—only a land of vague symbols. (The author calls one of his oriental parables a "symbolic short story.")[7] In other words, it amounts to a posthumous echo of a tradition that began with Hugo's *Orientales*, which at the turn of the century presented readers with a domesticated, ultraliterate Orient. This comparison has both shortcomings and advantages. On the negative side, the distinguishing feature of *Ariel* is not armed conflict but rather evolution; its constant disideratum is harmony, not contradiction. On the positive side, a ubiquitous aestheticism, emphasized by the author as the maximum value of life and culture, permeates the work. When years later Rodó was inclined to retrospectively contemplate *Facundo,* the pampa would transform itself into his frame and his novel's main character would lose his American gaucho traits and become the ghost of Macbeth. It is easy to see how, just as in *Ariel,* Rodó returns here to a Shakespearean theme. This is his way of viewing the American scene through the great prism of art, a device that permits him to clothe a barbarous, Creole caudillo in the somber trappings of medieval feudalism.[8]

Rodó is conscious of the nature of his work, something that he frequently emphasizes. "The genre of sacred oratory," he explains, is the discourse of youth. The terms *unction, devotion,* and the varied theological gamut with which he praises the eternally youthful spirit, reinforce this idea. When speaking of Renan, he states, "Even in the rigor of analysis, he knows how to apply the unction of a priest" (Rodó 1957, 73). Could this lyrical and flowery use of religious rhetoric be simply an ideological facade? The workings of Rodó in this regard follow more closely a logic of complementary terms already expressed in the title of his early literary enterprise, the *Revista Nacional de Literatura y Ciencias Sociales,* published in collaboration with Pérez Petit and the Martínez Vigil brothers. In the title itself, we clearly see the dual concern for both literary methods and sociology. It is useful to keep in mind this imperative duality when we turn to *Ariel.* For thanks to this condition, Rodó's sermon and spiritual message together with his progressive projects and programs form an indiscernible whole. The interior rhythm, the aerial harmony, finds itself in the service of action, reform to a great extent, which, in any case, is sociopolitical at heart.[9] In this light *Ariel* represents one of the many attempts at synthesis that Latin America produced around the turn of the century. It is a synthesis of the scientific materialist positivism that was dominant in the last half of the nineteenth century and the philosophical idealism that took hold in the 1880s and 1890s.[10] It also includes falls between the secularism to which both education and public opinion irreversibly led and the religious fringe benefits that by necessity had to be conserved in order to maintain a stable society.[11] In that regard, *Ariel* put the finishing touches on such a synthesis. Sharpening and refining liberalism and giving it an interior dimension that it had never possessed, it is the crown and glory of the nineteenth century's liberal establishment. In *Ariel* Próspero does not symbolize the concrete prosperity that Sarmiento had desired for his country.[12] Rather, as Rodó suggests, "había, para el nombre, una razón y un sentido más profundos"(Rodó 1957, 22; There was for men a more profound reason and meaning). It is spiritual wealth, a treasure chest of culture, a prosperity of a different character.

As for the Uruguayan political environment that surrounded the publication of *Ariel*, we can say the following: situated between the military regimes of Latorre and Santos and the modernization schemes that would emerge a few years later under Batlle y Ordóñez, *Ariel* embodies the moderated liberal ideal of its author. In the antipodes of the violent radicalism of his coreligionists, the "Colorado" dictators (a bitter taste of a still recent past), Rodó would distance himself as well from the excesses of the Jacobins, to which an excessively plebeian Batllism could lead—as shown by his controversial 1906 pamphlet. As immediately evidenced by Rodó's leadership role in the attempt to unify the Colorado Party's opposing factions, from *Ariel* on, his preference would always lean toward fusion (see n. 9).

It would be erroneous, however, to evaluate *Ariel* from the vantage point of an already established Uruguayan democracy. Even though Rodó's optimism and creative genius may parallel other political currents that would soon find expression in the Batlle order, the real framework that saw the writing and publication of *Ariel* was one of political and personal crisis. On the political level, the civil war had not yet ended; sporadic fighting continued until the 1904 Aparicio Saravia uprising that took place at the beginning of Batlle's first term.[13] On a personal level, recent investigations in Rodó's archives have shown that he suffered a severe emotional crisis shortly before 1900, a period to which he would later refer as his "shipwreck."[14] Against this decidedly sombre backdrop, is it not possible to see the optimism and marblelike serenity of his narrative in a different light? Could it be possible that the symbol of *Ariel* would be better understood if linked to the first episode of Shakespeare's play, the shipwreck in *The Tempest*. From this perspective the spirit of the book acquires more density. It now is transformed into a life preserver and its characters are valued as survivors.

These suppositions reveal a double meaning that, in the light of the smooth and uniform nature of Rodó's narrative, can easily be overlooked. In other words, the terseness of his style diverts the reader's attention away from these constant incisions. Let us take, for example, this passage from the beginning of the work: "Ariel es . . . ; es el entusiasmo generoso, el móvil alto y desinteresado de la acción, la espiritual-idad de la cultura, la vivacidad y la gracia de la inteligencia; el término ideal a que asciende la selección humana" (22; Ariel is . . . ; he is generous enthusiasm, elevated and unselfish motivation in all actions, spirituality in culture, vivacity and grace in intelligence. Ariel is the ideal toward which human selection ascends 31).*

Intoxicated by the heady nature of his writing, the reader might miss the miniscule and seemingly transparent phrase: "the elevated and unselfish motivation (*móvil*) in all actions." If instead we refuse to darken it in with our own preconceived notion of Rodó's style, we are able to pause and contemplate its peculiarity. The principle terms are *móvil* and *acción*. Now then, it is possible to interpret this psychologically and naturally understand that Rodó is referring to the internal motivations guiding the actions of young people. But it is also possible, and as we will later see from other indications, not hermeneutically unthinkable, that "móvil" and "acción" have connotations derived from physics. If this be the case, then a "Newtonism," for lack of a better term, is present and active in Rodó's system. "Lo alto", then, ceases to be a purely spiritual domain, the plane of symbolic space. Rather now in the literal sense it will be the physical area of a particular type of action. It will represent the space and the medium in which the "móviles" circulate—a domain that Rodó will later call, "el aire libre de la acción"(24; the free air of action 32).

When one looks at *Ariel* from this perspective, it is helpful to begin with this cardinal paradox: How is it possible that such a spiritualistic text gives rise to a "Newtonian"[15] conception of physics, a concept that, at least in part, underlies and articulates it? What is the role of these fragments characterized by a physico-mechanical epistemology when linked to eminently idealistic actions? Furthermore, what implications do these fragments have? Approaching this question requires both an explanation of the concept of youth as well as proof that such a physicomechanical dimension exists in Rodó's work.

In order to further clarify this point, if by "youth" we normally understand the period of human life transpiring between the end of adolescence and the beginning of maturity, we will fail to find such a chronological delimitation in *Ariel*. His notion of youth follows other lines, the two principal ones being intimacy and naturalism. "Espíritu

---

* All translations of *Ariel* come from the English version *Ariel* edited and introduced by Gordon Brotherson, Cambridge: Cambridge University Press, 1967.

de la juventud"(24; young mind), "juventud del alma"(31; young soul), and similar expressions tend to accentuate intimacy. On the other hand, youth conceived as nature, which eventually ends up transformed into instinct and biological spontaneity (38), unfolds with the rhythm of the seasons and gives rise to a series of metaphors related to the earth and plant fertility ("inmortal vegetación", p. 24; see also p. 136). Less conventional than youth as intimacy, this version, instead of an illusory *élan,* contains objective aporias. It is as if in the depths of youthful intimacy, Rodó discovered an instinctive root; and fearful of finding it sterile, he deifies it ipso facto, giving it supreme stature: "la sugestión divina de la Naturaleza"(38; Nature's divine suggestion 39).

In order to prove the existence of epistemological vestiges active in Rodó's ideology, I have chosen this initial formulation in which he describes youth in great metaphorical prolixity: "La juventud que vivís es una fuerza de cuya aplicación sois los obreros y un tesoro de cuya inversión sois responsables. Amad ese tesoro y esa fuerza" (25; The youth you are now living is a form of power; it is you who must employ it. And it is a treasure: it is you who must invest it. Cherish that treasure, that power 33).

Curiously enough, this definition, which closely resembles a moral maxim, is nestled in another definition, apparently tautological, with which it heads up both the paragraph and the aforementioned passage of Renan. It is interesting, above all, to observe the interactions produced among the three formulas in terms of the various schema of an incipient conceptualization.

The first one establishes youth as an object of faith. This initial equation essentially maintains that youth is faith in youth itself. Consequently, we see that Rodó already addresses the theme of youth with a systematic implementation of terms loaded with religious and evangelical meaning. What's more, the introduction of faith serves another implicitly philosophical purpose. It opens the experience of youth, exteriorizing it; in Hegelian terms, it weakens it, and in the process transforms it from a concept *in itself* to something *from* and *for* itself. We have here the particular use that Rodó makes of these types of terms. The display of theological virtues is by no means fortuitous or capricious in *Ariel.* On the contrary, it is equivalent to a theology by virtue of the display, a form that gives dynamism to the notion of youth and sets it in motion. First of all, faith establishes a relationship between youth and itself in relation to the mediation of moral duty. Secondly, hope is the relationship between youth and the ideals that generate the future.

Lastly, charity (the love mentioned so many times in the book) is the blending of these same relationships into a single beam of light. It is the radiation that consolidates the expansive character of youth at the same way that it refines, as we will later see, a latent substratum of energy and power. Clothed in this theological garb, youth begins to show itself as a process through which it manifests its own being.

When comparing the formulas of Rodó and Renan, one easily sees up to what point the student builds on his master, subjecting him from now on to a constant interplay of inflections. While it is clear that Renan was interested in underlining the dimension of knowledge, Rodó emphasizes the link with the effects of action: *fuerza, aplicación, responsables.*

The definition that I have transcribed carefully avoids giving "youth" a determined sociological profile. Instead it tries to institute a nonsynthetic, unreal conciliation of two opposing points: youth will be a laborer and an investor at the same time. It will use power, but at the same time it will manage its own capital. The lyrical and sentimental ideal of Darío here acquires some measure of reality that brings it closer to the sphere of human action (a humanized "divino tesoro" that goes against modernist tastes) and at last makes possible the relationship between this approach and the situation of the enlightened middle-class intellectuals on whose shoulders rests the management of the future. Having said this—and it is worth insisting on this point—this is not the problematic focal point of *Ariel.* The nuts and bolts of the reflection in *Ariel* consists of the effort to explore the ways and means of spiritual influence, the distinctive "how" of artistic activity that seeks to exist and produce in society. According to what I have already pointed out, *Ariel's* landscape is "the free air of action" through which moral and aesthetic forces circulate. One would like to direct these forces into a trajectory that would both carry them *to* as well as allow them to project themselves *over* society in its totality.[16]

This conceptual and lexical network is present from the beginning of the book, but it becomes more and more intense as we draw closer to and finally enter the sphere of actions in the North American realm. Here, in the section that is destined to evaluate both the obverse and the reverse of the United States in the course of human progress, what were once small forces, levers here and there (Rodó 1957, 28, 29) and improvised actions,[17] will come to full maturity. Let us examine a few examples of this system of forces that occur in the text:

Se ha observado más de una vez que las grandes evoluciones de la
historia . . . son casi siempre la resultante de dos fuerzas distintas y
coactuales que mantienen, por los concertados impulsos de su
oposición (104; More than once it has been observed that the great
epochs of history . . . are almost always the result of contemporane-
ous but conflicting forces 73) *En el principio la Acción era.* (110; *In the
beginning was Action* 77)

La relación entre los bienes positivos y los bienes intelectuales y
morales es, pues, según la adecuada comparación de Fouillée, un
nuevo aspedto de la cuestión de la equivalencia de las fuerzas que, así
como permite transformar el movimiento en calórico, permite
obtener también, de las ventajas materiales, elementos de superior-
idad espiritual. (133; The relationship between material good and
moral and intellectual good is, then, according to an analogy offered
by Fouillée, nothing more than a new aspect of the old equivalence of
forces; and, in the same way that motion is transformed into heat, elements of spiritual excellence may also be obtained from material benefits 89)

The passages hail from diverse sections, but they all have a common orientation. These passages are the parallelogram of forces that contains
the centralized instruction of statics, the laws of equilibrium and,
according to the Galileo of the *Discorsi* (1638), the principle of the composition of force; the Faustian motto that Rodó reproduces from
Goethe; and the final description that applies the first principle of ther-
modynamics to Culture. All of these selections consecrate a vision based
on either notions extracted from the material sciences or on a hypostasis
of human energy.

Curiously enough, this criticism, which in the name of idealism
seeks to condemn moral materialism (the dominant utilitarianism of
the North), constantly returns to the terminology of scientific materialism for support. Moreover, in truth, deep down these material processes
(almost always physical but also thermodynamic or pertaining to the
theory of gases) are the ones that provide Rodó with a unique model to
facilitate the propagation of his ideas.[18] The force-ideas (*idées-forces*) of
Alfred Fouillée, whom I have just cited, were probably present, due to
the fact that they were influential and gave rise to a long-lasting pattern
of configuration in the last third of the nineteenth century.[19] And the
reader of *Ariel* perhaps will remember the several pages that are dedicated to the phenomenon of propaganda—to the diffusion of intellec-

tual works—when obviously the word *propaganda* still lacked its present negative connotation.

> En el carácter de los pueblos, los dones derivados de un gusto fino, el dominio de las formas graciosas, la delicada aptitud de interesar, la virtud de hacer amables las ideas, se dientifican además con el "genio de la propaganda"—es decir: con el poderoso don de la universalidad. Bien sabido es, que en mucha parte, a la posesión de aquellos atributos escogidos, debe referirse la significación *humana* que el espíritu francés acierta a comunicar a cuanto elige y consagra. Las ideas adquieren alas potentes y veloces, no en el helado seno de la abstraccioón, sino en el luminoso y cálido ambiente de la forma. Su superioridad de difusión , su prevalencia a veces, dependen de que las Gracias las hayan bañado con su luz". (67–68; In the character of a nation, the gifts derived from refined taste, the mastery of gracious modes, the delicacy of altruism, the virtue of making ideas attractive, are also identified with the "genius of propaganda"; that is, with the all-powerful gift of universality. It is a commonplace that, to a large degree, to possess these select qualities is to possess the *humanity* the French impart to the things they choose to consecrate. Ideas acquire strong, swift wings not in the icy bosom of the asbtract, but in the warm and shining atmosphere of form. Whether they are widely disseminated and long lasting depends on whether the Graces have bathed them in their light 54–55)

There is, then, a categorical and explicit postulation of force and energy in the section that deals with the North. In the section on Latin America, on the other hand, in which the Latin American world—the "other" America that, in its tendency to blindly imitate (another form of gravitation) the United States, finds itself susceptible to losing its Latin heritage—we discover a lesser, almost euphemistic treatment of the theme. This Latin American euphemism will be the kingdom of air and light, which in a constrainedly prerelativistic panorama, crowns rather than opposes the Newtonian paradigm. The act of viewing, the domain of air and its vibrations of light, far from being a mere concretion of utterances or intimacy, creates an ad hoc epistemology for Latin America, an interval of experience in which actions separated by distance in Newtonian dynamics find a new application. They accomplish this task by influencing and affecting other masses on which they ultimately depend, but which do not destroy the illusion of an untouched spirit.

The sequence of terms helps to soften both the energy and the mechanical aspects by permitting the neutralization of the corresponding terms' semantic weight: "La juventud, que así significa en el alma de los individuos y de las generaciones, luz, amor, energía"(28; youth, which symbolizes light love and energy, for generations, and also for the evolutionary process of society—does exist 34).

Although we may read this as a climactic sequence by virtue of the preceding words *luz*, and *amor*, the term *energía* is relative, and for lack of a better explanation, loses its energetic character. And this, which one can find in other examples, permits us to read in perhaps a nontraditional manner *Ariel*'s well-known denouement. Enjolras, Prospero's young disciple, pronounces:

> Mientras la muchedumbre pasa, yo observo que, aunque ella no mira al cielo, el cielo la mira. Sobre su masa indiferente y oscura, como tierra del surco, algo desciende de lo alto. La vibración de las estrellas se parece al movimiento de unas manos de sembrador. (155–56; As I watch the passing throng, I notice that although people are not gazing at the sky, the sky is gazing at them. Something is descending from above upon these indifferent masses, dark as newly turned earth. The scintillation of the stars is like the movement of the sower's hands 101)

Here, the most unbearable aspects of Rodó's idealism begin to accumulate. They seem to culminate in a straightforward Platonic hierarchy: the stars above, the earth below; darkness here, light there; our herdlike and gregarious nature. Platonic thought, which in *Ariel* started out as a tripartite psychology *à la* Walter Pater (Rodó 1957, 22)—which thereafter came to be an idealistic modification of the Comtien law of the three estates (142–43)—ends up forging this cosmological happy ending in the midst of the urban night. It is important, however, to recognize both the communicative processes that are established between the two spheres and the manner in which they materialize. A "vibración", which is a prototypic version of a spiritual deed, intercedes between the "estrellas" and the "masa." This is the communication of ideas: a gentle force, a luminous energy in which intellectual influence shows through. The stars twinkle, showering their light upon the ignorant masses that wander through terrestrial streets. In this new modulation of liberal progressivism, Platonic sensibility and the Newtonian universe are inextricably joined.[20] If doubts still remain about this question, one only has to return to an earlier passage and relate it to the denouement:

> La ciudad es fuerte y hermosa cuando sus días son algo más que la invariable repetición de un mismo eco, reflejándose indefinidamente de uno en otro círculo de un eterna espiral; cuando entre las luces que se encienden durante las noches está la lámpara que acompaña la soledad de la vigilia inquietada por el pensamiento y en la que se incuba la idea que ha de surgir al sol del otro día convertida en el grito que congrega y la fuerza que conduce las almas. (138–39; A city is strong and beautiful when its days are more than the unvarying repetiton of a single echo circling and circling in an eternal spiral; when there is something in it that rises above the crowd; when among the lamps it lights by night is the vessel that accompanies the solitary wakefulness incited by thought, the vigil that incubates the idea that at the dawn is born as the cry that summons and the strength that leads human souls 92)

The panorama is the same; the elements are similar. In the midst of the big city, in the middle of the urban night, the stars come alive: the light of thought and of the street lamp. In Rodó's intense ascensional vision, the night's creative powers find themselves in service to the following day, at the disposition of the sun's activity and energy. The sequence of terms *idea, grito,* and *fuerza* speaks for itself, in the same way that it meticulously explains the sometimes poorly understood ulterior symbol of Esperanza's "gráfico grito"(Rodó 1957, 153).[21] In this triad, by virtue of which the idea is transformed into a force, the "grito" effectively consolidates Rodó's spiritualistic Newtonism by bridging the gap between solitude and society. "The strength that leads human souls" is the best expression of this paradoxical system. This system, however, is the only one that allows him to explain the action and mechanics of his ideas.

In spite of all of this, it is curious that, after having paused for a while in the modern city, Rodó returns to images of an agrarian environment. These "hands of the sower" that appear at the close of *Ariel* reveal quite a lot by renewing the Georgian tenacity that, from Bello onwards, aspires to reflect the reality of the ground-level Latin American struggle in the nineteenth century. Reiterating the idea of youth as natural fertility, they make visible—painfully visible in Latin American society—the distance from which this intellectual project of education, enlightenment and culture was conceived and implemented. This "sowing from above," on the part of an urban elite that had reaped from rural areas an "astrological" knowledge, then showed itself as a "sowing from a distance." In this way, Rodóian youth began to determine what would be, in the course of the coming century, the destiny of a great part of Latin American intellectualism: futile tilling of the air.

Discounting this aspect, without which one could not justly accuse Rodó (the Mariáteguis and the Mellas had not yet surfaced, and Recabarren and Sandino belonged to very different social groups), it is clear that in *Ariel,* Rodó poses a very real problem: How does one influence social groups? What is the nature of intellectual activity? How is it possible to orient and direct the masses? and, more restrictively in Rodó's mind, How does one carry out actions that fulfill humanistic requisites and at the same time avoid being guided by utilitarian ends? It is at this juncture that the correlated notions of both the ideal and the future come into play, thereby establishing a notably rigorous conceptual framework.

More than half of the last section of *Ariel* refers to and develops the structure of the future. According to this vision, the future is neither simple nor homogeneous, for its texture contains the following intertwined notions: a reaction to the status quo, a strong dimension of posterity, and lastly, the perception of the future itself as the distant goal of youth's actions.[22] These pulsations of the future, each wave larger than the last, form a temporal scheme in which actions separated by distance, instead of being valueless, confirm their importance as a distinctive trait of the task of culture. In fact—and this is vital for a thorough understanding of *Ariel* there exists no diametrical opposition between *human* and *utilitarian* values,[23] rather one finds either a diminution or increase of a temporal magnitude. In utilitarian actions, there exists no interim interval of time—interest is generated by the actions' relative immediacy in regard to their effect. On the other hand, for human and humanistic actions, as Rodó understands them, temporal distance is a determining factor. The more extended the parabola, the greater the projection of the goal into the inaccessible future; the more it will tend to coincide with the disinterested essence that is supposed to distinguish it. In utilitarian actions, time tends to converge towards the limit zero thereby showing that there is always a propensity toward the infinite in humanistic activity: divergent variables in the economy of actions; different modules; incommensurable units of measurement. Detached from immediate concerns, filtered and sifted by posterity, actions directed toward the future are the only ones capable of creating a truly human present. This gravitation of the future towards the present, the present's affinity with the future is an inherent characteristic of cultural life. This justifies and gives legitimacy to human actions as understood by *Ariel* and Rodó.

The magnitude that establishes this separation between immediate concerns and the future's attraction is the ideal. The ideal bridges the gap; it is the great curve that fixes the mobile in the most distant point on the horizon. It is not, as in Sartre's definition, an end without the means. In Rodó the ideal is simply ideal actions, actions carried out by and through ideas. It seems to me very probable that when composing this section Rodó had in mind the most privileged example of this phenomenon: the material and ideal nature of the printed word, a mobile that exerts its influence at a temporal and spatial distance.[24]

In this way the relations among the analyzed concepts neither fit into nor correspond to a simple grammatical proposition. Youth is not a collective subject, whose verb is action, directed towards the future as an ultimate goal—thanks to the effective complement of the ideal. On the contrary, one can better understand this group of relations in terms of linear algebra—a matrix, for example—in which all of its elements are interdependent variables: the variation of each one has an effect on the rest. The greater the tension of the ideal, the greater the future's power and presence. If the ideal conscience of the future increases, youth's actions become more possible and efficient. In this sense, the four aforementioned terms are only dimensions of the same process of cultural movement that renews the present in order to make way for a new phase in the evolution of ideas.

In this way, Rodó creates a certain "physics of ideas" that is destined to recognize and appraise the power of ideas in the functioning of societies. "Neoidealismo", as he accurately calls it, thus accepts and gathers together the results of the preceding positivism whose founder had conceived sociology as a type of "physique sociale." And if this sociology is precarious, since it constantly oscillates between organicist rudiments (groupings, hierarchies, order), the nomenclature of evolutionism (example, type species), and the discrete mumbling of the "free races" and the "thinking races," it also helps to profile the cultural dynamics that Rodó elaborates and proposes. Opposed to identifying society's concrete supporting structures, this sociology describes the phenomenon with an elegant and rigorous abstract purity that looks to delineate the action and the effects of cultural influence. If in *Ariel* we find its mechanics and its optics, in the *Motivos de Proteo* we are witness to an impressive attempt at calculus—as if one were trying to pinpoint the infinitesimal instant of change. In *Ariel* this reflection upon culture and society, upon ideas and social movement, leads to a very simple and categorical formula that has both the power of an evangelical apothegm as well as the simplicity of a scientific enouncement. Plainly stated, youth has an obligation to move the masses. We may or may not like the prescription, but whatever the eventuality might be, one would have to admit that it had an unquestionable influence for almost three decades. During that time it generated a varied gamut of arielisms in almost all of Latin America and was also able to manifest itself (not to mention the "arielist" groups by antonomasia, the typical university students) all the way from the squabbles in grade school teacher unions to more than one presumptuous presidential harangue.[25] Lastly, it would be a good idea to ask oneself if, among those who tried to stay afloat in the sea of independence and those who in this century have labored in a land in flames, there has not also been (perhaps more than one would be ready to concede) a good portion of arielisms—at least in the sense that I have tried to set forth.

Translated by Jeff Havlin

Addendum

The apologue of the Eastern monarch, which occurs in the second section of *Ariel* has given rise to multiple commentaries. Here is another in accordance with the ideas I have proposed.

The passage is divided into two parts, one describes the king's communion with his subjects and the other shows his inexpungable isolation. The first phase is organized (at least as far as their direction is concerned), in accordance with two opposing forces: "hospitalidad" and "liberalidad." Now then, this "inmensa reciprocidad de confianzas" (Rodó 1957, 50) is described as both a free-fall ("a desvanecerse tendía . . ., *como por su propio peso*, toda desventura") (48; any misfortune seemed to disappear in the boundlessness of his mercy as if *sinking of its own weight* 45) and in relation to the forces of attraction ("La naturaleza sentía también la atracción de su llamado generoso") (49; Nature, too, felt the attraction of the King's generosity 45). The topoi, the magical of Orpheus and the miraculous of St. Francis, culminate in an image that reminds one of Newtonian tides: "Empinándose desde el vecino mar, como si quisieran ceñirle en un abrazo, le salpicaban las olas con su espuma" (50; Waves from the nearby sea sprayed its walls with their foam, as if wishing to enfold the castle in their embrace 46).

The reclusive and interior retrenchment phase begins with an echo of Uhland (land of Uh-topia), which *significantly* charges the powerful sentence that closes the passage: "aislado en la Ultima Thule de su alma" (52; alone in the Ultima Thule of his soul 47). According to the Colombian legend, Thule is the unknown land prophesied by Seneca and located far away in the extreme northern regions of the planet. At that time it was both pole and center; before that it was the center of attraction; now it is a repelling pole. But what is worth noting here is not so much the separation between the exterior and the interior (which, after all, is obvious), but rather the fact that both find themselves situated on the same terrestrially or geodesically oriented axis of tension. The center of attraction, in order to avoid being contaminated by the attracted mass, distances itself until it is converted into a pole. This is nothing other than the center of actions separated by distance that in this manner "isolates" itself. But the island—the "Ultima Thule de su alma"—is nothing more than the preexisting idea of America. Rodó's idealism is never more physical than in this "symbolic short story" that has very little to do with a unilateral exaltation of intimacy.

Notes

1. The sentence, however, continues to be mysterious. To my knowledge no one has found it in any of Renan's numerous works. For example, Brotherson, in his excellent annotated edition, does not indicate its source.

2. An image such as this, in which the "vision of a regenerated America" is compared to the "vast rose window that radiates light above the austere nature of the somber walls" (Rodó 1957, 143–44) of a Gothic nave, should have been agreeable to those who frequented Masonic lodges. In accordance with both the traditional origins and the institution's name, the contrast between the light and shadows implants itself in the heart of the Masonic temple.

3. Renan's quotation, just transcribed, occurs in a well-structured paragraph that opens with the verb "to conquer" and concludes with "the visions . . . of the conquerors" (Rodó 1957, 25–26). The connection with the Spanish enterprise, obviously called forth by the association between the discovery and the conquest, adds a note of "hispanidad." However, what is the meaning of the equivalence between youth and the conquerors? In the absence of a historic pretext, one has, perhaps, seen it as pioneer rhetoric in the guise of a hymn or a

march; as the force of will in the experience of exploration and colonial expansion. If reality is absent, then utopia is the next best option!

4. From Alberto Zum Felde, see his first treatment of the subject in *Crítica de la literatura uruguaya,* and later, with modifications, from his well-known *Proceso* and *Indice.* From Carlos Real de Azúa, see his more mature treatment in the "Prólogo a *Ariel",* pp. ix–xxxv.

5. On Rodó's obsession with the ERRATAS, see Víctor Pérez Petit, p. 98ff. The first edition of this well-documented biography of Rodó was published in 1918 (Montevideo: Imprenta Latina). The edition that I have cited, although it is not dated, was published in 1937. It is considerably larger—512 pages, as compared to 325 in the first edition.

6. In preparing *Motivos de Proteo,* Rodó cites the New Testament: "para los que están en la parte de afuera, todo se hace por vía de parábolas" (Mark 4:11). Half of this citation, slightly modified ("Todo se trata por parábolas"), was used as the epigraph of the 1909 edition (cf. J. E. Rodó, *Obras Completas,* under the charge of Emir Rodríguez Monegal [Madrid: Aguilar, 1957], pp. 35, 301).

7. Included in the summary (written by Rodó himself) that heads up section II of *Ariel* and usually not present in ordinary editions (see *Obras Completas,* cit., 208).

8. "Como Macbeth en páramo siniestro, surge a la acción del drama la sombría figura de Facundo" (cf. "Juan María Gutiérrez y su época", *Obras Completas,* 705; in the earliest version, p. 780).

9. There is a perfect continuity (and coherence in my opinion) between Rodó's brief stint as a political journalist for the daily *El Orden* (1898) and, a little while after the publication of *Ariel,* his efforts as an organizer—almost leader—in the attempt to unite the Colorado Party (see. V. Pérez Petit, 201). This is without mentioning his later parliamentary projects, above all those that had to do with academic reform and university life in Uruguay (see "Discursos parlamentarios" in J. E. Rodó, *Hombres de América,* 250ff.). In reality, as Juan Marichal aptly mentions, all of Rodó's activities, intellectual as well as practical, revolve around the "problem of the relationship between culture and democracy" (cf. Marichal, 80).

10. Regarding the philosophical aspects in Rodó's work, see Arturo Ardao, *La filosofía en el Uruguay en el siglo XX,* 25–44; especially his excellent 1950 essay "La conciencia filosófica de Rodó", in *Etapas de la inteligencia uruguaya,* 241–69.

11. As is commonly known, Rodó studied for a while in the secular school "Elbio Fernández" that, according to Zum Felde, was "for a few years ... the most respected center of instruction in the Republic" (*Proceso Intelectual del*

Uruguay, 3d ed., 173; the first edition of this important work was published in 1930).

12. "Prosperity, riches, lights" is the constant triad in Sarmiento's *Facundo* and represents both his basic desire for Argentina as well as the essential requirements of his utopian capitalism.

13. See Tulio Halperín Donghi, *Historia contemporánea de América Latina*, p. 324.

14. His personal or intellectual crisis occured in 1891 and 1894, although another may have taken place in 1897. See Penco, *José Enrique Rodó*, pp. 8–10, 73–74.

15. I would like to make clear that I do not understand "Newtonism" as either a reading of Newton or his direct influence upon Rodó. Newtonism is better stated as the intellectual movement (translations, ideas, schema of thought and imagination) that took shape in France during the first half of the eighteenth century and that constituted a decisive vein in the history of the Enlightenment (see Pierre Brunet, *L'introduction des théories de Newton en France au XVIII siècle*). This knowledge, codified and mainstreamed, entered into manuals and permeated theological, political and scientific vocabulary in general (see Keith M. Baker, *Condorcet: From Natural Philosophy to Social Mathematics*, 7ff.; and Helen Metzger's already classic text, *Attraction universelle et religion naturelle chez quelques commentateurs anglais de Newton*). As for his own work, the North American historian Richard Hoffstader has spoken of the "mechanical metaphors" frequently used by the proponents of independence in *The American Political Tradition*, p. 10. The first edition was published in 1948.

16. Rodó said of U.S. books: "It has been a while since the wings of their books have reached an altitude where it would be universally impossible to descry them" (1957, 121).

17. What Rodó writes at the beginning of the book is curious: "Este programa . . . que se reserva otras veces para ser revelado en el mismo transcurso de la acción" (24; this individual agenda . . . which sometimes may be formulated or written but sometimes is revealed only during the course of action itself 33). How should one interpret this sentence: in a predialectic, semidialectic, or a decidedly antidialectic way? These kinds of ambiguities come from the following basic sources: Rodó leans toward a certain right-wing Hegelianism. His readings of Hegel are selective (Pérez Petit, 291), and, although he does not show a dialectical understanding of the relationship between theory and practice, he sees the need to reform the democracy. The whole *quid* consists of this.

18. About Poe and his position in the North American scene, Rodó writes: "Su alma escogida representa una *partícula inasimilable* del alma nocional, que no en vano *se agitó* entre las otras con la sensación de una soledad infinita. Y, sin embargo . . . cuando ideó a Ligeia, la más poderosa y adorable de sus criaturas, Poe simbolizó en la *luz inextinguible* de sus ojos el himno de triunfo de la Voluntad sobre la Muerte" (12; my emphasis; he is of the elect who resist assimilation into the national soul, a person who successfully, if in infinite solitude, struggled among his fellows for self-expression. And yet, as Baudelaire has so tellingly pointed out—the basic characteristic of Poe's heroes is still the superhuman persistence, the indomitable stamina, of their will. When Poe conceived Ligeia . . . he symbolized in the inextinguishable light of her eyes the hymn of the triumph of Will over Death 77–78). Differing from Sarmiento, for whom molecular movement (particles, agitation) expresses a barbaric and Asiatic materialism, Rodó emphasizes the process of a *particle vibrating* to an *inextinguishable light*. . . . Poe is a luminous body—a point of light in the middle of an environment dominated by energy.

19. In his edition of *Ariel*, G. Brotherson aptly points out the influence of Fouillée (n. 1, 4ff.).

20. As for the remainder, they are perfectly compatible, as A. Koyré pointed out some time ago in his classic text, *From the Closed World to the Infinite Universe*. One of the chapters on Newton is significantly titled "God and the World: Space, Matter, Ether, and Spirit" (206ff.). The difficulty experienced by the era's principal philosophers and scientists in accepting the notion of "actions separated by distance" is well known. Leibniz, his greatest opponent, ironically and expressively called it the "perpetual miracle."

21. The reader will remember that "hope" is in an "old coin" that was seen in a "museum" (Rodó 1957, 152). All of the ideological dilemmas center around this point: the structure of a noble era and a renovating ideal, a coin that is treasure rather than productive investment. Clearly, hope in the museum would be excessive sarcasm that Rodó does not deserve. I'm not sure why I got side tracked here.

22. This only permits the open challenge of Rodríguez Monegal's unilateral, exclusively utopian interpretation (see "El cincuentenario de Ariel", in Rodríguez, *José E. Rodó en el Novecientos*, 43–45).

23. The underlined selection is from Rodó (1957, 136). In a strict sense, I think that in Rodó there exists no categorical conflict between a intrinsic and instrumentalist concept of values. (I believe that, in some ways, Francisco Romero read *Ariel* in this manner.) Although this reading is not incorrect and indeed to a certain point is natural, it seems to me that Rodó's emphasis falls upon differences of degree, magnitude, and the spatial and temporal distance

between actions and their goals. *Ariel's* conceptual framework is not axiological, but rather sociocultural.

24. See note 16, where it is clear (or implicit) that a book should be a kind of mobile, with the spiritual coefficient of *Ariel*. See also *Ariel's* dedication, written by Rodó himself, sent to the Venezuelan César Zumeta: "Yo quisiera que este trabajo mío fuera el punto inicial de una propaganda que cundiera entre los intelectuales de América" (my emphasis; the quote comes from Carlos Real de Azúa's aforementioned "Prólogo . . . ", p. xxi; cf. n. 4).

25. Latin America's arielisms are still waiting for their historian. They are a fascinating chapter of our cultural heritage as well as a extremely complex theme in the history of ideas. From the vast bibliography (which for practical reasons I cannot include here), I will point out the recent and useful recompilation *El Arielismo en el Ecuador,* Quito, 1986. The president to whom I refer is the intermittent and vital appointee José María Velasco Ibarra who is represented in this book by two anthological pieces.

Works Cited

Ardao, Arturo. *La filosofía en el Uruguay en el siglo XX.* México: FCE, 1956.

———. *Etapas de la inteligencia uruguaya.* Montevideo: Universidad de la República, 1971.

Baker, Keith M. *Condorcet: From Natural Philosophy to Social Mathematics,* Chicago: University of Chicago Press, 1975.

Brunet, Pierre. *L'introduction des théories de Newton en France au XVIII siècle.* Paris: Blanchard, 1931.

Halperín Donghi, Tulio. *Historia contemporánea de América Latina.* Madrid: Alianza, 1979.

Hoffstader, Richard. *The American Political Tradition.* New York: Vintage Books, 1973.

Koyré, Alan. *From the Closed World to the Infinite Universe.* Baltimore: Johns Hopkins University Press, 1957

Marichal, Juan. *Cuatro fases de la historia intelectual latinoamericana.* Madrid: Ediciones Cátedra, 1978.

Metzger, Helen. *Attraction universelle et religion naturelle chez quelques commentateurs anglais de Newton.* Paris: Hermann, 1938.

Penco, Wilfredo. *José Enrique Rodó.* Montevideo: Arca, 1978.

Pérez Petit, Víctor. *Rodó. Su vida. Su obra.* Montevideo: Caludio García y Cía., Editors, 1937.

Real de Azúa, Carlos. "Prólogo a *Ariel*". *Ariel* y *Motivos de Proteo.* Caracas: Ayacucho, 1976.

Rodó, José Enrique. *Ariel.* Edited with an introduction and notes by Gordon Brotherson. Cambridge: University Press, 1967.

————. *Obras Completas.* Edited by Emir Rodríguez Monegal. Madrid: Aguilar, 1957.

————. *Hombres de América.* Barcelona: Editorial Cervantes, 1920.

Rodríguez Monegal, Emir. *José E. Rodó en el Novecientos.* Montevideo: Número, 1950.

Zum Felde, Alberto. *Proceso Intelectual del Uruguay.* Montevideo: Ediciones del Nuevo Mundo, 1967.

————. *Crítica de la literatura uruguaya.* Montevideo: Max García, 1921.

8

Jaime Balmes Redux: Catholicism as Civilization in the Political Philosophy of Pedro Albizu Campos

ANTHONY M. STEVENS-ARROYO

In the first quarter of the twentieth century, philosophical concepts of nation and culture first developed by the Catalán cleric and Catholic apologist, Jaime Balmes (1810–1848), were resurrected in Puerto Rico, half a world away in an island that Balmes scarcely mentioned in his writings. This phenomenon can be explained by careful examination of philosophical ideas that unfold against a background of changing political circumstances.

The Linkage

The book that links Puerto Rico to Balmes is *El protestantismo* (Stevens-Arroyo 1975). In this work, the Catalán apologist demonstrated the values of Catholicism and Spain over those of Protestantism and Northern Europe. It was his response to Guizot's premise that Scholasticism, Catholicism, and the Middle Ages were inferior to the Enlightenment. Balmes's later works, *El criterio* and *Cartas a un escéptico* amplified themes found in this major work.

Balmes contrasted the harmonious hierarchy of Medieval Christendom to a Europe torn by war and social conflict in the middle of the nineteenth century. For him, individualism, private enterprise, and rationalism were products of Protestantism's distortion of Christian civilization. On the other hand, the Spain of 1840 served as model for social organization. The privileges of the nobility were necessary, he argued, because this class formed a buffer between the absolutism of the monarchy and the chaos of the peasantry (chap. 59). Considering divorce a form of prostitution, Balmes asserted that courtly love in the Middle Ages was the apex of respect for femininity (chaps. 25–27). He stated that the Spanish Inquisition was lenient towards most Jews, punishing only heretics (chaps. 35–36).

Although these opinions fall on the right-wing side of contemporary thinking, Balmes is difficult to dismiss as a reactionary. Modern communications, public projects of assistance to the poor, increased medical research, and modern methods of education were humanistic causes he favored. Protestant apologists generally claimed that such policies originated with the Reformation and Enlightenment, attributing only obscurantism and reactionary views to Catholics. Balmes did not so much condemn modern progress, but rather claimed that the origins of all good things were to be found somewhere in the Medieval Catholicism. For instance, he thus argued that the Catholic Church had always suggested abolition of slavery, but in a gradual and organic way, rather than by legislative fiat. The Catholic approach to abolition, according to Balmes, sought to modify the customs of people, rather than impose norms of positive law that could prove destructive of social harmony (chaps. 15–19, 31).

Nor was he a blind believer in ecclesiastical privilege or in papal prerogatives. He defended, for instance, the Catalán right to dissent from the Pope (chap. 56) suggesting that "the Supreme Pontiff, as a particular person, can fall into heresy." The essential contribution of Catholicism was its exalted moral purpose, since for Balmes, progress without morality was not progress at all (chaps. 47, 67–71). Dedicated to reconciling Catholic traditionalism on the one hand and Spain's aching need for modernity in education, economic development, and political institutions on the other hand, Balmes saw in the corporate harmony of Medieval Spain a model to be imitated.

Balmes's apologetic style introduced long citations from original sources: Aquinas and Bellarmine, as well as the sixteenth-century Spanish Jesuits, Francisco Suárez and Juan de Mariana. From Suárez, Balmes defined the origin of social authority (chap. 54). From Juan de Mariana, he dwelt upon the reasons to legitimate the deposition of a tyrant (chap. 52). With these and many other citations, he attempted to justify a democratizing and progressive historical role from Catholicism in world history. But this role differed from that of Protestantism because of its moderation and tendency to work through institutions rather than with individuals.

The Spanish scholar of Iberian philosophy José Luis Abellán, separates Balmes's thought from the ultraconservative, nor even an apocalyptic Catholic one like that of Donoso Cortés (1809–1853), whose contemporary he was. Abellán considers Balmes, rather, as one in a long line from Catalán thinkers noted for a school of Common Sense, deriving in part of a Scottish empiricism to balance with Scholastic *a priorism* (Abellán, 346–48). In the words of Menéndez Pelayo, where Donoso Cortés was synthetic in thought and extremist in application to contemporary events, Balmes was analytic and moderate.

Balmes's great gift—and the basis for much of his popularity—was founded upon his ability to stitch together familiar customs and experiences with grand philosophical themes. Out of the texture of daily Spanish experiences common to his readers of ordinary sophistication, he wove a great tapestry in which Spanish traditions stood as evidence of superior civilization. For example, in *El protestantismo* he addressed the civilizational meaning of the bullfight in Spain (chap. 31). With ample erudition he essentially proved that rather than be apologetic to non-Spaniards about what is called a barbaric sport, aficionados of bullfighting were linked to a centuries-old tradition that had been elevated to high moral purpose by Spanish Catholicism.

During his lifetime the political importance of Balmes has always outweighed the originality of his philosophical contributions. Balmes wrote for a general public, and his articles were published in magazines and newspaper commentaries. Surpassing a merely esthetic admiration for Catholicism as a cultural expression, Balmes was strongly committed to the faith as a believer. His advocacy of religion was intended as part of a moral renewal among the people for the difficult task of creating a future for Spain.

I see in Balmes's approach to politics the germs of what is modern political populism. The 1840s saw the emergence of a party system in Spain and writing for a common public was an innovation. There can be little doubt that he wanted substantial change in Spain. His use of Catholicism was intended to make such change evolutionary rather than revolutionary. The restraining moderation based on continuity with the past that Catholicism represented was an antidote to a rapid and radical introduction of industrialized society, by either unbridled capitalism or revolutionary socialism. Balmes's moderating message, his use of common experiences, and his confidence in the basic virtues of Spanish civilization made his ideas very attractive to the people of his time.

Balmes's immense popularity was soon eclipsed, however. The reactionary course adopted by Pius IX after his disastrous flirtation with liberalism was one chief cause. While Balmes had written in 1848 in his last work of how Pius IX epitomized Catholic progress, the pontiff came to symbolize just the opposite. His 1864 Syllabus of Errors and the encyclical, *Quanta Cura* were capped with the declaration of Papal Infallibility in the First Vatican Council (1869–1870). Few could pretend that the Catholic Church stood in favor of any kind of progress after the harsh attacks of Pius IX against religious tolerance, democratic government, civil rights, or economic reform. Moreover, the rise of Krausism in Spain provided a temporary refuge against the extremes of either feudal absolutism or revolutionary socialism in mid-nineteenth-century Spain (Abellán, 394–511).

The end of the nineteenth century provided a resurrection of sorts for Balmesian thought. Leo XIII, who had met Balmes before assuming the papacy, issued the *Rerum Novarum* in 1891, and provided a new progressive stance for the Church that superseded the reactionary Pius IX. When Spaniards turned approvingly to such Catholicism during the generation of 1898 or during the Franco years, Balmes was *redux*.

Balmes was situated historically to link medievalist conceptualizations of Spain that arose in the seventeenth century with those of the twentieth century. He interpreted Suárez and Mariana about Spanish civilization in such a way in the 1840s that he could be repeated with them after 1898 and again during the Franco years. Thus, for instance, during the apogee of the generation of 1898 Baroja's book, *El arbol de la ciencia* ridicules Balmes by creating a caricature of triumphalist strain in Spanish society after the loss of the last of the colonies in the War in Cuba. Triumphalism surfaced again after the Spanish Civil War. Franco's Spain hosted frequent contests and school essay competitions about Balmes as part of a general policy of harmonizing a corporatist state with the twin notions of Catholic traditionalism and simultaneous material progress at a proper pace.

The Puerto Rican Balmes Redux

Life in Boston for a Puerto Rican mulatto who had came to the United States for the first time in 1913 on a Masonic scholarship proved to be a traumatic personal experience for Pedro Albizu Campos. Whether it was the sole cause for his transformation into an irreconcilable foe of American power in Puerto Rico is not clear (Stevens-Arroyo 1975, 10; Austin, 91–92; compare Hackett).[1] Faced with disillusionment (*Entzauberung*) of Weberian dimensions (cf. Swatos, 327), Albizu underwent an intellectual crisis. We know from his biographers that he confided in a priest, Father Luis Rodes (Ribes Tovar, 23). In a 1976 study, I verified that the readings that converted the young Albizu to Catholicism were from the works of Jaime Balmes.[2] It should be noted that Albizu's conversion to Catholicism was more of an intellectual matter than a religious experience. In Kavolis's terms, Albizu's embrace of Catholicism was a form of "religious revitalization" rather than religious revival (205). Although he professed belief in Catholic culture, Albizu was never regular in the practice of his rediscovered religion, following the general model for most Latin American men of his time. His political perspective on Catholicism allowed him to criticize aspects of church policy while exalting the faith. For instance, he denounced the Redemptorist missionaries from New York for using the Church to Americanize Puerto Ricans, the Catholic schools for teaching in English (Torres I, 270–71), and Cardinal Spellman for his patronage of the rich and anti-Communist at the Catholic University in Ponce (Díaz Ramírez, 168, n.53). But these observations should not be interpreted as detracting from the sincerity of his conversion: he was steadfastly committed to Catholicism as he understood it.

The Political Applications of Balmes's Philosophy

Much like Balmes, Albizu Campos made his greatest contributions to politics, not academic philosophy. Four volumes of Albizu's intellectual production have been published from the lifelong work of editing undertaken by the late Benjamín Torres. In his speeches and newspaper articles, Albizu demonstrates the same ability of Balmes to tie common Puerto Rican cultural customs to the grandeur of Iberian civilization. There is no direct mention of Jaime Balmes in any of the recorded speeches and writings of Pedro Albizu Campos. But this does not prove that he did not cite Balmes. The fragments of speeches by don Pedro in newspaper accounts, for instance, will cite that he spoke in "a long philosophical digression" (Torres I, 223), or that his speech lasted three hours (Torres I, 174).

But lack of direct testimony by Albizu of his indebtedness to Balmes, is not proof that don Pedro was not influenced by the Catalán's writing. I have taken pains to show textually, elsewhere (Stevens-Arroyo, 1975, that when Albizu quoted Mariana he quoted *Mariana as cited by Balmes*; when he cited Suárez, he repeated the Suárez he knows through Balmes. In a sense, Balmes was a mirror in which Albizu found the profiles of political philosophy, but his attention was to the outlines of that philosophy. The principal use of Balmes's thought by Albizu Campos was for its function as a political philosophy binding together ultraconservative Catholicism with a progressive social advancement for the nation. One must understand that Balmes was the point of departure for Albizu's Catholicism. Other Catholic thinkers and themes were adapted by Albizu and included in his speeches and articles (cf. Ferrao, 267–69). Balmes Redux came to Puerto Rico as part of a current of the times, swept along with others sources, such as the Arielistas (Zavala, 33–34) and José Vasconcelos.[3]

The Irish Connection

The Spanish-speaking world was not the only instance of political leadership turning to Catholicism as a bridge between conservatives and revolutionaries in the forging of a nation. In 1913, the year of the Albizu's conversion, James Connolly led the general strike of linen workers in Dublin. Connolly,who had lived for a while in the United States, had attempted a synthesis of Aquinas and Marx (Greaves; Ellis) as a basis for Irish revolt against British rule of the Emerald Isle. While Connolly's intellectual efforts were not as successful as his political leadership, he was not the only Irish leader to feel that Catholic identity had revolutionary potential in Ireland. Terence McSwiney, the Lord Mayor of Cork, who died in 1920 after a hunger strike while in prison, cites Balmes over and over in *Principles of Freedom* published in 1921. This matching of pro-Catholic philosophy with anti-Protestant speeches may have been the result of a centuries-old practice of sending prospective Irish priests to seminaries in Spain. But it should be noted that Balmes found grist for his anti-Protestant polemic in the speeches and essays of contemporaries, including Irish patriots (cf. Balmes, *El protestantismo*, chap. 7). Thus, not only Albizu Campos, but also Hibernians anxious to free their homeland from British rule had found in Jaime Balmes a philosophical voice for their cause against oppression by a Protestant nation.

Although the Irish influence is certain (Corretger 1969, 43–45; Silén, 41 n.; Fulton, 214), what is in doubt are the contours of this influence. Albizu's critics use the Irish connections as a mode of attributing terrorism in the mode of the Irish Republican Army to the Nationalists and their successors. Luis Angel Ferrao, who is sympathetic to the Nationalist cause, nonetheless considers Albizu's equation of the Irish and Puerto Rican struggles a political error. Ferrao assesses the weak connection between institutional Catholicism in Puerto Rico with nationalism, believing it different from nationalism's influence with Irish Catholicism and its native clergy.[4] Ferrao categorizes Albizu's Catholic emphasis as a form of exhibitionism (Ferrao, 258–59). While these criticisms ought not be dismissed summarily, the selection of Irish nationalism as a primary model for the Puerto Rican Nationalist Party can be traced to Albizu's encounter with Balmes while undergoing his intellectual crisis in Boston during the gestation of the Irish rebellion of 1916. The Spanish cleric quoted Irish patriots approvingly in *El protestantismo* (chap. 7) and also in other writings. He initiated the comparative link between the grandeur of Spanish civilization and the Irish struggle for independence. The function of Balmes's philosophy was to elevate a small and insignificant nation in political terms, into a participant in a major world civilization that rivaled Anglo-protestant hegemony. This I call the "argument of grandeur," and it was intrinsic to rallying support for the virtually impossible military task of confronting a major imperial power through a popular uprising on a Catholic island. The effect was the same in Puerto Rico as in Ireland.

The nationalisms of China and India during the 1920s exercised a certain influence upon Albizu after his conversion. But it should be noted that these are huge, densely populated nations, whose civilizations were characterized by native religions. Restoration of Puerto Rico's native Taíno culture, would have been alien to the argument of grandeur. Puerto Rico and Ireland, on the other hand, are small islands whose native religions survived only in folk tradition. Political leaders of the early twentieth-century rebellion sought to graft Irish and Puerto Rican nationalism onto Spanish civilization. This explains, I think, why Albizu preferred Irish nationalism to the Indian movement under Gandhi, even though the Puerto Rican leader had personally met Rabindranath Tagore, who promoted Ghandian principles as a way of subverting colonialism (Stevens-Arroyo 1975, 17–19). Finally, it should be noted that by identifying Spanish civilization and culture primarily with the Catholic religion, its defense acquired a sacred character.

Internationalism as a Political Weapon

The utility of identifying island culture with an age-old civilization provided political leverage for the independence movement. Balmes provided a window on the internationalist philosophy of nations in Suárez as well as the justification for a just war of independence as found in the Scholastics, and especially Juan de Mariana. These themes run through the Irish struggle for independence. As I have shown previously (Stevens-Arroyo 1975, 35–36), Albizu utilized the notion of nationhood as a marriage between the citizens and the motherland to imbue the nationalist cause with a sense of the sacred. This was taken from Suárez's, *De Legibus*, where he had explained that individual human freedom was constrained by social commitments to the nation much in the way that marriage freely consented to nonetheless imparts contractual obligation upon the parties (Balmes 1968, III 3: 2). Whereas Locke and the British philosophers saw the social contract as a fiduciary trust analogous to a business arrangement, Albizu, as influenced by the Catholic Suárez, described it as a sacred bond.

> The homeland must be loved as one loves a woman, spiritually and physically. He who does not suffer shame upon seeing it abused, is not a patriot, he is not even a man. (Ribes Tovar, 192)

The right of a nation to sovereignty was likewise given a sacred meaning. Suárez insisted that a nation could never renounce the right to sovereignty (Balmes 1968, III, 9: 2). While in actuality (*in actu exercito*) a nation could be without its own government, it always had the right (*in potentia*). A majority vote against sovereignty would not nullify the right, according to Suárez, since the democracy and freedom come from God. Contrary to Rousseau, the majority cannot make right what is objectively wrong, nor is the majority infallibly right (see Scannell, 55; Stevens-Arroyo 1975, 37–38).

Suárez also developed the notion of just war against a tyrant that is found in Aquinas and scholasticism. Suárez asked who would be justified in acting against the tyrant, thus applying the abstract principle of Aquinas to a very real European situation in which the religious hostilities between Protestants and Catholics had made civil war against authorities a palpable historical reality. Suárez reasoned that the tyrant could be deposed by the public, even violently, with the "general deliberation of its community and leading men" (Suárez, Def. Fid. VI 4: 14). This was amplified by Juan de Mariana.

The War for Freedom and Legitimate Assassination

Laudatory of medieval Spanish institutions, the Jesuit Juan de Mariana had considered his country the chief defender of Christendom against attacks by Protestantism. For Mariana, war against the Reformation was a continuation of the Reconquista waged against Islam by Spanish knights (see Albizu in Torres I, 255–56, 272). The fervor of the Jesuit led him to praise the assassination of the French Huguenot king, Henry III, whereupon he was censured by the General of the Society.[5]

Mariana's redress against tyranny served as a blueprint for the Nationalist Party. When the body of the Republic had been deprived of its soul, that is liberty, said the Jesuit, several men of prominence in the society must bring equal force against the tyrant and deprive his body of its soul, that is assassination. Mariana felt that as long as at least some in the nation opposed a tyrant, the rights of freedom were guaranteed.[6] Moreover, this opposition was the equivalent of war in which assassination was legitimate.

There are limits to the rebellion, however, each deriving from the code of the Spanish crusader. At all costs, the rebellion must not be seditious (Hansen Rosas, 320). The mercenaries of the evil ruler are also targets for violence. But just as the declaration of war against the king must be open and without subterfuge, so too the attacks on his hirelings must be in the nature of the knightly code of honor.

Martyrdom as Valor

According to Mariana, the principal purpose of attack was not victory on account of superior force, but demonstration of a more noble morality (Hansen Rosas, 321). For the Nationalists, the role of the assassin was intended to conclude either with death or with apprehension by the authorities and incarceration. In a sense, each mission was intended to bring about a form of martyrdom. Hence, religious self-immolation, rather than a suicidal death wish, best explains the party's tactics (cf. Marqués, 40–43; Silén, 88). In fact, Albizu realistically stated that the Nationalists could not hope to militarily defeat the United States, but that by trying they would unleash a public opinion that would lead to victory (Torres, 173; Torres II, 118). This tactic of self-immolation offers parallels with Ghandi's campaign in India (Corretger, 1972, 116–17; Lewis, 1974, 186–87), and ought not to be linked, as Clarke attempts to do, with "crazies." Most particularly, it echoes Connolly in Ireland. After his conviction and sentencing to death in 1916, the Irish leader explained his purpose in his last words before execution:

> We went out to break the connection between this country and the British Empire and to establish an Irish Republic. We believed that the call we then issued to the people of Ireland was a nobler call, in a holier cause, than any call issued to them during this war, having any connection with the war. We succeeded in proving that Irishmen are ready to die endeavoring to win for Ireland those national rights that the British government has been asking them to die to win for Belgium. As long as that remains the case, the cause of Irish freedom is safe. Believing that the British government has no right in Ireland, never had any right in Ireland and never can have any right in Ireland, the presence, in any one generation or Irishmen, of even a respectable minority, ready to die to affirm that truth, makes that government forever a usurpation and a crime against human progress.
>
> I personally thank God that I have lived to see the day when thousands of Irish men and boys and hundreds of Irish women and girls were ready to affirm the truth and to attest it with their lives if need be. (cited in Greaves, 421–22)

The notion of bravery *despite the inevitability of failure*, a frequent theme of Albizu's speeches,[7] is echoed in the statement delivered to the FBI by the Nationalist Oscar Collazo who was found guilty of attempted assassination of President Harry Truman in 1950 (cited in Stevens-Arroyo 1987.

Connolly in Ireland had organized the Citizens' Army in 1913, not as a clandestine terrorist organization, but as a public paramilitary force (Greaves, 329, 358). It was to act *as if sovereign*, anticipating Irish emancipation. In fact, the Citizens' Army already possessed legitimacy because it was the voice of an Irish sovereignty, which could never be renounced. The success anticipated in the founding of this Irish organization consisted in merely "being there." Military victory and international recognition of Irish sovereignty was a long-range goal, logically subordinated to first asserting via the Citizens' Army that it existed (Ellis, 203–7).

Albizu, like Connolly, imposed Mariana's formula for the legitimate revolution, including the somewhat impractical norms derived from chivalry. Thus, the Nationalist Party, in imitation of Connolly's Citizens' Army, held political meetings in open air plazas, practiced military maneuvers in public, and announced demonstrations and pickets against the government *before* the fact, although such announcements enabled the authorities to frustrate party activities. For instance, when the Nationalists carried guns and made no effort to conceal the fact, gun control legislation was easily passed in order to harass the party members (Corretger 1969, 76; Maldonado Denis 1972a, 197–98). The Nationalists observed Mariana's rules for chivalrous warfare. They never attacked any of the U.S. civilians in Puerto Rico. Despite frequent provocation, only members of the U.S. armed forces and government officials were victims of Nationalist violence (Corretger 1969, 116–17; Maldonado Denis 1972a, 34–39; Lewis 1974, 186–87; Cripps, 63–87).

Such a philosophic purpose, I would suggest, framed Pedro Albizu Campos' insistence on founding the paramilitary Cadetes de la República as a part of the Nationalist Party in 1933. It was the goal of acting as if sovereign that was imitated from the Irish experience. Likewise, the issuing of bonds in the name of a forthcoming "Republic of Borinquen" and the formal declaration of war against the United States by the Party, fit into this pattern of acting like a nation in order to become a nation. These notions came from Suárez and the Irish experiences as mediated by the contact with the thought of Jaimes Balmes. Thus, on the one hand, Pedro Albizu Campos repeated the philosophical framework, while imitating the Irish tactic of resistance on the other. But in both cases, the theoretical and practical were unified by the originality of Albizu's insight into Puerto Rico's reality.

Before concluding this description of the Irish connection with Albizu's nationalism, there is one other key notion to be listed. Irish Republicans maintained that "Englands' misfortune is Ireland's opportunity" (Stevens-Arroyo 1975, 56). This strategy was based on the belief that only outside world events could force a stubborn British government into a concession as monumental as Irish independence. Indeed, the king's proclamation of Irish freedom on 6 December 1922 is generally seen as London's recognition that it could not prolong fighting in Ireland after the end of World War I (Curran, 16–22; Townshend, 29, 205–6).

Albizu believed that as World War II grew more likely after 1935, it was imperative to develop a paramilitary potential that could threaten the U.S. in the Caribbean if and when it went to war in Europe. Placed in straits to fight aggression abroad and nationalism at home, the U.S., it was believed, would seek to settle just as England had done in Ireland and was to do in Egypt and India. In this insight, Albizu was correct (see Torres I, 211–12, where the Philippine experience is examined by Albizu). The U.S. offered such an agreement to the Philippines in exchange for resistance against the Japanese. Even in Puerto Rico, there is evidence that the Puerto Rican leader in 1940 before the war believed that eventually the United States would have to grant independence (Anderson, 52–53, 63). Yet, because he was feared, Albizu was deprived of his freedom in the campaign of the U.S. to discredit him and dismantle the Nationalist Party. Incarcerated in 1936, Albizu spent the war years in prison, leaving the way open to Luis Muñoz Marín's Popular Democratic Party to reap the benefits of Puerto Rican militancy at a time of crisis in the United States.

The Functions of Balmesian Catholicism

The establishment of the Puerto Rican independence movement was not an *ex nihilo* creation. In the waning years of Spanish rule, two opposing classes of *criollo* leadership had gained political legitimacy: conservative Catholics opposed to home rule; and free thinkers and anticlerical liberals, urging autonomy or even separation from Spain. When the United States' appointed governors assumed political control of the island, they encountered these groups scrambling for power.

But the first fifteen years of U.S. rule on the island had caused many of the free thinkers and anticlerical liberals to reconsider their admiration for the "modern United States." Much as the *Arielistas* elsewhere in Latin America, the Puerto Ricans began searching for a special character or soul to distinguish themselves from the United States. Thus, gradually emerged the nucleus of independence advocates who included *both* conservative Catholics opposed to a Protestant United States and freer thinkers resisting capitalist corporations. This group was a minority, largely because the power of the North American institutions, including a foreign Catholic clergy, thwarted any organized opposition to U.S. rule. It was only with the founding of the Nationalist Party in 1922, that there was a political alternative to seek separation from the United States.

Such was the party that don Pedro Albizu Campos inherited when he assumed its presidency in 1930. He faced the unenviable political task of keeping united two philosophically opposed groups of elite leaders, while simultaneously seeking to convince the public of the need for independence. In some ways, his need to speak popularly to the masses while walking a delicate line between conservative Catholics and liberals, was the same challenge that Jaime Balmes had confronted in Spain in the 1840s. Just as Balmes joined conservatives with progressives by suggesting that Catholicism understood as a modernizing force would bind together all the people, so did Albizu apply the same function to Catholicism in Puerto Rico. This is not to suggest that don Pedro consciously studied Balmes as a moderating force. I suspect that the utility of Balmes's arguments in his time maintained cogency for Albizu, and the Puerto Rican leader simply repeated from Balmes what he found applicable to his own situation.

The Balmesian notion that progress without morality is not progress at all can be found repeatedly in the writings and speeches of Albizu (Torres I, 272; II, 118–19; III, 66–67). I expect that this was the key message Albizu intended for the free thinkers in his party (cf. Ferrao, 289–93). But likewise, his paeans of praise for Spanish civilization were targeted upon the conservative Catholics like the Perea brothers (cf. Ferrao, 265), who formed another wing of the party's leadership.

Like Balmes before him, Albizu recognized the need to provide social justice in a new order for the island. His systematic analysis of Puerto Rico's economy embraces key notions about limiting the power of foreign corporations and the need for local land ownership (Torres I, 111–65). And even if such reforms advocated a return to power of small-landholders—the rural bourgeoisie—that is much criticized by modern commentators (Silén, 48–49), it is consistent with the evolutionary rather than revolutionary stance borrowed from Balmesian political philosophy. When pressed by the socialists within his party for a more explicit social agenda, Albizu insisted on the necessity of obtaining independence first, via a united populace, rather than risk dividing the party along ideological lines. Thus his party was focused precisely upon a "Nationalist" agenda, subordinating other considerations to the achievement of sovereignty.

Yet this does not imply that Albizu was partisan of the state-central-
ized notions of nationalism characteristic of Fascism. Albizu's arguments were in favor of restoring Catholicism as a civilizing force rather
than arguing that the party was the arbiter of national purpose. Once
independence was achieved, the mission of Nationalism would be
ended (cited in Ferrao, 299, n. 60). His militancy, as suggested above,
was directed against the instruments of an illegitimate foreign power.

The focus of Nationalist energies was upon establishing a just order.
This required not the fashioning of a new state or a new economic order,
but in restoring recognition among the Puerto Rican people of their
own dignity and in the international community of Puerto Rico's right
to sovereignty. Injustice in Puerto Rico, said Albizu, was the result of
conflict between two cultural systems, each contradictory to the other.
In my opinion, Catholicism for Albizu and the Nationalists approxi-
mated the Weberian function of "ethos," which highlights how value-
concepts derived from religious premises foster collective social action
(Weber 1949, 159–60; Bendix, 259–61).[8]

Albizu's conviction that a Catholic ethos guaranteed a correct moral
and political agenda has been summarized by his life-long compatriot,
Juan Antonio Corretger:

> his Catholicizing action was a conscious act of conserving what
> Puerto Rico has been in the fact of the North American policy of forc-
> ing Puerto Rico to stop being itself. If Imperialism, based on the lib-
> eral principle of freedom of conscience and worship fomented the
> proliferation of Protestant churches . . . , and of Masonry, as factors
> disintegrating the psychic unity of Puerto Rico, 'Let us foster Cathol-
> icism!' said Albizu Campos himself, 'in order to preserve what the
> invader wants to destroy.' (Corretger 1969, 45)

He articulated symbols that linked the aspirations of the Puerto
Rican common man to an elaborated vision of the world that hitherto
had been the domain of the educated elites. Utilizing the grievances of
both upper and lower classed in Puerto Rico, Albizu attributed Puerto
Rico's woes to United States' rule. His movement was the first truly
"nationalist" organization in Puerto Rico, consciously binding together
separate classes with a common call to one collective personality (Lewis
1974, 177–78, 186–89; Silén, 38–42, 91–99). Albizu found in Balmesian
Catholicism the social premises for interclass cooperation he believed
sufficient to create a Puerto Rican Republic.

Albizu's indebtedness to Balmes's political philosophy is reflected in his speech of April 14, 1931, commemorating the fall of the monarchy and the establishment of the Spanish Republic. The free thinkers and socialists in the Nationalist Party were overjoyed at the end of Monarchy that had come to symbolize both the dominance of Catholicism as well as Spain's reactionary political and economic systems. According to Corretger, who confesses his own difficulty at the time in understanding Albizu's reasons, the Nationalist leader argued against the antimonarchist sentiments of most of the those at the rally. Albizu declared that the Spanish Republic would not succeed if it destroyed the institutions that had developed in Spain over the centuries (Corretger 1969, 51–53). Such a speech, I would contend, echoes the use of Catholicism as a unifying force. Within the Nationalist Party, Albizu sought to satisfy two different wings, by rejoicing for the Republic on one hand, but providing a warning about the need for cultural continuity on the other.

Moreover, not only was this an appropriate stance for a Puerto Rican political leader, it was an accurate political diagnosis. This warning in 1931, before the emergence of Franco, proved to be prophetic, even if it was borrowed from Balmes's same political stance in the nineteenth century.

Catholicism and Fascism

Did Albizu's affirmation of a Catholic ethos make him into a Fascist? In the world of Puerto Rican scholarship, this is a question frought with political implications and has become a way of discrediting not only Albizu Campos but the movement for Puerto Rican independence. Like the accusation of "Communist" during the Cold War, "Fascist" conveys undesirable ideological tendencies. However, there is an inherent contradiction labeling the same person both "Communist" and "Fascist" at the same time, because the ideologies are conflictive of each other. Nonetheless, Albizu Campos was described as a "Fascist" before World War II and a "Communist" after it (Ramírez Barbot in Hackett)—even though he had spent all of the intervening years in a federal prison.

It would be remiss for a scholarly work not to address this issue of such vital importance to Puerto Rican assessment of its political ideologies. Moreover, a philosophic analysis of the sources of Albizu's thought has been missing from the general debate. The majority of current studies are focused upon historical questions or issues from the concerns of political science. Thus, for instance, Albizu's strong statement against despots like Machado in Cuba and Somoza in Nicaragua and elsewhere in Latin America (Stevens Arroyo 1975, 12–13) are offered as proof that he belonged to the anti-Fascist left (Maldonado Denis 1972b, 17–20). I am not certain, however, that the issue can be settled on the basis of association. Are Albizu's denunciations of U.S.-supported dictators in Latin America merely anti-American statements, meant to incorporate foes of the United States to the Puerto-Rican cause? When Albizu rejected right-wing authoritarianism supported by the United States, was his hostility primarily against United States' policy, or against an ideological posture?

José Luis González has advanced the thesis that Albizu was so conservative as to be anti-Franco because he was a Carlista (cited in Ferrao, 307, n. 68), and advocated the most reactionary form of Catholicism. While most commentators do not agree with González on this point, in varying degrees they do equate the support of the *Falange* by some members of the Party, the antipathy to Communism, and the adoption of Fascist organizational trappings as evidence of Fascist sympathies.

I would suggest, however, that the question should be addressed from a philosophical basis. The issue cannot be decided merely by tracing the influences upon the Nationalist Party in Puerto Rico by other Nationalist movements such as that of Mussolini in Italy. Nor should the accidentals of black shirts, banners, paramilitary activity, and so forth, be substituted for the substance of a political philosophy. Ferrao falls into this trap and concludes that at heart Albizu supported the Falange (326–27). He cites a letter Albizu wrote to his wife in the first year of his incarceration at Atlanta as proof that Albizu participated in the Franco's vision of Spanish Fascism.

> La Madre Patria de la civilización moderna, España, resurgirá en su gloria y poderío pristinos, cumpliendo su deber como depositaria de la civilización cristiana. (cited in Ferrao, 326–27, n. 91)

Yet this same citation could have been written by Balmes in the 1840s! Spanish Fascism adopted Balmes's political philosophy, not vice-versa. Hence, it becomes crucial to define the question of Albizuan sympathies as whether he was citing Balmes or the Falange. That both the Puerto Rican Nationalists and the Spanish Fascists used the same philosophical source does not make Albizu a fascist. The corporatist statement about society defended by Franco in the 1930s can be found clearly stated in the papal encyclicals of Leo XIII and Pius XI on economics, and was the basis for articulate clergy support for Franco, Mussolini, and even Hitler, but these events do not make Catholicism inherently Fascist (Germani, 275, n. 21; see Fulton, 212, citing Gramsci on the same point).

I reiterate that the purpose of Albizu's Catholicism was identical to that of Jaime Balmes: A unifying cultural ethos in which to introduce scientific progress and political modernization. The conservative Catholic wing of the Nationalist party was personified by the Perea brothers and Paniagua Serracante, and Albizu's declarations of the Spanish Catholic grandeur were intended to satisfy the conservative segment of Puerto Rican Nationalism. Advocacy of paramilitary action and a reformed socioeconomic system was targeted toward the left-leaning radicals and socialists in the party. But like Balmes's curious blend of conservative and progressive Catholicism, the ideology of Albizu Campos was constituted by the juxtaposition of both trends, rather than the domination of one or the other. Advocates of ideology instead of nationalism, like Vergne Ortiz or reactionary Catholics like the Perea brothers, were expelled from the party (Ferrao, 330, 333). Thus, reviewed as a coherent corpus of pronouncements with a philosophical basis, Albizuan thought contains elements that resonate both with Fascism and Communism, but which are neither. Rather than clarity, detailed analysis of the issue suggests that Albizu's ambiguity towards Spanish Fascism and anti-imperialism was intentional.

The statement of the party on the Spanish Civil War, one of the last official acts taken while Albizu was president and before his imprisonment after 1936, demonstrates not the Fascist sympathies but Balmesian moderation. After offering prayers for "the restoration of peace and the reconciliation of the Spanish Mother Country," the Party concluded,

> todos los españoles, sin distinción de creencias o credo político, en España, son defensores de la independencia de Puerto Rico. (Ferrao, 326, n. 90)

The stricture then proceeded to restrict direct participation by Puerto Rican Nationalists as combatants on either side. Ferrao points out that this reprimanded José Enamorado Cuesta, who had jointed Loyalist forces, but the party's decision also refused support for the Falange, something Ferrao neglects to mention in suggesting that the Nationalists supported Franco. This statement of neutrality and call for reconciliation of all Spaniards of both sides fits a Balmesian notion of Spanish national unity.

Conclusions

Albizu's politics for Puerto Rico were much like those of Balmes for Spain. In both countries, *mutatis mutandis*, oligarchical elites and their land-holding economic base were in the process of replacement by rapid industrialization and the introduction of political populism. The open-ended ambiguity of the Catholic political and religious symbols advanced a social agenda that promised to maintain harmony among classes. Restoration of the Catholic ethos, however, was also advocacy for a progressive introduction of scientific innovations. Under the aegis of Catholicism, the nation could unify both conservative and liberalizing tendencies during a transitional political period. In this, there was little difference in the basic philosophical cast between Albizuan and Balmesian thought.

When Albizu began his political stewardship of the Nationalist Party, however, the need to adopt pragmatic measures to advance his political agenda intruded upon his philosophical premises. The Irish experience after 1916—which had played such a key role in Albizu's conversion while in Boston—dictated action at the time of world war as a necessary condition for independence. Only in this way could a small country hope to force a world empire into granting independence. Not incidentally, Balmes's notions of a grand Catholic civilization transformed island culture into civilization and its preservation into a sacred duty. This was as true in Puerto Rico as in Ireland.

In addition to its Irish impulse, the Party acquired the trappings of other nationalist movements of the time, including those of Fascism. These were symbols to unify forces in Puerto Rico with a worldwide affirmation of political nationalism, rather than evidence of an ideological dependency upon Fascism.

On the basis of Albizu's concept of Catholicism as a unitary force in mediating Nationalism, his philosophy approximates religion. Although not a theologiam, Albizu Campos's charismatic leadership linked religion to politics by casting both as liberating expressions of Puerto Rico's inherited Catholic ethos. Albizu's system was designed to inject moral purpose and humanistic social focus into economic development. His was not a conservative and reactionary Catholicism. Rather, like Balmes, he sought material progress under the moderation of a spiritual renewal.

If Puerto Rico had gone on to establish an independent republic in the late 1930s or early postwar years, at least one of his followers believes

Albizu would have developed a clear program of Christian Democracy by borrowing from Jacques Maritain and some of the post–World War II European experiences (Corretger 1969, 42). Albizu's choice of Catholic symbol built an authentic, if precarious, synthesis that was properly his own. He was a pioneer in viewing religion as a source of political mobilization of a people.

In this sense, Albizu created a "conservative" Catholic political radicalism with creation parallels to the Peronist Justicialismo (Stevens-Arroyo 1988, 10, n. 1). Reliance on the hierarchical structures of the Church in the 1930s made his model reactionary, even at the same time it was anticapitalist. Nonetheless, Albizu's adoption of the Catholic ethos may also be considered a forerunner of contemporary Liberation Theology on account of a parallel call to inject morality into a political agenda (Stevens-Arroyo 1980, 58–59).

Albizu has had lasting influence on Puerto Rican politics because his emphasis of particularity accompanied by a linkage to a grand historical tradition and an attendant anti-imperialist worldwide movement. Thus, his defense of Puerto Rico was not a lapse into a defensive, self-demeaning profession of inferiority and insulation against the world but an option for solidarity with an anticolonial struggle. Because he adopted the "semiotic universalism" (Kavolis, 214–15) of Balmesian thought, Albizu made the labyrinth of Puerto Rican politics an example of a more general struggle in civilizational history.

Notes

1. Mistreatment of the blacks in the United States was definitely a factor in the conversion to the independence cause of Rosendo Matienzo Cintrón, like Albizu, a Rosicrucian (Hornik, 104–5).

2. My paper was shared with Harold Lidin, then a reporter with *The San Juan Star,* who was preparing a history of the independence movement of Puerto Rico (subsequently published in 1981). He showed my paper to Don Juan Antonio Corregter, lifelong disciple of Albizu in the Nationalist Party and his companion during the years of imprisonment in the Atlanta Penitentiary. He verified my deduction and, in a subsequent personal interview, told me that in the Atlanta prison Albizu read parts every day of two books he kept with him. These were Balmes's *El protestantismo* and a copy of Suárez's *De legibus,* that is, *Tratado de leyes.* Unfortunately, I have no correspondence to document the book choice, nor am I certain on whether the Suárez's edition was in Span-

ish, Latin, or a bilingual version; although I am virtually certain that Albizu had never studied Latin.

3. The philosophical connections between the Mexican Vasconcelos and the Puerto Rican Albizu Campos merit further exploration. It should be noted, however, that Albizu had as much impact upon Vasconcelos as the other way. See Vasconcelos's own testimony in Indología: "en Ponce, nos recibieron los nacionalistas. El jefe local, Pedro Albizu Campos, me conquistó de primera intención y me ha seguido cautivando. Posee una preparación sólida. ¡No sé cuántos años en Harvard! Así que conoce a fondo la cultura rival y nadie como él para exponer sus secretas debilidades y sus astutas maquinaciones. Pocos hombres me han enseñado tanto, en sólo un día, como me enseñó Albizu Campos" (xxiv).

4. By failing to distinguish between folk Catholicism, or the religion of the people, and institutional Catholicism, Ferrao falls into the error of overestimating the support of the official Church for Irish nationalism. The Irish hierarchy generally scorned the cause of militant Irish nationalism (see Greaves, 225–26).

5. In 1609, his criticism of Spanish imperialist policies—because they prejudiced domestic well being—provoked the Inquisition, which jailed him and destroyed many of his works so that, in 1913, there was only one English copy of Mariana's works available in the United States—in the Boston Public Library (Stevens-Arroyo 1975, 39–41).

6. See again Albizu's statement about the need to oppose statehood in 1948, which led to the Jayuya rebellion of 1950 (Corretger 1969, 111–15).

7. For Albizu, independence for Puerto Rico from the United States was equivalent to Spain's Reconquista against the Moors (Torres I, 255–56; II, 110–11; III, 77–83). Martyrdom was an essential component of such struggle.

8. It is not my intention here to debate the subtleties of Weber's thought. Besides this notion of a religious ethic that influenced social behavior, the Weberian notion of charismatic leadership may also be useful in analyzing Albizu Campos (Weber 1947, 358–63). Also see Fulton (211–12) for the notion of Antonio Gramsci on Catholic ethos as civiltá cattolica.

Works Cited

Abellán, José Luis. Historia crítica del pensamiento español, 4 vols. Madrid: Espasa-Calpe, 1984.

Anderson, Robert W. Party Politics in Puerto Rico. Stanford: Stanford University Press, 1965.

Austin, Dolores Stockton Helffrich. "Albizu Campos and the Development of a Nationalist Ideology," 1922–1932. Master's Thesis, University of Wisconsin–Madison: Department of History, 1983.

Balmes, Jaime. *El Protestantismo comparado con el catolicismo.* Madrid: Biblioteca de Autores Cristianos, 1968, 2d ed.

Bendix, Reinhard. *Max Weber: An Intellectual Portrait.* Garden City: Doubleday, 1962.

Clarke, James W. *American Assasssins: The Darker Side of Politics.* Princeton, NJ: Princeton University Press, 1982.

Corretger, Juan Antonio. *Albizu Campos.* Montevideo: El Siglo Ilustrado, 1969.

———. *El líder de la desesperación.* Guaynabo: n.p, 1969.

———. *La lucha por la independencia de Puerto Rico.* Guaynabo: n.p, 1974.

Cripps, Louise L. *Human Rights in a United States Colony.* Cambridge: Schenkman, 1982.

Curran, Joseph M. *The Birth of the Irish Free State, 1921- 1923.* Tuscaloosa: University of Alabama Press, 1980.

Díaz Ramírez, Ana María. "The Roman Catholic Archdiocese of New York and the Puerto Rican Migration. 1950–1973: A Sociological and Historical Analysis" (Ph. D. dissertation, Fordham University, Department of Sociology). Ann Arbor, MI: University Microfilms, 1983.

Ellis, P. Berresford. *James Connolly: Selected Writings.* London: Monthly Review Press, 1973.

Fernández, Ronald. *Los Macheteros: The Wells Fargo Robbery and the Violent Struggle for Puerto Rican Independence.* New York: Prentice Hall, 1987.

Ferrao, Luis Angel. *Pedro Albizu Campos y el nacionalismo puertorriqueño.* San Juan: Editorial Cultural, 1990.

Fulton, John. "Religion as Politics in Gramsci: An Introduction." *Sociological Analysis* 48, 3 (Fall 1983): 197–216.

Germani, Gino. *Authoritarianism, Fascism, and National Populism.* New Brunswick: Transaction Books, 1978.

Greaves, C. Desmond. *The Life and Time of James Connolly.* London: International Publishers, 1971.

Hacker, Frederick J. *Crusaders, Criminals, Crazies: Terror and Terrorism in Our Time.* New York: W. W. Norton, 1976.

Hackett, William H. *Report to the House of Representatives on the Nationalist Party.* Washington, DC: Government Printing Office, 1951.

Hansen Rosas, Christian. *Ensayo sobre el pensamiento político del P Juan de Mariana.* Santiago: Universidad Católica de Chile, 1959.

Hornik, Michael Sam. "Nationalist Sentiment in Puerto Rico from the American Invasion Until the Foundation of the Partido Nacionalista, 1899–1922" (Ph. D. Dissertation: SUNY, Buffalo, Department of History). Ann Arbor, MI: University Microfilms, 1972.

Kavolis, Vautaytas. "Contemporary Moral Cultures and the 'Return of the Sacred.'" *Sociological Analysis* 49, 3 (Fall 1988): 203–16.

Lewis, Gordon. *Puerto Rico: Freedom and Power in the Caribbean.* New York: Harper Torchbooks, 1963.

———. *Notes on the Puerto Rican Revolution.* New York: Monthly Review Press, 1974.

Lidin, Harold. *History of the Puerto Rican Independence Movement.* San Juan: n.p, 1981.

Maldonado Denis, Manuel. *Puerto Rico: A Socio-Historical Interpretation.* New York: Vintage Books, 1972a.

———. *La conciencia nacional puertorriqueña.* Mexico: Siglo 21, 1972b.

Marqués, René. *The Docile Puerto Rican.* Translated by Farbara Bockus Aponte. Philadelphia: Temple University Press, 1976.

Quintero Rivera, Angel G. *Conflictos de clase y política en Puerto Rico.* Río Piedras: Ediciones Huracán, 1976.

———. "Clases sociales e identidad nacional; notas sobre el desarrollo nacional puertorriqueño". *In Puerto Rico: identidad nacional y clases sociales.* Río Piedras: Ediciones Huracán, 1979, pp. 13–44.

Ramírez, Barbot, Jaime. "A History of Puerto Rican Radical Nationalism, 1920–1965" (Ph. D. Dissertation, Ohio State University, Department of History). Ann Arbor, MI: University Microfilms, 1973.

Ribes Tovar, Federico. *Albizu Campos: Puerto Rican Revolutionary.* New York: Plus Ultra, 1971.

Robertson, Roland. "Globalization and Societal Modernization: A Note on Japan and Japanese Religion." *Sociological Analysis* 47, S (March 1987): 35–42.

———. "Globalization Theory and Civilization Analysis." *Comparative Civilizations Review* 15, 2 (Fall 1987): 20–30.

————, and Joann Chirico. " Humanity, Globalization, and Worldwide Religious Resurgence: A Theoretical Exploration." *Sociological Analysis* 46, 3 (Fall 1985): 219–42.

Scannell, Brother Leo. "Principles Operative in the American and French Revolution in the Light of the Doctrine on Revolution of Francisco Suárez" (Ph. D. Dissertation, New York University). Ann Arbor, MI: University Microfilms, 1955.

Silén, Juan Angel. *Pedro Albizu Campos.* Río Piedras: Editorial Antillana, 1976.

Stevens-Arroyo, Antonio M. "The Political Philosophy of Pedro Albizu Campos." Masters Thesis, New York University, Caribbean and Latin American Studies Center, 1975.

————. *Prophets Denied Honor: An Anthology on the Hispano Church.* Maryknoll, NY: Orbis Books, 1980.

————. "Puerto Rican Independence as a Catholic Crusade: The Nationalist Party and Armed Resistance." Paper presented at the SSSR Convention, Louisville, Kentucky, 1987.

————. *Cave of the Jagua: The Mythological World of the Tainos.* Albuquerque: University of New Mexico Press, 1988.

Swatos, William H., Jr. "Enchantment and Disenchantment in Modernity: 'The Significance of Religion' as a Sociological Category." *Sociological Analysis* 44, 4 (Winter 1983): 321–38.

Torres, Benjamin. *Pedro Albizu Campos: Obras Escogidas: 1923- 1936,* 4 vols. San Juan: Editorial Jelofe, 1975–1981.

Townshend, Charles. *The British Campaign in Ireland, 1919–1921.* London: Oxford University Press, 1975.

Vasconcelos, José. *Indología: una interpretación de la cultura ibero-americana.* Paris: Agencia Mundial de librería (between 1920–1929).

Weber, Max. *The Theory of Social and Economic Organization.* New York: Free Press, 1947.

————. *Max Weber on the Methodology of the Social Sciences.* Translated and edited by E. Shils and Henry A. Finch. New York: Free Press, 1949.

————. *The Sociology of Religion.* Boston: Beacon, 1963.

Zavala, Iriz M., and Rafael Rodríguez, eds. *The Intellectual Roots of Independence.* New York: Monthly Review, 1980.

9

Reality and Desire of America in Luis Cernuda

SANTIAGO DAYDÍ-TOLSON

In the brief introduction to his *Variaciones sobre tema mexicano* (*Variations on a Mexican Theme*), published in 1952, the Spanish poet Luis Cernuda calls attention to the lack of interest among his compatriots for Latin America and anything related to it. Choosing two Spanish writers representative of modern Spain as good examples of this lack of interest, Cernuda (1975) comments upon the silence that was kept, relative to the Latin American nations, by even those Spanish intellectuals who had been most aware of Spain's cultural weaknesses:

> ¡Ni Larra ni Galdós, quienes, aunque tan diferentes, tenían una conciencia igualmente clara, se preocuparon nunca por estas otras tierras de raigambre española. Ante su desgarramiento peninsular, Larra, contemporáneo, Galdós, casi contemporáneo, guardan silencio. ¿Por qué? A la visión nacional que uno y otro nos ofrecen, le falta así algo; algo que históricamente había sido parte de nuestra vida, y que se desintegra de ella durante el siglo mismo en que ambos vivieron y escribieron. (*Prosa*, 113)

> (Neither Larra nor Galdós, who, although so different from each other, had an equally clear conscience, paid attention to these other lands of Spanish roots. Faced with their uprooting from the peninsula, Larra, a contemporary, and Galdós, almost a contemporary, keep silent. Why? Thus, something is missing in the national views each one of them gives us; something that had been historically a part

of our lives, and breaks off from it during the century in which they lived and wrote.)

The absence of America in the view that both nineteenth-century intellectuals have on the Spanish culture seems inexplicable to Cernuda, who, from his then recently acquired American perspective wonders: "¿Cómo entender ese silencio?" ("How to understand such silence?"). Without even trying to offer an answer, Cernuda insists, with two examples, on the historical continuity of a general attitude of Spanish intellectuals who, from the very moment of the discovery and the annexation of the new continent, showed no interest in America:

> Unas primero, otras después, en brevísimo espacio, todas estas tierras se desprenden de España. Ningún escritor nuestro alude entonces a ello, no ya para deplorarlo, ni siquiera para constatarlo. Si la accesión de ellas halló tan pocos ecos en nuestra literatura clásica, es lógico que su separación hallara menos en nuestra literatura moderna. (*Prosa,* 113)

> (One after another, in a brief lapse of time, all these lands break apart from Spain. No writer among us alludes to it then, not to deplore it, not even to take notice of it. If the annexation of these lands had so little effect in our classical literature, it seems logical that their separation had less effect in our modern literature.)

These are very true observations and very significant commentaries coming from someone like Cernuda. However, Cernuda was also at fault because of his ignorance and his lack of interest in the new continent up to the moment of his first visit to Mexico in 1949. It was this trip that prompted him to write his *Variations on a Mexican Theme,* to return to Mexico in following years, and eventually, to take up residence in the Latin American country. His critical comments with respect to his own silence and that of the other Spaniards make manifest a cultural reality well known to most Latin Americans but mostly unnoticed by Spaniards. With implacable judgement Cernuda confirms categorically the absolute disregard for anything American in the Spanish mind:

> España, pues, no había sido, ni era para la mayoría de nosotros, sino el territorio peninsular. . . . Acaso a los españoles no nos interesaron nunca estas otras tierras, que durante tres siglos fueron parte de nuestra nación. (*Prosa,* 113)

(Spain, then, had not been, and was for most of us nothing but the peninsular territory. . . . Perhaps we Spaniards were never interested in these other lands that for three centuries were a part of our nation.)

The terms *territory, lands* and *nation* in this quotation point to the center of the issue. While peninsular Spain is given the attributes of "territory" (a clearly defined land) and "nation" (the abstract concept of a national identity), Latin America is designated less precisely as "lands" that are distinctly recognized as "other." As an exiled Spaniard visiting Mexico, Cernuda gained a direct knowledge of that other Hispanic place and saw and understood for the first time the attitude of Spain with respect to America: a lack of a feeling of belonging to that distant continent, to those "other lands," those of other peoples. But even then, he fails to truly change his own perspective on Latin America.

Symptomatic of the strong hold of the detached attitude among Spaniards is that Cernuda, the poet who realized the significant magnitude of the problem, manifests the same Spanish characteristic in his own direct confrontation with Latin America. In presenting his writings about the Mexican experience, he makes direct reference to the lack of interest among Spaniards for the new continent. He has been surprised by his own ignorance and feels the need to change his attitude and that of all Spaniards who, like himself, are unaware of their limited views. But although he tries to address the intellectual interests of those who would like to see Spain tightly united to America, he is unable to correct the defect that he has described so well. This duality in Cernuda's approach to his Mexican experience—the realization of a long-held, mistaken attitude and the inability to change it—bespeaks a seemingly basic impossibility for the Spanish mind to see Latin America as a reality.

A first indication of this duality in Cernuda is the fact that *Variations on a Mexican Theme*, the work in which he tries to solve the deficiency, was written as a very personal and emotive account of a rather late experience in life. Before his first visit to Mexico at almost fifty years of age, Cernuda had never touched the subject of Latin America; during most of his life he was not interested in it and consequently he completely ignored it. In this he was no different from most Spaniards. In the same introduction to *Variations on a Mexican Theme*, Cernuda admits to the general and total ignorance among Spaniards of a reality that only the direct experience of exile made evident to him, as well as to many others:

En tu niñez y en tu juventud, ¿qué supiste tú, si algo supiste, de estas
tierras, de su historia, que es una con la tuya? Curiosidad, confiésalo,
no tenías. Culpa tuya, sin duda; pero nada en torno podía tampoco
encaminarla. (*Prosa*, 114)

(In your childhood and in your youth, what did you know, if you ever
knew anything, about these lands, about its history, that is one and
the same with yours? Curiosity, admit it, you had not. No doubt it was
your fault; but nothing around you could have directed it.)

His sense of guilt, toned down by the fault of many, is not enough to save
him from his mistake, and even if in his late life and in few works he
seemed to embrace the Latin American context, in essence he continued
to be interested only in his European intellectual tradition. Different
from the many Spanish intellectuals who took residence in a Latin
American country immediately after the Civil War, Cernuda decided
late in life to live in Mexico. He had left Spain in 1938, with an invitation
to lecture in England. He never returned to Spain, and he did not visit
an Hispanic country until eleven years later, when, having already lived
in the United States for two years after his long stay in England, he took
a trip to Mexico in the summer of 1949. That brief visit to the Latin
American country after so many years away from the Hispanic world
had a decisive effect on the poet. After the experience of being in a Spanish-speaking country again, Cernuda seemed to be incapable of living
happily in the Anglo-Saxon world he had admired so much and in
which he had lived exiled from Spain, oblivious of the Latin American
countries. "Vine a México por vez primera en el verano de 1949" ("I
came to Mexico for the first time the summer of 1949"), he writes in
"The Story of a Book," "y, contra mis presunciones, el efecto resultó
considerable; tanto que la vida en Mount Holyoke se me hizo enojosa"
(*Prosa*, 932) ("and, against my presuppositions, the effect was considerable; so much so that life in Mount Holyoke College became annoy-
ing"). "No pensaba sino en la vuelta a México" ("I thought only of going
back to Mexico"), he confesses, recognizing the unreflective nature of
his situation: "Hoy veo que era la mía una situación donde mis reac-
ciones primeras, no controladas por mí, iban dominándome contra
toda reflexión y todo sentido común" (*Prosa*, 933) ("Now I see that my
situation was one in which my first reactions, not controlled by me,
were taking control of me against all reflection and all common sense").
"Téngase en cuenta [he adds in the same text] que yo llevaba algunos
años de vivir *vicariously* (a eso alude el título de 'Vivir sin estar vivi-

endo')" (*Prosa*, 933) ("One has to take into account that for some years I had been living vicariously [that fact is alluded to by the title 'Living without Living']"). He was fascinated by Mexico; the newly discovered Hispanic country attracted him as the place where he could recuperate all he had lost, where he could truly live in his own world.

Thus, after several trips to Mexico in the "successive summers" of 1950 and 1951, Cernuda took permanent residence in Mexico in 1952. But this was not a decision without problematic consequences, as the poet himself suggests in "The Story of a Book":

> Me instalé pues en México en noviembre de 1952, decidido, como era natural, a no dejar la responsabilidad de mi proceder en otros hombros que los míos. No digo, sin embargo, que luego, en no pocas ocasiones, no me haya arrepentido de lo hecho. (*Prosa*, 937)

> (I settled myself in Mexico in November of 1952, determined, as it was natural, not to leave the responsibility of my act on anybody's shoulders but mine. I am not saying, though, that later, on few occasions, I did not repent of what I had done.)

The first emotional impression that led him to decide to leave the United States and settle in Mexico, that ideal place where he could live authentically, was not enough to satisfy the need Cernuda felt for a sense of belonging. His decision to live in the Latin American country not only came too late in his life but was also ineffective, since it could not satisfy the exiled poet's need to be in his own world. His infatuation with Mexico did not last and the poet never developed an intellectual interest in Mexican reality. Cernuda was thus unable to understand the Latin American world.

Save for the brief texts in prose from his *Variations on a Mexican Theme*, written before taking up residence in the country, Cernuda wrote practically nothing about Mexico, and he did not seem to be at all interested in its culture. His intellectual occupations while living in Latin America have little to do with his new cultural circumstances, and in his last years he even returned on several occasions to the United States (Ruiz Silva, 153–54), disenchanted with his life in Mexico. Only three poems—"El elegido" ("The Chosen One") (*Realidad*, Cernuda 1964, 292–93), "El viajero" ("The Traveler") (*Realidad*, 294–95), and "Otra fecha" ("Other Date") (*Realidad*, 301–2)—and three articles— "Aire de la Habana" ("Havana's Air") (*Prosa*, Cernuda 1975, 1099–1102), "Reflejo de México en la obra de José Moreno Villa" ("The Reflection of Mexico in the Work of José Moreno Villa") (*Prosa*, 1394–1403), and "Experimento en Rubén Darío" ("Experimentation in Rubén Darío") (*Prosa*, 994–1005)—account for his passing interest in Latin American subjects while living in Mexico. Not much more about Latin America can be found in Cernuda's work written before *Variations on a Mexican Theme*. These include only one poem—"Quetzalcoatl" (*Realidad*, 208–12)—one article—"Rubén Darío" (*Prosa*, 1434–38)—and very few passing references in essays, letters, and interviews. These few examples, together with the prose texts of *Variations on a Mexican Theme,* give a good idea of some characteristics of Cernuda's attitude toward the subject of Latin America. First of all, it must be said that when Cernuda was young he had, as did many young Spaniards of his generation, an interest in North America as a fascinating country that represented the ideals of an emerging new society under new values:

> La afición al cine hacía que me interesaran los Estados Unidos, ya que las películas norteamericanas eran las más cotizadas entonces, y la vida allá la que más cercana parecía al ideal juvenil sonriente y atlético, que no pocos mozos se trazaban entonces. Nombres de ciudades o de estados de aquél país dieron pretexto a algunos de mis versos. No se olvide, por otra parte, que los países "artísticos", como Italia, habían caído en descrédito entre muchos de nosotros. (*Prosa,* 910)

> (My fondness for the movies made me take interest in the United States, since the North American films were then the most highly considered, and life there was the one that seemed to be nearer to the smiling and athletic youthful ideal that not few lads set for themselves in those days. The names of cities or states in that country gave a pretext for some of my verses. One must not forget, on the other hand, that the "artistic" countries, like Italy, had fallen out of grace among many of us.)

When some years later, having already passed his fortieth birthday, Cernuda accepted an invitation to teach at Mount Holyoke College and traveled for the first time to the United States, he was hoping to satisfy his interest of years before: "Los Estados Unidos fueron, como ya dije, entusiasmo juvenil mío, que no llegó entonces a obtener satisfacción visitando el país, y puede suponerse si la propuesta me atraería" (*Prosa,* 928–29) ("The United States were, as I already said, an enthusiasm of my youth that was not satisfied then with a visit to the country, and one can surmise if the proposition attracted me or not"). Such interest in the United States might have been increased also by Cernuda's knowledge of the literature of the English language that he studied and admired during his exile period in England. His life in the United States, though, did not satisfy him; quite the opposite, he felt that the America he had imagined and idealized as a young poet in the twenties did not correspond in any way to the real America where he came to work as a college professor.

There is no corresponding curiosity for Latin America to Cernuda's curiosity of Anglo America. While he seriously studied the literatures of Spain, England, and the United States, he was totally oblivious of the literature of the Spanish-speaking continent. This lack of interest is maintained even after having been in a Latin American country he claimed to love. In an interview given after having taken up permanent residence in Mexico, Cernuda avows with direct sincerity his ignorance about Latin American literature: "Reduzco el alcance de su pregunta a la poesía moderna española—he points out before answering a question about the characteristics of contemporary poetry in Spanish—ya que conozco mal la de los demás países de nuestra lengua" ("I reduce the aim of your question to Spanish modern poetry since I do not know well the poetry of other Spanish-speaking countries" (*Prosa*, 1452).

In his studies on contemporary poetry he devoted only two essays to a Latin American poet: "Rubén Darío", written in 1941, and "Experimentation in Rubén Darío", written in 1959. And if he writes about the Nicaraguan it is only to deny him any influence on Spanish poetry. Casting doubts about the poetic value of much of Darío's aesthetic accomplishments, he admits greatness in his work only when the Latin American poet turns to the Spanish tradition:

> Es curioso que cuando Darío comprende mejor lo español sea cuando escribe la parte mejor de su obra. Y es que los *Cantos de vida y esperanza* los escribe olvidando efímeras modas literarias, compenetrado con la tradición más propia de su espíritu y hostigado por el afán de admirar e iluminar el futuro de su tierra, la América que habla español. Su "Letanía a Nuestro Señor Don Quijote", la visión más original e intensa de nuestros días sobre el héroe de Cervantes,¿no marca el momento culminante de su obra poética? (*Prosa*, 1437–38)

> (It is curious that when Darío better understands the Spanish tradition it is when he writes the best part of his work. And this is because he writes his *Songs of Love and Despair* forgetting the passing literary

fashions, imbued with the tradition to which his spirit properly belongs, and inspired by the desire to admire and enlighten the future of his land, the Spanish-speaking America. Doesn't his "Litany to Our Lord Don Quixote," the most original and intense view of Cervantes' hero in our days, correspond to the highest moment in his work?)

Likewise, the only reference to another Latin American poet—just a passing comment in an interview—makes reference to the improbable influence of the poet within Spanish poetic developments: "Neruda, por razón de su fuerza poética y de su estancia en España antes de la guerra civil, tal vez haya dejado eco entre algunos poetas más jóvenes que los de mi generación" ("Neruda, by reason of his poetic strength and of his stay in Spain before the civil war, perhaps has left an echo among some poets younger than those of my generation") (*Prosa*, 1453–54). The reference to the "stay in Spain" must be interpreted as a confirmation of the absence of Latin American literature in Spain; it is recognized as existing only when the Latin American poet himself makes it evident with his physical presence. Even before knowing Mexico, when there are no indications in Cernuda's critical writings of an interest in the Latin American reality, he writes a poem of an apparently Mexican theme, "Quetzalcoatl" (*Realidad*, 208–12). This poem, however, is only coincidentally related to a Latin American subject as it follows a poetic technique Cernuda learned from English poetry. In "The Story of a Book" he explains:

Algo que también aprendí de la poesía inglesa, particularmente de Browning, fue el proyectar mi experiencia emotiva sobre una situación dramática, histórica o legendaria (como en "Lázaro", "Quetzalcoatl", "Silla del rey", "El César"), para que así se objetivara mejor, tanto dramática com poéticamente. (*Prosa*, 923)

(Something that I also learned from English poetry, particularly from Browning, was to project my emotional experience into a dramatic situation, either historical or legendary [as is the case of "Lazarus." "Quetzalcoatl," "King's Chair," "Cesar"], in order to better objectivize the experience, both dramatically as much as poetically.)

In the case of the poem that evokes a pre-Hispanic America, Cernuda uses the monologue of one of Cortés' soldiers to express his own worries as an expatriate Spaniard. This text represents the moment when the poet admits to himself the impossibility of returning to Spain. In spite of the title, it is not Latin America that really matters in this

poem, but rather the emotion of a Spaniard who is far from his homeland and after many marvelous experiences in a foreign country, realizes
that he can only await death in a foreign land. The image of America
does not represent the reality of the continent but only the symbolic
value for what is different and incredible outside of one's own country:

> Cuando en una mañana, por los arcos y puertas
> Que abrió la capital vencida ante nosotros,
> Onduló como serpiente de bronce y diamante Cortejo
>   con litera trayendo al rey azteca,
> Me pareció romperse el velo mismo
> De los últimos cielos, desnuda ya la gloria.
> Sí, allí estuve, y lo vi; envidiadme vosotros.
>   (*Realidad*, 211, vv. 82–88)

> (When, one morning, under the arches and doors
> That the vanquished capital opened in front of us
> Fluttered as a bronze and diamond snake
> The entourage with a sedan chair carrying the Aztec king,
> It seemed to me as if the very veil
> Of the ultimate skies was ripped, glory finally naked.
> Yes, I was there, and I saw it; do envy me.)

This poem has no relationship to Latin America, in spite of the title
and the dramatic anecdote. At most, it shows that Cernuda was aware
of the existence of the pre-Hispanic world and felt some attraction to its
value as a representation of an alien world that transforms itself from
illusion to reality; in the process it loses all interest to the foreign conqueror who, unable to adapt to the new circumstances, feels nostalgic
sorrow for the loss of his own land. In response to a question about the
possible influence of Latin American art in Spain, Cernuda makes
known his admiration for pre-Columbian art:

> La exposición de arte mexicano en Europa debió causar a muchos
> gran impresión, si juzgo por la mía; aunque hubiese visto en el Museo
> Británico algunas muestras de arte precolombino, sólo al visitar el
> Museo Arqueológico de México comprendí la grandeza de dicho arte,
> que una vez entrevisto no se puede olvidar. (*Prosa*, 1455)

> (The European exhibition of Mexican art must have produced great
> impression to many, if I judge by my own reaction; although I had

seen some examples of pre-Columbian art in the British Museum, only when I visited the Museo Arqueológico de México did I understand the greatness of such art, an art that after having been seen cannot be forgotten.)

Although he admits having felt an attraction to pre-Columbian art, it is obvious that his knowledge of Latin America, his recognition of it as a true entity, seems to happen only with direct contact with it. This contact has strong emotional connotation in Cernuda, as is shown in both his *Variation on a Mexican Theme* and in two poems written in Mexico—"The Traveler" and "Other Date"—which deal with the emotion of recognizing the original land in the new continent.

These poems deal directly with the identification of the Latin American landscape with the landscape of a nostalgic and idealized view of Spain. In "Other Date" the reference to the almost complete recuperation of the original place in Mexico is direct and explicit:

¡Aires claros, nopal y palma,
En los alrededores, saben,
Si no igual, casi igual a como
La tierra tuya aquella antes.
                    (vv. 1–4)

(Clear airs, prickly pear and palm tree,
In the surroundings, they feel,
If not equally, almost equally as
Your land of before, there.)

In "The Traveler" what matters is the finding of that place never reached before coming to a Latin American country. After offering a brief view of the foreign land where the poet finds himself now—"cálido aire" ("warm air") (v.2), "hojas/Perennes" ("perennial/Leaves") (vv. 3–4), "palma oscura" ("dark palmtree") (v. 9)—comes the almost rhetorical question and the recognition of a finding:

Lo que ves ¿es tu sueño
O tu verdad? El mundo

Mágico que llevabas
Dentro de ti, esperando

Tan largamente, afuera
Surge a la luz.
(vv. 11–16)

(What you see, is it your dream
Or your truth? The magic

World you carried
Within yourself, waiting
For so long, outside
Appears in the light.)

This emotive experience is explained in the preliminary words to *Variations on a Mexican Theme*, words that, being the confession of a personal and collective fault, are also the admission of a personal revelation and a change of attitude (albeit a temporary one) as will be proven by Cernuda's later evolution:

> Esa curiosidad fue la vida con sus azares quien mucho más tarde la provocó en ti, al ponerte frente a la realidad americana. Y tras la curiosidad vino el interés; tras el interés la simpatía; tras de la simpatía el amor. (*Prosa*, 114)

> (Life with its happenings was the one that provoked that curiosity in you much later, when it puts you in front of Latin American reality. And following curiosity came interest; after interest came sympathy; after sympathy, love.)

In Spain, the love of America usually does not come from knowledge. Cernuda was one of the few poets to be interested in knowing America. However, after his initial interest, he soon became more distant. In his 1955 article, "Reflections of Mexico in the Work of José Moreno Villa," Cernuda quotes Moreno Villa, another Spanish poet exiled in Mexico, the sensitivity of which could easily be attributed to himself. Like Moreno Villa, who "con su inteligencia, su sensibilidad, su cultura y buen gusto supo ver a México y expresar esa visión en diversas obras" ("with his intelligence, his sensibility, his culture, and good taste he knew how to see Mexico and how to express such vision in several works") (*Prosa*, 1399), Cernuda finds himself also "en el período del amor a México, lo que quiere decir que ha pasado la fase de la sorpresa" ("in a period of love for Mexico, meaning that the period of surprise had already passed") (*Prosa*, 1400).

It has to be remembered also that Cernuda's decision to leave the economic and job security of the United States to establish himself in Mexico was motivated mainly by the love of a Mexican. This adds a new and significant dimension to his love of the country:

> Como poseído por un demonio, no vacilé en tirar a un lado trabajo digno, posición decorosa y sueldo suficiente, para no hablar de la residencia en un país amable y acogedor, donde la vida ofrece un máximo de comodidad y conveniencia. Pero el amor tiraba de mí hacia México. Con tanta más fuerza cuanto que siempre padecí del sentimiento de hallarme aislado y que la vida estaba más allá de donde yo me encontraba; de ahí el afán constante de partir, de irme a otras tierras, afán nutrido desde la niñez por lecturas de viajes a comarcas remotas. Y sólo el amor alivió ese afán, dándome la seguridad de pertenecer a una tierra, de no ser en ella un extranjero, un intruso. (*Prosa*, 936–37)

> (As if I was possessed by a demon, I did not hesitate to throw away a dignified job, a decorous position and a sufficient salary, not to mention the residence in an amiable and friendly country where life offers a maximum of comfort and convenience. But love was pulling me to Mexico. With much more force because I always suffered from the sentiment of being insulated and of life being further away from where I was; so the constant desire to leave, to go to other lands, a desire that since boyhood was fed by readings of travels to far away regions. And only love satisfied such desire, giving me the security to belong to a land, of not being a foreigner there, an outsider.)

Although Cernuda is not referring in this text to the love he felt for Mexico, it is not impossible to understand how he could have confused his love for an individual with the love for the country. In both cases there is a sense of belonging. In finding love in Mexico the Spanish poet thought for a moment that he also found that sense of identity he had been missing during his exile in the English-speaking world. This identity is shown in *Variations on a Mexican Theme* with the recuperation of several elements from the lost world of his youth.

The article on Moreno Villa, written after Cernuda already knew Mexico well, is of much interest to the analysis of these recuperations as treated in *Variations on a Mexican Theme*. In that article Cernuda comments on Moreno Villa's *Cornucopia de Mexico* (*Mexican Cornucopia*), and touches upon subjects that coincide with the subjects Cernuda developed in his book of observations about Mexico. What the cultural critic analyzes rationally, Cernuda experiences emotionally. His adoption of the Mexican reality is not the result of intellectual knowledge but, rather, of the emotion of a vital experience—the feeling of being in a world very similar to that of his native Andalusia. The idealization of the abandoned land of birth and his desire to return to it finds a resolution in Latin America, a place where exile seems to cease. The recuperation of what had been lost up to then is almost complete in Mexico, and the poetic prose texts of *Variations on a Mexican Theme* represent this recuperation as a vivid experience of both reality and desire.

The main recuperation is language. Thus, the variations on the experience of Mexico begin with "La lengua" ("The Language") (*Prosa,* 117–18), a composition in which, through a dialogue with himself, the poet who has first arrived to the Latin American continent asks, "Tras de cruzada la frontera, al oír tu lengua, que tantos años no oías hablada en torno, ¿qué sentiste?" ("After crossing the border, upon hearing your language, which you had not heard around you in so many years, what did you feel?") (*Prosa,* 117). He does not ask for what he thought about the experience but for what he felt emotionally at the sound of his mother tongue. In his comments on the treatment of the subject of the Spanish language by Moreno Villa, he alludes again to his emotions: "la impresión tan honda y entrañable que el español puede sentir al oír su lengua hablada por otros pueblos al otro lado del mundo" ("such deep and affectionate impression the Spaniard could feel upon hearing his language spoken by other peoples on the other side of the world") (*Prosa,* 1400). It is surprising, though, to discover that the feeling of the poet is that of "orgullo al escuchar hablada nuestra lengua . . . por otros pueblos al otro lado del mundo" ("pride upon hearing our language spoken . . . by other peoples at the other side of the world") (*Prosa,* 117), pride that finds its secure basis on the egocentric personal pronoun, by which the Latin American speakers of Spanish are designated as "ellos" ("they"), who "a sabiendas o no, quiéranlo o no, con esos mismos signos de su alma, que son las palabras, mantienen vivo el destino de nuestro país, y habrían de mantenerlo aun después que él dejara de existir" ("knowingly or not, wanting it or not, with those same signs of their souls, which words are, keep alive the destiny of our country, and would keep it even after it had ceased to exist") (*Prosa,* 117). The Spanish language spoken in Mexico is the indelible cultural legacy of "quienes cuatro siglos atrás, con la pluma y la espada, ganaron para ella destino universal" ("those who four centuries ago, with the pen and the sword, gained for it a universal destiny") (*Prosa,* 118). The view held by the exiled Spaniard is rather that of the conqueror: Latin America is nothing but an extension of Spain.

But the poet feels sympathy for the new land and looks for a means to close the gap that divides it from his own land. In successive texts of *Variations on a Mexican Theme,* he details the positive aspects he sees in Mexico, those aspects in which he finds a coincidence with Spain. This is because Latin America occupies in Cernuda the place left empty by his departure from the land of his youth. And in such recuperation the sustaining pillars are, besides the language, the people who speak it and the landscape; that is, the land as concrete reality, as a physical body, object of desire and possession. Because of this, the prose poems on Mexico insist on the sensuality of concreteness—bodies, voices, objects, climate, landscape—at the same time that they claim spirituality as the essential difference between Latin America and the rest of the lands of exile.

In Latin America, the America that speaks Spanish, Cernuda finds alive and concretely in existence the world he could only evoke in nostalgic dreams. Latin America is Spain, at least for a while. During this period of love for Mexico, Cernuda cannot understand how the Spanish people continue to be uninterested and ignorant in matters related to Latin America. He cannot explain this phenomenon, yet he only suggests a solution: make possible the sympathy and love that come after knowledge. The last words of his book, though, seem to indicate his lack of confidence in the possibility of reaching that knowledge and the consequent interest and love. Faced with the uncertainty about the possibility of his countrymen understanding and accepting the reasons for his own love for Latin America, the poet comments, almost dreamingly:

> Lo que yo quería, insisto, era simpatizar. Qué ocurra luego con el don de esa simpatía, no me concierne. Como el niño que juega a lo que sueña, con su mismo ensimismamiento, he lanzado mi barco de papel, que ha de perderse de todos modos, a la corriente. (*Prosa*, 162)

> (What I wanted, I insist, was to sympathize. What will happen afterwards with this sympathy is not of my concern. Like the boy who plays back his dreams, with the same concentration, I have let go my paper boat which, in any case, will have to be lost to the current.)

Whether Cernuda had any influence in a change of attitude among Spaniards toward the Latin American continent is not to be discussed here. It should be, however, the subject of a critical inquiry that might try to understand why the knowledge of America, and the sympathy and love for it, have been mainly absent from the Spanish mind, as is so clearly shown by Larra and Galdós. These two representative figures were so aptly selected by the Spanish poet who himself could not go beyond an initial interest incited only by his mistaken view of the new continent as the object of his desire.

Works Cited

Cernuda, Luis. *Prosa completa.* Barcelona: Barral Editores, 1975.

————. *La realidad y el deseo.* 4a. Augmented edition. México: Fondo de Cultura Económica, 1964.

————. *Variaciones sobre tema mexicano.* México: Porrúa y Obregón, 1952. Reproduced in *Prosa completa,* 111–62.

Ruiz Silva, Carlos. *Arte, amor y otras soledades en Luis Cernuda.* Madrid: Ediciones de la Torre, 1979.

10

Hispanist Democratic Thought versus Hispanist Thought of the Franco Era: A Comparative Analysis

MARÍA A. ESCUDERO

Introduction

In 1957, Alberto Martin Artajo who served for more than eleven years as Minister of Foreign Affairs with the Franco government, adhering to the words of Argentine writer Mario Amadeo, wrote in *Cuadernos Hispanoamericanos* (hereafter, *C.H.*):

> Spain is also a European nation, and as such, has interests and obligations that link her to the continent. But Spain would be incomplete without an intimate understanding with Spanish-America.... For this reason we strongly believe that the position of Spain in Europe . . . would be considerably strengthened if she projected herself as the European bastion of a great transnational community. (*C.H.*, 97 1957, 332)

Twenty-five years later, Spain's King Juan Carlos I, upon receiving the Carlo Magno Prize in Aquistran on May 20, 1982, affirmed that

> Spain, a radically European nation, is transeuropean. Since her birth as a nation-state she has projected herself beyond our continent: she

is an Hispanic nation, one of the members—certainly the original
and oldest—of a community of independent Hispanic nations.[1]

The amazing similarity between the two quotations seems to indicate
that there is a clear continuity in the Hispanist discourse during this
twenty-five-year period. Nevertheless, scholars of Hispanist thought as
well as politicians representing the different Spanish democratic
administrations, have made an effort to convince us that in these last
twenty-five years, there has been a radical transformation in the Hispanist discourse as a result of the political transition from the Franco
regime to democracy.[2] Consequently, the purpose of the present study
is to see if, indeed, this transformation has taken place and, if so, what
the characteristics of this process are.

In this study I have chosen *Cuadernos Hispanoamericanos*—a peri-
odical that is considered the voice of the Americanist policy of the
Franco regime from 1948 to 1975[3]— as the source of Francoist Hispanist thought. To represent democratic Hispanist thought I have chosen
the speeches of politically relevant figures such as the king, prime ministers, ministers of foreign affairs, and so forth.

The texts with which this work opens show two of the fundamental
aspects of Hispanist thought, whether Francoist or democratic: the first
is the notion of the Hispanic Community of Nations and the second the
role that Spain plays—or ought to play—in this community. These two
concepts will be the foundation of my analysis.

Hispanist Thought

Hispanist thought is understood in this study as the movement that
aimed to use the common ties of language, culture, and religion as the
basis to draw the Latin American countries closer to Spain. This current of thought also known as *Hispanismo* was not started by the
Franco regime. Although it is difficult to determine the exact starting
point for the Hispanismo movement,[4] its origin lay in the new imperialistic currents of thought in late-nineteenth-century Europe (Hobsbawm, 56–59).

This movement, called by Pike "lyrical Hispanismo,"[5] did not have
a clearly defined ideology and its postulates were extremely vague. Both
in Latin America and Spain, Hispanismo resulted from the development of an ambiguous relationship between Spain and the Latin Amer-

ican republics, which permitted different interpretations by different political tendencies.[6] However, this notion of Hispanismo should not be confused with the idea of Hispanidad that prevailed during the Franco regime. According to Bonilla, Angel Ganivet was the first to use the term *Hispanidad* in 1897 (Bonilla, 247–54). Later, in the early 1930s, the term was used by some writers such as Unamuno without a political-ideological purpose (Morodo, 270–75). In 1934, Zacarías de Vizcarra was the first person to give the word an explicit ideological meaning that was popularized by Ramiro de Maeztú.[7]

The concept of Hispanidad took some of the foundations of conservative Hispanism such as the defense of Catholicism, race, and the Spanish language, as well as the idea of the *Madre Patria*, and defended the need to develop closer ties with Latin American republics in order to create an ideal Hispanic Community. Franco's regime used the idea of Hispanidad during the Spanish Civil War, both as a way to give coherence and purpose to its own supporters and as a political-ideological weapon against the Republicans. Hispanidad was also the ideological foundation of the regime's foreign policy toward Latin America. Thus, Hispanidad was not just a movement—as was Hispanismo—but a policy. During the first years of the Franco regime—from 1936 until 1941—this policy was implemented in Latin America through one of the factions that compound the government: the Falange.

In 1940, the Francoist government created an institution entirely dedicated to promoting the relations between the Latin American republics and Spain: the *Consejo de la Hispanidad*. This institution, as well as the foreign policy, was under the control of the Falange. The rhetoric used by the Falange to expand this concept was rather agressive inside Spain and slightly less, but still provocative, inside the Latin American Republics. The Hispanic spirit that the Falange wished to see prevail throughout the Hispanic world was the strongly Catholic, antiliberal tradition of the Spanish Empire of the sixteenth and seventeenth centuries. The constant reference to the idea of the empire was the least acceptable principle to the majority of public opinion in Latin America.[8]

Once the Axis powers lost World War II, the Franco regime was in an extremely precarious situation. Its main immediate task was to prove that it was different from the fascist regimes of Italy and Germany. Thus, the imperial rhetoric towards Latin America was one of the first topics to be avoided. Therefore, the *Consejo de la Hispanidad* became the *Insti-*

tuto de Cultura Hispánica, on 31 December 1945, with autonomy from the Foreign Office.[9]

This way, *Cultura Hispánica* appeared as a nonpolitical institution whose main purpose was to tighten the cultural links between Spain and her "sisters," the Latin American Republics, in a purely "spiritual" manner. Within this new frame of thought, the Panamerican policy of the United States was no longer a problem because the projects were different levels and did not exclude but, rather, complemented each other. This reorientation was easily implemented thanks to the ambiguity inherent to the concept of Hispanidad and to the different tendencies that supported it. The Catholic conservatives were still less agressive than the Falangists and were stronger supporters of a purely cultural Hispanidad (Morodo, 271).

I. The Hispanic Community of Nations

Origin and Historical Justification

Since 1945, Hispanists have attempted to justify the existence of a Hispanic Community of Nations by establishing its origins, foundations, and destiny. Hispanist discourse situates the origin of the Hispanic Community of Nations in the Spanish conquest and colonization of Latin America. But trying to justify the existence of a supposedly fraternal community on the basis of a series of historical events brought about over three centuries of imperialist domination is as hard a task for the representatives of the democratic regime as it was for the representatives of the Franco regime.

Consequently, the democratic regime, in an effort not to offend the Latin American listener when dealing with the conquest and colonization, advocates that history be accepted. According to King Juan Carlos I:

> In this new phase our people, made brothers by blood and language, are also bound by a similar and transcendental endeavor: that of accepting their history, with its mishaps, its successes, and its failure, in order to mould for themselves a calm and peaceful coexistence.[10]

But, as we will see, this desire to accept history is not new. It starts to be systematically expressed in 1957, once the Franco regime succeeds in getting international recognition. Hispanist scholars find themselves with more freedom to try to initiate reconciliation. This reconciliation was based on the Francoist disposition to accept the errors committed during the conquest as well as the glories of independence, so long as Latin Americans were themselves also willing to accept the glories of the conquest and the errors of independence. The first step toward acceptance was to admit that both events were part of a common history:

> historic Spain is not the exclusive patrimony of the Spaniards of today, but belongs to the common traditions of all Hispanic countries . . . therefore it is neither right for Spaniards to take as their exclusive heritage the glory of the conquerors, nor for some Americans to emphasize the human defects of the conquerors as something completely foreign to themselves. In this order of things it is logical as the Minister of Foreign Affairs states, that Spain "feel as a partaker in the everlasting glory of the captains of the American emancipation." (*C.H.*, 95 1957, 135)

Accepting both the "glory" and the "human defects" of the conquerors, the responsibility for the conquest is shared. As a compensation, Francoist Hispanism lends itself to accepting "the everlasting glory of the captains of the American emancipation," thereby equating what is glorious in both events. But to what can the "defects" of the conquerors be equated?. These defect" will be equated to the "infidelity" of the "American daughters" that led them to their independence. Considering both events as consequences of the imperfection of human nature, Hispanist thought of the Franco era was ready to take the first step toward reconciliation by acknowledging that

> if it is hard, very hard, for parents to get over the pain caused by a parting son, the paternal Spanish house had already overcome the pain and was happy with the return of the glorious son. (*C.H.*, 142 1961, 11)

With the metaphoric use of the prodigal son parable, the Franco regime intended to show Spain's good intentions and generosity by taking the first step, but without relinquishing her status as "mother." Thus, Spain became the understanding mother who opened her door to reconciliation, that is the formation of the Hispanic Community of Nations. This led to the conclusion that what the wars of independence had accomplished was not a separation but, rather, the opposite: "the intimate and indissoluble relationship between Americans and Spaniards . . . that of the victors and the defeated, . . . will always be enveloped in the same haze of glory."[11] This reinterpretation of history reinforces even further the idea of belonging to a community, making everyone participant and coauthor of the same history. The argument comes to an end and the community acquires its definitive justification when it makes Simón Bolívar, one of the fathers of independence, the "champion" of Hispanidad.[12] Franco himself, upon inaugurating a monument to Simón Bolívar, says,

> You come as the high civil and military representatives of a group of brother countries of America to participate in the homage paid by Spain to Simón Bolívar, one of the greatest heroes of the American emancipation and a brilliant synthesis of this, our race, creator of people for liberty. (Franco 1970)

Thus, what the Francoists proposed was not simply to accept history, but rather to accept the Francoist version of history.

The democratic regime, without rethinking the origin or the ideological implications of this reinterpretation, integrates it into its discourse and uses it for the same purpose that the Franco regime used it: to justify the origin and existence of the Hispanic Community of Nations. Like King Juan Carlos I emphasized in 1983:

> Once the sufferings of the separation were forgotten, and the ideals and even the disillusions of Simón Bolívar were purified, there still remained as a collective heritage his great hope for a community, the ideal of the unity of all Hispanic countries.[13]

However, this is not the only way in which the Franco and democratic regimes manipulate history when making reference to the origins of the Hispanic Community of Nations. By trying once again to elude the topic of the conquest and colonization, both discourses overlook the past, thus situating the present ahistorically. Both rhetorics use various methods to accomplish their objective. First, they resort to impersonal forms, such as "was created," "originated from," and "was started," which avoid making reference to the subject that generates the action: "we pray so that the community, which was initiated four centuries ago, does not suffer a weakening, but on the contrary, becomes consistently stronger."[14] Phrases such as the one quoted from the Franco Minister of Foreign Affairs, Fernando María Castiella in 1964, are frequent in the democratic discourse (*Actividades*).

Another way to avoid reference to the historical origin of the community is by attributing the responsibility of the actions to impersonal and abstract subjects such as history or the past: "We believe that these particular ties, which are woven by history and which continue to persist today with regularity, are an important element" (*El País*, 05–20–82). In this way, it is history itself—and not the individuals that made it—that "wove" the ties that, according to Francoist thought, unite the member countries of the community.

Finally, metaphors are also frequently used. Thus, when the Minister of Foreign Affairs, Fernando Morán, speaks in 1983 of the Hispanic Community of Nations as a "community of independent nations that has sprung from a common stalk,"[15] he is only recycling a metaphor already used by Hispanist scholars thirty years earlier: "International solidarity—always desirable—is a principle that cannot be declined when it comes to nations with a common root and affinities as profound as those that unite Iberoamerica."[16] In this way, direct references to the polemic origin of the community are avoided while, at the same time, the shared history becomes one of the factors that determines the existence of the community.

Foundations and Destiny of the Community

According to Hispanist scholars, there are factors other than history that give cohesion and sense to the community. In 1976, King Juan Carlos I lists these factors:

> Our unity [is] based on biological traits; [it is] in solidarity vis-à-vis the basic beliefs about man, his dignity and his destiny; [it] is heir to a cultural heritage that possesses not only the glory of the past, but also the vitality of the present.[17]

If we bear in mind that, for the Hispanist of Franco's times, the Hispanic community was the synthesis of "the historical, ethnic, and spiritual essences—including within the last two, language, a common idea about man, and the habit of feeling and thinking,"[18] we see that, with the arrival of democracy, the factors of cohesion for the community have not varied substantially. The ethnic, historical, and cultural aspects, as well as the notion of a community of basic beliefs about man, remain unchanged.

But next to these historical factors there is another element that gives cohesion to the community. In the words of former president Adolfo Suárez, this element is "shared destiny" (Suárez, 33–34). For the democratic regime, this destiny consists in taking advantage of the theoretical existence of the community in order to posit itself as a "third power." Felipe González clearly expressed this in 1983:

> The Iberoamerican Community of Nations . . . could contribute to relaxing international tensions; to taking the world away from bipolar action; to the making of a multi-polarity that would balance international tensions and would give its countries a space to stop being each day more dependent on the plans of the great powers.[19]

The notion of the Hispanic community as an alternative capable of bringing the world out of a "bipolar action" already appears in the Hispanist discourse of the forties. The Francoists postulated the existence of a "crisis of civilization" in which two models, the capitalist or Western model and the Communist or Eastern one, would confront each other and destroy humankind. They saw the Hispanic Community of Nations as the only alternative possessing the spiritual values necessary to save the world from the crisis:

> The world is dividing its forces, and one of the banners that will arise at the right time will be raised and defended by Hispanic men before anyone else. There is only one power capable of confronting and overcoming all contingencies of history, and the Hispanic arm is, par excellence, the master of that power.[20]

This self-justification of the Francoist regime at a "spiritual" level is reinforced by a series of practical considerations concerning the future of the Latin American republics:

> because of their economic and human potential, [the republics] constitute a political and cultural unity called upon to occupy a leading position in the destiny of the world and to decisively intervene in favor of world peace in order to correct the political evils that the antagonism of the imperialist nations has unleashed upon the people of the earth.[21]

In this first stage, Hispanidad comes through as anti-Communist as much as anti-Capitalist, but once the first phase is overcome and Spain becomes a part of the "Western block"—when the cold war reaches its peak—the Francoist regime adopts an increasingly pro-Western posture against the so-called Communist threat. The fundamentally Catholic and anti-Marxist spiritual essences of Hispanidad are emphasized: "The role of Spain and of Hispanidad, [are] greatly significant and of undeniable influence within the current battle for the survival of the West."[22] Thus, from the Francoist point of view, the Hispanic Community ought to be aligned with the "Western" block, although always preserving its own "idiosyncrasy."[23]

But in time, the ideological-political concern posed by the threat of the expansion of Communism is followed by an economic concern produced by the magnification of the economic crisis in Latin America in the late fifties. It is increasingly evident that along with the West-East ideological split there is another division of great scope that affects the Hispanic countries equally: the North-South economic division. The awareness of one's own economic weakness in an increasingly polarized economic environment leads to viewing unity as the only means of survival. As the Minister of Foreign Relations, Castiella, indicated in 1959: "Either we save our common personality through unity, or we disappear drowned by more vigorous currents in the loud torrent of History."[24]

The democratic discourse continues this line of thought with Adolfo Suárez who in 1980 indicates that for Spaniards and Latin Americans, "[the] dream was to walk together or perish."[25] In this manner, the democratic discourse, echoing the Francoist discourse, presents unity as an economic necessity to counteract the action exerted by the great powers. But the democratic regime does not abandon the idea that the Hispanic Community of Nations should play the political role of mediator in world society. In 1983 King Juan Carlos I, declares:

> And that spontaneous proximity, created by a common past, language, and culture, could be elevated to a flexible institutional level, one that would allow the community of Hispanic nations to perform a mediating role in world society, between the north, an industrialized center, and the south, or periphery. Setting in motion the human potential and mobilizing the economic resources of that community would contribute to the ensurance of equilibrium among the great powers, or to put it in the words of the Liberator, to the equilibrium of the world.[26]

The community of shared language, culture, and history from which spontaneously springs—eluding once more the topic of the conquest—the necessity to institutionalize this community, and the role of the community as mediator between antagonistic blocks in order to

reach worldwide equilibrium, are concepts already present in the Hispanic discourse of the Francoist regime. These concepts have prevailed
over the disintegration of the system of blocks, the source of the Capi-
talist-Communist antagonism that gave origin to these concepts in
Francoist rhetoric. In October 1990, the Spanish Secretary of State for
the International Cooperation, Luis Yañez Barnuevo, wrote:

> The Ibero-American community, of which Spain feels a part, must
> formally organize itself into an international lobbying group willing
> to utilize all of its influence inside and outside the great institutions
> and pursue a worldwide balance based on policies that fight against
> the grave North-South iniquities that generate conflict and insecu-
> rity. (Yañez Barnuevo, 10)

Now, in order for this community to attain some international influence, it must transcend mere rhetoric. But, in the opinion of the democratic regime, what features should the materialization of such community include? In 1985, the director of International Relations for the
Spanish Socialist Labor Party, Elena Flores, wrote:

> The Socialist government did not want to create a bureaucratic super-
> structure or attempt any sort of integration from above, but rather
> achieve a growing network of relationships in all spheres, going
> beyond the indispensable political and cultural aspects as well as tech-
> nology, commerce, and trade, to include what might be termed the
> realm of affection. (Flores, 97)

We see that the community put forth by the Spanish democratic regime
encompasses the cultural as well as the political, economic, and technological aspects. In this way, the democratic discourse retrieves the character granted to the community by the Francoist regime. As the Minister
of Foreign Relations, Fernando Mª Castiella affirms in 1964:

> our bond with the Ibero American countries transcends the level at
> which the political, economic, and even cultural relations unfold
> because it is based on a community of spirit and blood, on the unde-
> niable evidence of an authentic fraternity. (C.H., 180 1964, 415)

The democratic regime repeatedly expresses its desire to contribute to
the development of Latin American governments with democratic
character, but it does not clearly establish what are the political bonds
that will unite the countries that compose the Hispanic community. In

fact, the democratic regime admits that the community is above the political regimes of the countries that constitute it: "Beyond the social systems, beyond the different political options, solid, spiritual, and historical fact, has united and will continue to unify the destinies of Spain and *Iberoamerica*."[27] In this sense, the democratic discourse is a prolongation of the Francoist discourse. In the words of the Minister of Foreign Affairs, in 1963, "each one should seek and find in the political, the social, and the economic their peculiar solutions, to build—in mutual respect—the one and varied edifice of Hispanidad."[28]

II. The Role of Spain within the Hispanic Community

Having analyzed the origin, the foundations, the destiny, and the character of Spanish Hispanist thought attributed to the Hispanic Community of Nations as a whole, we must determine the role assigned to Spain within this community. With respect to the democratic regime, it is King Juan Carlos I who tells us that "the vocation of Spain is to offer itself as a bridge between *Iberoamérica* and Europe, and we are willing to attempt this and to be a factor of integration."[29]

The idea of Spain as a "bridge" between Europe and Latin America already appears in the Hispanist discourse of the 1940s. It establishes that Spain is a part of Europe in both a cultural and geographic sense and declares that Spain, through colonization, opened America to Europe, making the Latin American republics an extension of "Europeanness." As a result of this, Latin America will not be able to succeed without relying on Europe. But in order to have access to Europe, Latin America must go through Spain.[30]

The notion of Spain as mediator and as a liaison remains present in the Socialist rhetoric, even though the word *bridge*—harshly criticized by some Socialists[31]—does not appear explicitly in the discourse. An example of such role is the reiteration by the president of the Spanish government of Spain's willingness to contribute

> to the rapprochement of America and Europe, and to the strengthening at every level [of all ties] with the Ibero-American countries, to which [Spain] is linked by unquestionable historic and cultural ties as well as a solid and cordial friendship. (*Actividades*)

Another role that Hispanist thought assigns Spain with respect to the Ibero American republics is that of "the model." At the beginning, the

Franco government presents Spain as a model of political stability attained through a regime of nationalist character.

> In this grave historic juncture it would do Iberoamerica well to turn its eyes towards the Mother Country, if only to see how men of the same race, language, and beliefs have struggled under similar circumstances and have tried to look for a political solution and a standard of conduct authentically national.[32]

Later, in the early seventies, Spain presents itself as a model of economic development:

> To you, Americans of historic ancestry, there is no greater pride than being partakers of the same historical tradition and brothers of people such as the Spanish who have been capable of reemerging from their ashes in the last years and who now contemplate you with enthusiasm, hope, and love. (Franco 1970)

Finally, the democratic regime portrays Spain as a model of political transition towards democracy: "Spain could also provide an attractive example of Western development and democratic processes among Spanish-speaking people."[33] While the characteristics whereby Spain is presented vary over the twenty-five-year period analyzed here, what remains constant in the discourse is the notion of superiority implicit in the model. As a bridge, as much as a model, Spain is presented as a leader of the community.

According to the Hispanists of the Franco era, this superiority derives from the very fact of discovery, since Spain was the country to which God "entrusted the mission" of conquering and colonizing Latin America. Spain was thus the country chosen to allow Latin America to enter history, "into civilization, into the universality of humankind."[34] Spain was therefore the Mother.

During the Spanish Civil War and in the first years that followed, the idea of the "Mother Country" was used profusely. But since the mid-forties, efforts were made to progressively substitute this term with the notion of "brotherhood" to avoid any doubt regarding the political intentions of the Franco regime and its desire for supremacy. However, toward the end of the fifties, when Spain witnesses her own economic recovery and the Francoists saw themselves free from international pressures, the concept of Mother Country surfaces again:

> Today, precisely because Spain does not shelter any hegemonic polit-
> ical or economic ambition toward America, and because it exhibits a
> special title—a historic, traditional, or sentimental one, if you wish—
> that of "Mother Country," Spain can and must assume the task of
> consolidating her sincere attempts to accomplish the Hispanic super-
> nationality, since this is like the desire to unite a conglomerate of
> countries on the basis of ideals and not on the basis of interests or fear
> of threat.[35]

Spain once again is considered the "center of the system."[36] Currently,
even though the democratic regime avoids the use of the term *Mother
Country* and talks continually of brotherhood, it has not been able to
avoid the notion of superiority that remains latent in the discourse
through euphemism. This is clear in the statement by the king of Spain
quoted at the beginning of this analysis: "[Spain] is an Hispanic nation,
one of the members—surely the oldest, the original one."

Or in the description that Luis Yañez Barnuevo makes of what he
assumes to be the participation of Spain in the Hispanic Community:
"the presence of Spain in this community will grant to the whole a European dimension, 'a northern one,' that can yield, as well, numerous
practical benefits to the integrationist effort" (Yañez Barnuevo, 10). The
two quotations cited above clearly show how, even in the rhetoric of the
democratic regime, Spain distinguishes herself from the other Hispanic
nations by her antiquity, her origin, her Europeaness, and by the fact
that she belongs to the "north," that is to the center and not to the
periphery of the system.

Conclusion

The analysis above allows us to affirm that—although the evolution of
the internal political situation of Spain, as well as that of the international context have brought about a certain reorientation of Hispanist
thought—it is not possible to speak of a radical transformation.

The democratic regime retains practically intact the final Francoist
notion of what the Hispanic Community of Nations is, and what it's role
should be in the international context as well as the role Spain should
play in this community. Furthermore, the democratic regime has inherited the internal contradictions of Hispanist thought of the Francoist
regime, such as (1) claiming that history be accepted while manipulat-

ing that very history; (2) wanting to create a Hispanic Community of a fundamentally political character, while member countries have internal regimes that differ from each other; and (3) pretending to give the appearance of equality while maintaining a rhetoric based on the notion of Spain's superiority.

Having established these conclusions, the immediate question is: How is it possible that a structural change of the dimension of that undergone by Spain's political regime does not bring along with it a parallel change in the Hispanist conceptions that were so closely linked to Francoist ideology?

The answer appears simple: Hispanist discourse, as stated, continues to be useful for the current Spanish government, above all for its policy of attempting to gain prestige in the eyes of the United States and Europe. Spain, as a bridge between Latin America and Europe—or as a mediator in the triangle of Latin America-Europe-United States—acquires, in the international context, an importance that she would not have by herself.

Now, how is it possible for this discourse of Francoist origins not to come into conflict with the ideals of the democratic regime? Two factors seem to explain this paradox: the discourse, as pronounced by a democratic government, polishes its content with a democratic gloss, and then the effort made by the sources emitting the democratic discourse to convince public opinion of the "novelty" of their Hispanist discourse, by stressing the contradictions between the current discourse and the Hispanist discourse of the first Francoist years. In this manner, the democratic discourse has appropriated many of the changes that the Hispanist discourse had undergone between the sixties and 1975.

Clearly, the Spanish democratic regime, in fifteen years of existence, has not been capable of finding new sources from which to replenish Hispanist thought so as to make it truly democratic.

Notes

1. Speech of Juan Carlos I in Aquistran upon receiving the Carlo Magno Prize (05–20–82), *Actividades, textos y documentos de la política exterior española.* Ministerio de Asuntos Exteriores (MAE), OID (Madrid, 1982).

2. See Howard J. Wiarda, ed., *The Iberian-Latin American Connection: Implications for U.S. Foreign Policy* (Boulder, CO: Westview, 1986), 5ff.; Silvia Enrich, *Historia diplomática entre España e Iberoamérica en el contexto de las*

relaciones internacionales (1955–1985) (Madrid: Ediciones de Cultura Hispánica, 1989), pp. 151, 163; Frederick B. Pike, "Latin America," in *Spain in the Twentieth-Century World: Essays on Spanish Diplomacy, 1898–1978;* James W. Cortada, ed., (Greenwood, CT: Greenwood Press, 1980), p. 205; Elena Flores, "Spain and Latin America: Two Views I," *Spain: Studies in Political Security,* Raymond Carr, ed. New York: Praeger Publishers, 1985), pp. 93–100; José Antonio Martínez Soler, "Spain and Latin America: Two Views II," *Spain: Studies in Political Security,* Raymond Carr, ed. New York: Praeger Publishers, 1985), pp. 101–7.

3. Archivo del Instituto de Cooperación Iberoamericana (AICI) Arch. 1604, Carp. 5335 y Carp. 5338.

4. William B. Bristol considers the creation of the *Unión Ibero-Americana de Madrid* in 1885 as the first attempt to institutionalize the movement called "Hispanismo." See pp. 15–17.

5. Quotation taken from Howard J. Wiarda, "Interpreting Iberian-Latin American Interrelations: Paradigm, Consensus and Conflict," in *Occasional Papers Series* 10 (January 1985): 12. See also Fredrick B. Pike, "Latin America," Jaime Cortada, ed., *Spain in the Twentieth-Century World* (Greenwood, CT: Greenwood Press, 1980), pp. 181–212.

6. As Fredrick Pike points out, two different tendencies developed within the *Hispanismo* movement: a conservative, and a liberal one. See Fredrick B. Pike, *Hispanismo, 1898–1936: Spanish Conservatives and Liberals and Their Relations with Spanish America* (South Bend, IN: University of Notre Dame Press, 1969).

7. See Zacarías de Vizcarra, *La vocación de América* (Buenos Aires, 1933); Ramiro de Maeztú, *Defensa de la Hispanidad* (Madrid, 1941).

8. See "Imperio" in *Informaciones* (Madrid) (18 July 1940): 1; *El Universal* (Lima) (25 July 1940).

9. See Lorenzo Delgado Gómez-Escalonilla, *Diplomacia franquista y política cultural hacia Iberoamérica, 1939–1953,* (Madrid: C.S.I.C., 1988).

10. *España en el Mundo,* Discursos de S. M. el Rey: 1976–1979, OID (Madrid: 1979).

11. See *C.H.,* 263–64 (May–June 1972), Demetrio Ramos: "El cambio de mentalidad sobre la emancipación hispanoamericana", 450.

12. See *C.H.,* 211 (July 1967), Miguel Aspiazu Carbo: "La partida de bautismo de la Hispanidad. Simón Bolívar, su adalid", pp. 145–55.

13. Words of Juan Carlos I in Caracas at the awards ceremony of the Simón Bolívar Prize in *El País* (26 July 1983).

14. See *C.H.*, 180 (1964), p. 415. Speech by Fernando M. Castiella in Guernica (12 October 1964).

15. Speech by Fernando Morán in Habsburg (25 February 1983). *Actividades, textos y documentos de la política exterior española* (MAE), OID, 26 (Madrid: 1983).

16. See AICI. Arch. 2571. Carp. 7765

17. Speech by Juan Carlos I in Cartagena de India (12 October 1976).

18. See *C.H.*, 163–64 (July–August 1963), Julio Icaza Tigerino: "Tensión de la Hispanidad en el mundo actual", p. 56.; *C.H.*, 70 (1955) Pedro Laín Entralgo: "Lengua y ser de la Hispanidad", pp. 3–14.

19. Intervention by the President of the Spanish government, Felipe González, in the closing session of "Iberoamerica: encuentros en la democracia" (30 April 1983), *Actividades, textos y documentos de la política exterior española* (MAE), OID, 28 (Madrid: 1983). Taken from Enrich, Silvia (1989), p. 299.

20. See *C.H.*, 4 (1948), Juan Miguel Bargallo Cirio: "Voz hispánica en la futura evolución del derecho", p. 39; see also *C.H.*, 4 (1948), pp. 42, 110; and *C.H.*, 3 (1948); Julio Ycaza Tijerino: "España, el Plan Marshall y el bloque occidental", p. 562.

21. See *C.H.*, 3 (1948), "Unión continental iberoamericana en defensa de la paz mundial", p. 582.

22. See *C.H.*, 118 (Oct. 1959), "La Hispanidad y la supervivencia de Occidente", p. 246.

23. *C.H.*, 15 (May–June 1950), Laín Entralgo, Pedro: "Sobre el ser de España". See also *C.H.*, 58 (Oct. 1954), Rudolf Grossmann, "Balance espiritual de la moderna Hispanoamérica", pp. 16–23.

24. See *C.H.*, 119 (Nov. 1959). Text of the speech given by Fernándo Mª Castiella (12 October 1959).

25. Speech given by the President of the Spanish government Adolfo Suárez, as a visiting Chief of State, in the Memorial Ceremonies of the 150th anniversary of the death of Simón Bolívar in Santa Marta (Colombia) (18 December 1980) (MAE), OID, Nota i 141181. Taken from Enrich, Silvia (1989), 160.

26. Words of Juan Carlos I in Caracas in the reception ceremony for the Simón Bolívar prize; *El País* (26 July 1983).

27. Speech given by Juan Carlos I in the UNESCO (4 November 1983) (MAE), OID.

28. See *C.H.,* 163–64 (1963), p. 7.

29. *Discursos y declaraciones del ministro español de Asuntos Exteriores, Marcelino Oreja* (October 1987) (MAE) OID (November 1978).

30. See *C.H.,* 7 (1949), p. 103. See also *C.H.,* 8 (1949), pp. 239–60; *C.H.,* 23 (1951), p. 271; *C.H.,* 8 (1949), p. 367; *C.H.,* 15 (1950), p. 498.

31. See Fernando Morán, *Una política exterior para España* (Barcelona: Ed. Planeta, 1980), pp. 399–400.

32. See *C.H.,* 151 (July 1962), Antonio Ortiz García, "Las dos Américas", p. 107.

33. See José Antonio Martínez Soler, "Spain and Latin America: Two Views II," in *Spain: Studies in Political Security,* Raymond Carr, ed. (New York: Praeger Publishers, 1985), p. 103. See also, Fernando Morán (1980), pp. 396–97.

34. See *C.H.,* 7 (1949), p. 139; *C.H.,* 14 (1950), p. 261; *C.H.,* 54 (June 1954); Vintila Horia: "Indoamericanismo y realidad", p. 374.

35. See *C.H.,* 152–53 (Aug.–Sept.), Prieto Castro, Fermín: "La Supranacionalidad Hispánica", p. 257

36. See *C.H.,* 216 (Dec. 1967), Costas, Carlos José. "II Festival de Música de América y España", p. 645.

Works Cited

Actividades, textos y documentos de la política exterior española. Madrid: Ministerio de Asuntos Exteriores (MAE), OID, 1982.

Artajo, Alberto Martin. *Cuadernos Hispanoamericanos* 97 (1957): 332.

Bonilla, A. "Concepto histórico de la Hispanidad". *Cuadernos Hispanoamericanos* 120 (1959): 247–54.

Bristol, William B. "Hispanidad in South America, 1936–1945" (Ph.D. Dissertation in History, University of Pennsylvania, 1947), pp. 15–17.

Delgado Gómez-Escalonilla, Lorenzo. *Diplomacia franquista y política cultural hacia Iberoamérica, 1939–1953.* Madrid: C.S.I.C., 1988.

Enrich, Silvia. *Historia diplomática entre España e Iberoamérica en el contexto de las relaciones internacionales (1955–1985).* Madrid: Ediciones de Cultura Hispánica, 1989.

España en el Mundo. Discursos de S. M. el Rey. 1976–1979. Madrid: OID, 1979.

Flores, Elena. "Spain and Latin America: Two Views I." In *Spain: Studies in Political Security*, Raymond Carr, ed. New York: Praeger Publishers, 1985.

Franco, Francisco. *Mundo Hispánico* 273 (1970).

Hobsbawm, Eric. *The Age of Empire, 1875–1914*. New York: Vintage, 1989.

Martínez Soler, José Antonio. "Spain and Latin America: Two Views II." In *Spain: Studies in Political Security*. Raymond Carr, ed. New York: Praeger Publishers, 1985.

Morán, Fernando: *Una política exterior para España*. Barcelona: Ed. Planeta, 1980, pp. 399–400

Morodo, Raúl. *Acción Española: Orígenes ideológicos del Franquismo*. Madrid: Tucar Ediciones, 1980.

Pike, Fredrick B. "Latin America." In *Spain in the Twentieth-Century World*. Jaime Cortada ed. Greenwood, CT: Greenwood Press, 1980, pp. 181–212.

———. *Hispanismo, 1898–1936: Spanish Conservatives and Liberals and Their Relations with Spanish America*. South Bend, IN: University of Notre Dame Press, 1969.

Rey, Juan Carlos I. *Actividades, textos y documentos de la política exterior española*. Ministerio de Asuntos Exteriores (MAE), OID. Madrid, 1982. In Aquistran upon receiving the Carlo Magno Prize (20 May 1982).

Suárez, Adolfo. "La Comunidad iberoamericana: una utopía necesaria". In *En el camino de la historia*. México: Sociedad Cooperativa Publicaciones Mexicanas, S.C.L., 1988, pp. 33–34

Wiarda, Howard J. "Interpreting Iberian-Latin American Interrelations: Paradigm, Consensus and Conflict." In *Occasional Papers Series* 10 (January, 1985): 12.

Yáñez Barnuevo, Luis. "Iberoamérica, entre el Norte y el Sur". *El País* (12 October 1990): 10.

11

The Universal Exposition Seville 1992: Presence and Absence, Remembrance and Forgetting

MARINA PÉREZ DE MENDIOLA

The bridging is never done without cost.
—James Clifford

One of the most recent reminders of the "initial" bridging between Spain and Latin America was clearly the quincentennial and the many events commemorating it around the world. Among these events, the Universal Exposition Seville 1992, hosted by Spain, was the most elaborate, surpassing the others in size, scope, and in its exposure and funding. In the Proclamation Discourse of the Seville Expo '92 made public on January 12, 1986, King Don Juan Carlos I of Spain stated that this exposition would be different from other universal expositions. It would be truly universal "unifying all nations with good intentions," making sure that the commemoration "would not be foreign to any of its participants" (*Catálogo Oficial*, 3). This assertion came to be the motto of the exposition. Spain set out to renew the conventional exposition strategies centered around exclusion and marginalization, and hoped to introduce an alternative mode of "exposing." As a Spaniard and as a Latinamericanist, I am particularly interested in examining select aspects of the Latin American presence in this event. The study of selective forms of linking between Spain and Latin America on the exposition grounds raises the fundamental issues to be addressed in this chapter. First, how different was this exposition from previous world fairs and particularly from the 1893 World's Columbian Exposition and the 1929 Iberoamerican Exposition? Did the assumptions on which the organization of this exposition was founded allow for the stark contrast to previous exhibitions that Spain anticipated and promised? How significant was the representation of Latin America in this exposition for Spain? How present was Latin America, and how was this presence articulated? Although I do not intend to compare nor to review this exposition with previous ones, I would like to begin this analysis with a brief discussion of specific historical events and themes in other expositions that will help us interpret the idiosyncracies of Expo '92 and the logic behind its organization.

Of particular relevance to this study are the expositions held in North America at the turn of the century that involved Latin American countries: The World's Columbian Exposition of 1893 in Chicago, the Atlanta Cotton States (1895), the International Exposition of 1895, and the Pan American Exposition of 1901 at Buffalo. As Robert Rydell cogently showed in his book *All the World's a Fair*, the concept of exposition is hardly new. Rydell points in particular to the World's Fair "craze" that struck between 1876 and 1916, which he reads as an effort to contain a nation marked by a period of great social instability. According to his study, the United States government resorted to the ritual of expositions and fairs

> to alleviate the intense and widespread anxiety that pervaded the United States. The directors of the expositions offered millions of fair-goers an opportunity to reaffirm their collective national identity in an updated synthesis of progress and white supremacy that suffused the blueprints of future perfection offered by the fairs. (Rydell, 4)

The World's Columbian Exposition commemorating Columbus's chance arrival in the West Indies was the perfect occasion for North Americans to celebrate and show "American progress through time and space since 1492" (Rydell, 47). While it promoted "order and progress" for the world, the World's Columbian Exposition of 1893 in Chicago characterized itself by "ethnological underpinnings."

Indeed, the locations of different villages and stands on the Midway (the site of the amusement section of the fair) of nonwhite and non-Western cultures proved that the whole fair was "an utopian construct built upon racist assumptions" (Rydell, 48). If African Americans were hardly allowed to participate in such an exclusive event, American Indians were displayed as entertaining but alien others to the observer and the White City (main ground of the fair):

> Nearest to the White City were the Teutonic and Celtic races as represented by the two German and Irish villages. The center of the Midway contained the Mohammedan World, West Asia, and East Asia. Then we descend to the savage races, the African of Dahomey and the North American Indian, each of which has its place at the opposite end of the Plaisance. (Rydell, 65)

Interestingly enough, Latin American countries such as Cuba, Brazil, Guatemala, Mexico, Venezuela, Chile, Ecuador, Colombia, and Peru[1] sent many officially and privately funded representatives. The Latin American countries were not ostracized the way Asian and African countries were. For one thing, these countries were given space outside the Midway. Although some of the indigenous cultures from Latin America were represented in ethnological villages constructed by Western anthropologists and relegated to the Midway, this racial compartimentalization would not offend overmuch their national governments. Countries such as Mexico were at that time under the aegis of presidents who themselves considered its Indian population as a hindrance for expansion and civilization. Most of the newly formed Latin American countries had only recently claimed their independence from Spain, and were in the process of building their nations. They looked toward France, England, and the United States, anxious to assert themselves in the world of production. What prompted North America to include Latin American countries in the White City and, by the same token, in "the illustrated encyclopedia of civilization" (Rydell, 44) was the the opportunity for the United States to expand its commercial empire and open potentially huge markets in these new neighboring nations.

Similarly, the presence of Latin Americans at the Atlanta Cotton States (1895), and the International Exposition (1895) could only be seen in terms of North American growth. As the studies on the World Industrial and Cotton Exposition of 1885 or the Atlanta Fair reveal, "the exposition was intended to promote American capital investment in Latin America and to demonstrate its market potential for American surplus production. . . . *The New York Times* reiterated that the exposition would portray Latin America as a market for American products"

(Rydell, 91). A few years later, The Pan American Exposition of 1901 at Buffalo opened with the motto "Pax 1901." Its purpose reminds us uncannilly of the theme of the Expo '92 in Seville: to illustrate progress on the eve of a new millenium and to lay a strong and enduring foundation for international, commercial, and social unity of the world. However, "Pax 1901" revealed a great deal of what its partners understood by unity. In the same way that the 1893 Chicago Fair ostracized "the savage races," Rydell reminds us that

> as in the case of Africans, Afro-Americans, and Filipinos, the exposition also locked selected Latin Americans into villages with predetermined ideological contours. . . . Mc Garvie, who raised the money for the Mexican Village concession, romanticized the Spanish influence in Mexico, emphasized the potential for American investment in the Mexican economy, and stressed the inferiority of the other Mexican people. (147–48)

Different nations from Latin America became increasingly conscious that the "Anglo-Saxon" America, and the "Iberian or Latin" America were far from forming a united America. This relation of dominance would have an enormous and long-lasting impact on Spain and Latin American relations during the first three decades of the twentieth century.

This period also became known as a period of renovation, a period during which "Latin America resurfaced with great strength in the culture and in the collective sensibility of the Spanish people" (Ubieto, Reglá, et al., 921). Several Latin American countries, such as Argentina and Mexico, were willing to resume their ties on a friendly footing with the country that had dominated and subjugated them for centuries. The 1929–1930 Iberoamerican Exposition held in Seville, was the crowning achievement of a policy initiated in 1900 with the creation of the Iberoamerican Union (Ubieto, Reglá, et al., 921). It crystallized the efforts made on both sides of the Atlantic to engage in a new dialogue. The Iberoamerican Exposition is considered to be the first truly neocolonial fair and, as French art historian Sylvie Assassin explains, "it seems to be precursory of the Expo '92. This project was part of Primo de Rivera's politics of prestige and great works that originally also included the preparation of the 1928 Olympic Games" (Assassin, 69). Primo de Rivera's 1923–1930 dictatorship followed the constitutional crisis of 1917–1920, the dissolution of the parliamentary system, and the Moroccan Disaster of 1921, which could almost be seen as a reminder of 1898

when Spain lost her remaining "American" colonies in the Spanish
American war. Yet Primo de Rivera's government made use of and cap-
italized on Spain's neutrality during World War I and portrayed itself as
the only link between Latin America and Europe. In addition, Primo de
Rivera profited from the scarcity of raw materials in Europe, which, in
contrast, were abundant in Latin America during and after the war and
benefited as well from the enmity between Latin America and North
America. As the title of the Iberoamerican Exposition indicates, this fair,
unlike most expositions, was not intended to be universal. A Spanish
chronicler clarified this choice by writing that "the world is too large and
cannot fit in a single exposition" (quoted in Assassin, 17). Thus, Spain
limited the invitation to its former colonies as well as Morocco,[2] the
United States, and its neighbor, Portugal.

Primo de Rivera insisted that the pavilions representing Latin
American nations be conceived and built by Latin American architects.
His policies differ from those of the previous fairs like the 1893 Chicago
Exposition where "shackles of ecclecticism and archeological revivals"
prevailed. The invitation extended to Latin American countries to *represent themselves* in Spain, presumed relief from paternalism and from
the economic interests that elicited the invitation in the first place.
Despite the fact that Spain did not see the exposition as an act of self-
redemption, it was nonetheless the first country to "allow" its former
colonies and native architects to conceive and build their own pavilions.[3] For many countries in Latin America the twenties were considered a prosperous period; however, not all of these countries could be
present in Seville or could provide their own architects. Paraguay and
Bolivia were busy fighting the Chaco war. Panama, Nicaragua, Hondu-
ras, Costa Rica, and El Salvador reduced their participation to stands in
other commercial and industrial buildings (Assassin, 131). Among the
countries that participated and built their own pavilions, only Guatemala, Colombia, and Venezuela did not entrust the elaboration of their
pavilions to one of their own architects. The remaining countries, Peru,
Chile, Uruguay, Argentina, Brasil, Mexico, Cuba, and the Dominican
Republic,[4] were encouraged by the organizing committee to represent a
national style in their design. Except for Cuba and the Dominican
Republic, these Latin American countries shaped their pavilions in the
image of how they imagined their relatively new nations. The
Iberoamerican Exposition did not attract many visitors. For one thing,
there was little interest in Spain and in Latin America. Moreover, for
most Europeans in 1930, Spain seemed to be at the far corner of the

world, Seville being closer to Africa than Europe. Conversely, Expo '92 aimed at a rapprochement between the Iberian Peninsula and the rest of Europe hoping to break its secular isolation. Many efforts were once more made to bring Spain and Latin America closer; yet by choosing Seville, the door to the West Indies, as the host of the exposition, it was also Spain's way of saying that "Seville remains the symbol of our civilizing adventure" (quoted in Assassin, 27).

Sixty-two years later, Seville opened its doors again, this time welcoming the entire world to Exposición Universal Sevilla '92 or Expo '92. Expo '92 was erected on the Cartuja Island—on the west side of Seville, bathed by the Guadalquivir River—where Christopher Columbus once lived among the Cartujo Monks in the Santa María de las Cuevas Monastery, before sailing off to the Americas. To link the Cartuja Island with the rest of the world for this universal "encounter," four bridges were built between Seville and the Island; a high-speed train service and a new train station to house it were created between Madrid and Seville; additional highway networks were put in place and boats were able to berth at a quay next to the recreated Puerto de las Indias. The last universal exposition of this millenium, as the official catalogue of the Expo '92 proudly proclaims, was the largest in terms of the number of countries represented.[5] Conceived around the theme of "the human capacity to discover and its discoveries," the exposition wished to send "a message of peace, of coevalness, and solidarity as a base for a new world order for all the inhabitants of our common home, our fragile planet earth" (*Guía Oficial*, 18).

Despite the hype, there was a recurrent question among most Spaniards: Would there be life after 1992? Surely in 1992, Spain was the focal point of Europe and the world. Madrid was named the cultural capital of Europe, the Summer Olympics games were hosted by Barcelona,[6] and the Universal Exposition took place in Seville. But the spectre of the Conquest loomed on the horizon. Indeed, if the conquest of the "New World" enhanced the prestige of the Iberian Peninsula in times of strong Western economic expansion, 1992 placed it once again at the center of international attention. After the extraordinary and liberating quake that followed the end of the Francisco Franco's dictatorship, the quincentennial couldn't have been more timely. The *Movida*—a term used to define social and artistic effervescent activity as a result of Spain's new democracy—that agitated the early eighties paved the way for the economic and, above all, cultural boom that allowed Spain to concentrate all its energy in the "Great Works of '92." The most important goal was of course to become part of the European Economic Community; but Spain also hoped to improve its image, which since the "Siglo de Oro" had cut a sorry figure. Nevertheless, the revival of the spirit of the conquest—through the conquest of Europe—in the midst of the Spanish *perestroïka* was an irony that did not pass unnoticed, particularly on the other side of the Atlantic, in the Americas.

The polemic that started in the mid-1980s around the celebration or commemoration of the "encounter" of the two worlds has caused much ink to flow. Numerous groups of Indians in the Americas took initiatives to counter the celebration scheduled for 1992 wishing to see the quincentenary "as an opportunity to correct some old conceptions."[7] Their program included

> the commemoration of both the Indians placed in slavery by European explorers and colonists and the Indian nations that have disappeared since the arrival of Columbus; a public campaign to petition the King of Spain, Juan Carlos, to adopt an *Apology to Native People of the Western Hemisphere* based upon the historical Apology proposed by Bartolomé de Las Casas, and a mock trial of Columbus in which Indians of the Americas will charge him with crimes against Indians. (*Native Nations,* 11)

The Native American Council of New York City called for an "Indian Summer." According to the New York City-based Indian Organizations, the American Indian Community House (AICH), the Solidarity Foundation, and the American Indian Law Alliance sought to "challenge the current vision of consumption and destruction, and to remind the public that there exists the means and the will to change the troubled destiny of human kind" (*Native Nations,* 13). In Latin America, one could encounter the same degree of activity. In July 1990, a meeting entitled "Five Hundred Years of Indian Resistance" brought four hundred people together in Quito. They represented one hundred and twenty nations, tribes and organizations from North, Central, and South America and the Caribbean. Their aim was to "study and develop resolutions on the following issues: Human rights, land and natural resources, the five-hundredth anniversary of Columbus's land fall, legislation, women's organizations, education, and self-determination" (Selverston, 12). While the revisionist approach to this celebration went beyond the notion of "exploration" and focused more on how the devastating consequences of the Conquest can inform our societies and their future, the "official constituencies" reacted very differently.

For the most part, the majority of the turn-of-the-century fairs expressed exclusion, negation of plurality, and the isolation of certain cultures on "Midways." The aim of the Seville Exposition was "global participation," "global exchange" within the context of "development and humanism," to reach a level of representation that would "summarize planetary sensitivity at the end of this millenium" (*Guía Oficial*, 28). But what is substantially different almost a century later in the world of expositions?

Much work has been done on the notion of exhibition and the world of expositions.[8] This research shows that the entrance to civilization through the doors of these expositions has been possible only at a very high cost. As seen earlier, the expositions can be perceived as symptomatic elaborations of ideological constructs. Yet, although Expo '92 was conceived in the age of political correctness, the legacy of the previous fairs still hung over the blissful aura with which the organizing committee veiled the Cartuja Island. In spite of the organizers' claims, the Exposition '92 did not seem to be able to shun the ideology of exclusion around which the world exposition was conceived. That is to say, nations—namely modern Western nations—whose cultural, historical, and economic past, present, and future function as a symbol of success, partake in this formidable showcase in order to reassert their power without reassessing its problematic relationship to other cultures and histories. They only allow the rest of the world to raise itself—in an illusory fashion—to the level of those who orchestrated a simulacrum of unity in diversity. In this evanescent context anyone can pretend to be inclusive since the exposition represents, above all, modern Western nations' "perfected dream of themselves."[9] It is not without irony that the first country to express interest in participating in the fair—as early as 1987—was one of the poorest countries in the world: The Dominican Republic, the country where Spaniards erected their first settlement. Between the ethnological villages of the Pan American Exposition (1901) and, as Rydell puts it, "the affection and racist antipathy" surrounding it, to the benevolent and patronizing ideology of Expo '92, the cleavage (splitting?) is smaller than one would like to think. What especially interests me is how the prevailing attitudes of this event set the tone for future dialogues between Spain and the different countries of what I call—for lack of a better name—Latin America. After all, Expo '92 was conceived around the historical theme of 1492, and the importance given to the presence of Latin American countries in Seville is undeniable. But how was Latin America's presence "figured," and how important was its presence, and for whom?

For one thing, most of the Latin American and Caribbean countries were housed under the same pavilion in the Plaza de America Pavilion covering the largest surface area of the exposition—33,000 square meters. Yet, the (forced) cohabitation of Latin American and Caribbean countries under one roof seemed to spring more from economic necessity than from the desire to prove inter-American solidarity. Could the fair really help to improve cultural awareness with euphemisms such as "the small countries, those *in need* of solidarity, have *grouped themselves* around the Plaza of Africa, the Plaza of America, in the Pavilion of the Caribbean and in the Pavilion of the Southern Pacific Islands" (*Guía Oficial*, 37; my emphasis). Despite the fact that King Don Juan Carlos of Spain had hoped for a World Fair where "stereoptype and routine would have no place," we find again a world ruled and mapped out by an international economy. This is a world politically determined by those who can conveniently afford epistemic enhancement. Had Brazil, Argentina, Bolivia, and other countries been able financially to have their own pavilion as did Venezuela, Mexico, or Chile, among others, would they have opted for this type of representation that caters to the Western ideological "arsenal" behind the conceptualization of Expo '92? Or does this mean that those who were able to afford their own pavilion placed themselves outside of this "inter-American solidarity"? The question that must be asked, then, is What defines solidarity in Latin America? or, in a slightly different way, Who defines it? What role did Spain play in this "unifying" process? Might Spain still see itself as the only one capable of "unifiying" these former colonies? What underlies such an ideal of unity? How different is this association or division from the segregation those same nations faced a century ago?

Still, the official *Catalogue of the Exposition of 1992, Exposición Universal Sevilla 92: Una isla para el mundo*, insists under the title "112 Countries Representing Themselves," that the

> Plaza of America is more than a pavilion. This architectural ensemble has two converging goals that could at first be read as contradictory. On the one hand, it wished to emphasize the potential for unity of Latin America, rendered symbolically by the unity of the building and by the presence in the Pavilion of the Organización de Estados Americanos. On the other hand, the personality of each country is represented through well-defined *interior spaces.*[10] (*Catálogo Oficial*, 54; my emphasis)

James Kiernan, director of an office that coordinated the Quincentennial Commemoration of the Discovery of America: Encounter of Two Worlds at the OAS, stated that "this six-month celebration of the spirit of discovery, both past and future, is also a manifestation of the optimism with which the world faces the twenty-first century" (54). The homogenization that results from this "grouping together" of so many different countries and cultures raises more pessimism than does the oblivious optimism shown by the organizing committee of this exposition.

What remains crucial here is the much-debated issue of representation. The question, How are we being represented?[11] posed by the "peripheral" countries that participated in previous fairs, becomes in Seville How do we represent ourselves? Are these two significantly different questions? The sense of autonomy (or self-determination) implied in the idea of self-representation seems incompatible with the act of representation in the context of a world exposition where the notions of representing and of being represented are inextricably linked to the ideological apparatus of state power: "Behind spontaneity there lies a purely mechanistic assumption, behind the liberty a maximum of determinism, behind the idealism an absolute materialism" (Gramsci, 129). Within the logic of a universal exposition the concept of representation is inseparable from the notion of physical presence. The pavilion, the architectural structure, is what establishes this presence, its materiality being "a prerequisite to presence" (Benedikt, 14), and by extension, to representation. But what kind of presence are we referring to here? In Deconstructing the Kimbel, architect Benedikt reminds us of how presence often becomes idealized, grounding his interpretation of architecture in Derrida's philosophy of deconstruction. Summarizing Derrida's argument of "the idealization of presence," Benedikt writes that "the idealization of presence in Western metaphysics, causes all systems of distinctions and categories to be hierarchical, hierarchical in the sense that one term dominates by overshadowing or occluding the others with its extra presence" (16). This "extra presence" was doubly displayed in the Expo '92 , first by the event itself, the exposition as the commemoration of 1492 and the age of discovery (a celebration that the President of the Spanish government, Felipe González, considered "justified because of its magnitude"); second, by Spain itself as the host of the event, by its pavilion, and the additional seventeen pavilions representing the seventeen Autonomous Communities of Spain. These pavilions were centrally located on the Lago de España (Lake of Spain). The Spanish Pavilion was built on the west side of the lake facing the seventeen other Pavilions built on the east side, mirroring and redefining each other in a self-containing manner. Spain's "extra presence" managed to suppress the presence of the other participants, in particular the presence of those defined as minor, even though, as Benedikt puts it, "they are logically necessary and logically preconditional to the whole scheme" (17). Necessary, yes, but under the "*protection* of the organizer," and "governed by its organizational principal" as Buren underlines in another context (66). The "extra presence" of Spain particularly overshadowed the presence of the Latin American countries, this "idealized presence" without which Spain's extra presence could not have been possible. It works as a sort of "ground" on which hyperbolized presence depends.

Let us examine how this extra presence was further constituted. In *Exhibiting Culture*, Crew and Sims insist that "it is the event that is of ultimate importance, not the things or even our directed thoughts about them. And it is in the place/time of the event that the audience takes part, becoming cocreations of social meaning. Authenticity is located in the event" (Crew and Sims, 174). In the context of this exposition Crew and Sims's assertion is particularly pertinent. As mentioned above, Spain saw the commemoration of 1492 as the event that could allow the country to signal its radical transformation to the rest of Europe and the World:

> Spain is not different any longer. It is rather a country that participates in the elaboration of great international projects. We want our citizens to feel proud of their country and we want the foreigners to update the myths they have about Spain. The Expo is an operation of images . . . to help us shake off the idea that Spaniards do not know how to organize themselves. (Caballero, 4)

These words, spoken by Angel Luis Gonzalo (Commissioner of the Spanish Pavilion), indicate that Spain's main objective was to be in tune with the rest of the world and decided, after its first drive of expansionism, to "expand again the world limits." But at what cost?

Indeed, what matters is the image all countries present through their pavilion to fairgoers and to coparticipants. For Spain, of course, it would also have been a golden opportunity if not to "redeem" itself historically, at least to set a different tone for future expositions. Instead, Spain chose to follow in the tradition of previous world fairs that requires that the host establishes himself hierarchically as the "dominant term." The Spanish Pavilion is paradigmatic of Spain's failure to transform this logic. Seven rooms of the Spanish Pavilion guided the visitors through the topography, geography, and history of Spain. The first room welcomed the spectator to the routes of Spain's daily life and led to the second room where the visitor could travel back to Spain's past. The third room finally took the visitor to the Era of Discovery and was followed by the fourth room, dedicated to the Spanish Language, emphasizing the fact that 300 million people speak Spanish around the world. Finally, the fifth and the sixth rooms showcased Spain's technological advances, a requirement without which full membership in the European community is impossible. The first rooms set the tone for the rest of the Pavilion. One could feel that everything was made to avoid contentious issues. The descent towards past millenia reveals, as Antonio Caballero puts it, "an asceptic history that is, a history not 'positively global' any more—as the panegyrists of real socialism used to say in another context; instead it is totally positive, all light no shadows" (15). In the script supporting the visual material covering the past, no one "conquered," no one "invaded," the Jews were never "expelled," and once again, historical amnesia governed the discourse of the long-awaited Pavilion. No, Spain did not engage in a thorough study of its historical past because it was too preoccupied with "asserting its sovereignty as the universal ideal" (Chatterjee quoted by Bhabha, 293). Spain adheres to the universal exposition's predicate, which is to emphasize neither disagreements, confrontations between nations, nor past or present genocides.

The third room, The Room of Discovery, was no less disappointing and problematic. The script narrating the "encounter" between the two worlds, Europe and America, was offensively romanticized. One can accept the constant wavering of euphemisms such as "arrived" to replace "invade," "encounter" instead of "conquest"—euphemisms that replace the motives of expansionism with the rhetoric of affiliation— but the absence of Cortés, Pizarro, and many other embarrassing figures in the array of slides representing the event cannot go unnoticed. Furthermore, I can only agree with Caballero who, in his revisionist essay about the "Quincentennial Celebration," maintains that the omission of the word and notion of religion in the text supporting the visual display of 900 slides for this retrospective falls within the province of a "Faustian dilemma": "Without the mention of gold or silver, of religion or blood, the spectator will take with him the confusing impression that Spaniards traveled to the Indies on a strictly academic mission, that is to look for useful plants and to offer new agricultural techniques and domestic animals to the native people" (Caballero, 23). The Spanish Pavilion demonstrated that certain modes of remembering put stress on forgetting. Furthermore, it showed that, as Lyotard phrased it, "what the event makes absent is forgotten" (252). If, as Crew and Sims assert, "the vision of the historical events controls the direction and point of view of the exhibiting" (171), we could thus say that Spain wished to reinvent itself, its history, and above all, its place within the Western world through Expo '92, and particularly through the Spanish Pavilion. Shouldn't we read this Pavilion as an overarching frame guarding this process of reinvention, a process sustained primarily by a specular image (or an "operation of images"), itself contingent on imperialistic redefinitions?

Mexico was probably the only country to remind Spain, in admittedly symbolic fashion, that it did not come to the exposition to be conquered again. Mexico did so by framing the entrance to its pavilion with two sculptures, each eighteen meters high and representing an X. This X was sculpted to symbolize a forking path, the encounter between pluralities. Albeit, it was also a reminder that Mexico should always be *written* and *read* with an autochthonous X, and not with the Spanish *jota* (Méjico), a spelling the Spaniards gave to Mexico during the conquest. Going even further, one could see this X as a sign under which the Mexican Pavilion placed itself, as if "under erasure," a device, Benedikt recalls, which was "introduced by Heidegger, with *sous rature*, when a word is printed crossed out, with an X through it." Its legibility, he adds, "both physically and as a unit of meaning, is questioned even as it is used" (Benedikt, 13). With this X, Mexico may have been pointing to a "twofold play on presence and absence": although materially present, it questioned the celebration and jogged the memory back to almost five hundred years of absence.

Ironically, this exposition showed that what promoted the original "encounter" and later the different types of rapprochement between Latin America and the Iberian Peninsula, continues to determine the relationship between these two regions: Spain's desire to overcome its historical liminality within Western Europe and, by extension, its renewed influence on the Americas. Through the exposition, Spain wanted to break away from its marginality within Europe and earn its citizenship as a European country. Spain hoped to place herself at the fore, reminding her neighbors that it is "from Spain, in 1492, that sprung the grandest historical enterprise undertaken by Europe" (*Catálogo Oficial*, 16). As the catalogue asserts, this is what Spain wished to celebrate: "an event that should be noted with the magnitude and depth it deserves" (16). Spain wished to be remembered for its "illustrious and grandiose" (yet bygone) times, hoping that its past credentials would still constitute a valid passport to join the community of great nations and to establish a complicity with the rest of Europe. Spain required the "presence" of its former colonies to reaffirm itself, as a physical remembrance of its past accomplishments.

Spain showed its eagerness to compare itself with the most powerful economies in the world, such as Japan: "Since the exposition held in Osaka in 1970, no one had seen a larger and more impressive exposition than the 1992 Exposition" (*Catálogo Oficial*, 28). In fact, the official guide to the Expo dedicated several paragraphs to what appeared to be a blatant "courting" of Japan. It went so far as to describe at great length and approvingly the tremendous ecological progress represented by the construction of the Japanese Pavilion, emphasizing the fact that Japan brought back to our "postindustrial era" the prestige of wood by constructing the largest pavilion ever made out of wood. But what the catalogue fails to mention is that Japan, one of the largest importers of wood in the world, is also in great part responsible for the massive deforestation taking place in Indonesia, Brazil, and Central America. Many incongruities in this exposition, resulting in great part from Spain's unwieldy and ingenuous attempt to seduce those who are still reluctant to grant her full membership, would be worth pursuing. As for now, it is important to remember that, since 1992, Europe's financial and cultural turmoil has been cause for much worry in the Iberian Peninsula. In spite of the extensive efforts Spain has made in the last decade, it is still not recognized as part of what France and Germany called in 1993 "Europe in first gear." France and Germany seem to perceive Spain as a country running only in second gear, and once more it will be hard for the Iberians to move from their "vagón de segunda" to the "vagón de primera" (from second-class carriage to first-class carriage).

Spain's "liminal minority position" within Europe over the centuries, her attempt to reaffirm and reinvent herself, has had a great impact on the relationship between Latin America and the Iberian Peninsula. Yet, to conclude, I would like to venture that Spain is not alone in circumscribing the terms of its relationship with Latin America to a politically regressive order. By accepting the tendentious invitation to join the self-congratulatory World Exposition '92, Latin America has also missed the opportunity to undermine the universal rhetoric of "real participation." That is to say, it failed to show the world that the notions of "progress, global communication, cultural exchange, and solidarity" that fueled this exposition go beyond this transient staging during which everything is measured in terms of each country's ability to be ostentatious for this once-in-a-lifetime event. Finally, although the North American process of empowerment is considerably more recent than the Spanish one, its role and participation in mapping out the dynamics between these three parties is central.

It would be safe to say that North America's current manipulation of Spain's ontological and epistemological unsteadiness over the centuries could be a reminder of the Hispano-North American conflict in 1898, during which Spain lost her last overseas possessions to the benefit of the North American imperial power. While Spain is doing its best to relocate Latin American subjectivity formation within the Iberian Peninsula, North America capitalizes on Spanish mediation between the two Americas in order to facilitate the process of its "desatanization" (Fuentes's word as quoted in Delaney) in the eyes of Latin America. However, these types of opportunistic maneuverings originating from Spain and North America should not be seen only as an unsurmountable obstacle. Latin America could instead look at 1992 as the chance for a salutary, momentary distancing from its historical ties with Spain and North America. Spain and the Americas should be able to "bridge" their differences in a spirit of true intellectual debate, keeping in sight their respective historical, cultural, and economic roles from which yet "unimagined" ideas of exchange and cooperation can still emerge.

Notes

I wish to thank Panivong Norindr, Robin Pickering-Iazzi, and Carmen Cavallo for their insightful comments on this piece.

1. Jeanne Madeline Weiman in her informative study *The Fair Women*, documents also the participation of women from these Latin American countries. See in particular pp. 136, 276, 544–45, 145.

2. In spite of its defeat in 1921, Spain remained in control of the region of the Rif in the northern part of Morocco and, in the south, the Ifni and Tarfaya.

3. Assassin reminds us that Spain turned down France's invitation to its Colonial Exposition of 1931 held in Paris, either because of its concern to be consistent or its inability to come to terms with the end of its colonial dream.

4. These two countries had a very awkward status for a long time. The United States army occupied Cuba from 1899 to 1902. Later, despite its independence from Spain, it remained under the control of the U.S. until the Cuban revolution of 1959. The U.S. also maintained a tight grip on the Dominican Republic. Although independent since 1844, this country suffered from numerous North American interventions. It was thus difficult for these countries to think of themselves as independent.

5. One hundred twelve countries were represented, as well as the seventeen Autonomous Communities of Spain (Andalucía, Aragón, Asturias, Baleares, Canarias, Cantabria, Castilla-La Mancha, Castilla y León, Cataluña, Euskadi, Extremadura, Galicia, La Rioja, Madrid, Murcia, Navarra, Valencia).

6. The 1992 Olympics were a success. Spain won as many medals in these olympic games as they won in all the previous games combined.

7. See "1992 Alliance: A Coalition for Native Leaders of North America." *Native Nations* 1:1 (January 1991): 10–11.

8. Adolphe Demy's *Essai historique sur les expositions universelles de Paris* (1907) is still of great relevance today. More recent works include Edo Mc Cullough's *World's Fair Midway* (1976); Robert Rydell's *All the World's a Fair* (1984); James Clifford's *The Predicament of Culture: Twentieth-Century Etnography, Literature, and Art* (1988); *L'exposition imaginaire: The Art of Exhibiting in the Eighties* (1989), edited by Evelyn Beer/Riet de Leeuw, and Ivan Karp; and Steven Lavine's *Exhibiting Cultures: The Politics of Museum Display* (1991).

9. Here I borrow Peter Conrad's words. See his book *The Art of the City: View and Versions of New York* (1984), in which he deals with *New York World's Fair* of 1939.

10. While reading this chapter, Carmen Cavallo noted that the idea that Latin American countries have "interior" personalities follows the same logic that locates "essence" as interior; yet it also makes each country stand synecdochically as part of the Latin American whole that inheres only in the minds of the organizers.

11. Although, in 1929, Latin American countries were invited to represent themselves, they were strongly advised as to *how* they should represent themselves.

Works Cited

Assassin, Sylvie. *Séville: L'exposition ibéro-américaine 1929–1930.* Paris: Norma, Institut Français d'Architecture, 1992.

Benedikt, Michael. *Deconstructing the Kimbell: An Essay on Meaning and Architecture.* New York: Sites/Lumen Books, 1991.

Bhabha, Homi K. *Nation and Narration.* New York and London: Routledge, 1990.

Caballero, Antonio. "Dos mundos se encuentran". *Cambio 16* 1066 (April, 1992): 18–23.

Catálogo Oficial: Exposición Universal Sevilla 92: Una Isla para el Mundo. Sevilla, Recinto de la Cartuja: La Sociedad Estatal para la Exposición Universal Sevilla 92, S.A., 1991.

Conrad, Peter. *The Art of the City: View and Versions of New York.* New York: Oxford University Press, 1984.

Crew, Spencer R., and James E. Sims. "Locating Authenticity: Fragments of a Dialogue." In *Exhibiting Cultures: The Poetics of Museum Display.* Edited by Ivan Karp and Steven Lavine. London and Washington: Smithsonian Institution Press, 1991, pp. 159–76.

González, Felipe. "Presidential Greeting from H. E. Felipe González of Spain." *Encounters: A Quincentenary Review* 2 (Spring, 1992): 5.

Gonzalo, Angel Luis. "El objetivo principal es la imagen del país". *Cambio 16* 1066 (April, 1992): 4–5.

Gramsci, Antonio. *Prison Notebooks.* Edited by Quintin Hoare and Geoffrey Nowell Smith. New York: International Publishers, 1971.

Guía Oficial Expo '92. Sevilla, Recinto de la Cartuja: La Sociedad Estatal para la Exposición Universal Sevilla 92, S.A.,1992.

Kiernan, James. "A World Class Show: Expo '92 and Beyond." *Américas* 43, 3 (1991): 54.

Lyotard, Jean François. "Mémorial immémorial". *L'exposition imaginaire: The Art of Exhibiting in the Eighties.* Edited by Evelyn Beer/Riet de Leeuw. Rijksdienst Beeldende Kunst's-Gravenhage: SDU Uitgeverij's-Gavenhage, 1989, pp. 247–71.

Native Nations. "1992 Alliance: A Coalition for Native Leaders of North America." *Native Nations* 1, 1 (January 1991): 10–11.

Rydell, Robert. *All the World's a Fair: Visions of Empire at American Different International Expositions.* Chicago: University of Chicago Press,1984.

Selverston. "Looking back at Quito." *Native Nations* 1:1 (January 1991): 12.

Ubieto, Antonio; Juan Reglá; José Jover; and Carlos Seco. *Introducción a la historia de España.* Barcelona: Editorial Teide, 1979.

Weimann, Jeanne Madeline. *The Fair Women: The Story of the Woman's Building. World's Columbian Exposition Chicago 1893.* Chicago: Academy Chicago, 1981.

12

Cultural Identity:
The Aesthetic Dimension

OFELIA SCHUTTE

I

To speak of cultural identity is to attempt to place ones's discourse within the collective memory of a community or people. I propose to explain this concept in two parts. First, beginning with some observations on this subject by Nietzsche, I will point to the relation between a culture, especially its aesthetic dimensions, and the collective life of a community. In the first section of this chapter, I argue broadly that the collective memory of a community needs to be understood as having an imaginative as well a historical dimension, and I lay stress on the recognition of the imaginative component. In the second section of the chapter, I examine briefly one classic view of a Latin American cultural identity—that of José Martí in an essay "Nuestra América"—in the context of a legacy of affirmation of and solidarity with the spirit of self-determination of Latin American peoples. I try to show that Martí's perspective, by embracing the imaginative dimension of cultural identity, is able to surpass other perspectives that place doubt on the cultural integrity of the region. Finally, in section III, I note that the aesthetic dimension of Hispanic-American people's cultural identity deserves special attention today as a "new world order" in international politics comes into being, attempting to rank cultures primarily in terms of their scientific-technological achievements. This trend leads to fragmentation of nontechnologically oriented cultures unless strong unifying elements can be found within such cultures to withstand the technologically mandated pressure to declare their internal traditions outdated or void and their current social cohesion obsolescent.

In the opening remarks to his "untimely meditation" on history, Friedrich Nietzsche states:

> Consider the herd grazing before you. These animals do not know what yesterday and today are but leap about, eat, rest, digest, and leap again; and [they do] so from morning to night and from day to day, only briefly concerned with their pleasure and displeasure, enthralled by the moment and for that reason neither melancholy nor bored. . . . Man may well ask the animal: why do you not speak to me of your happiness but only look at me? The animal does not want to answer and say: because I immediately forgot what I wanted to say—but then it already forgot this answer and remained silent so that man could only wonder. (8)[1]

But, Nietzsche goes on to say that man "also wondered about himself, that he cannot learn to forget but always remains attached to the past; however far and fast he runs, the chain runs after him" (8). He is speaking here of European man, who distinguished himself from the animal by positioning himself on the side of reason and history, yet who is burdened excessively by such a demand. He longs to escape from the burden of historical time in the fleeting pleasure of the moment, but in so doing he only adds to his burden by resisting it in the wrong way. For Nietzsche, the healing force that will deliver man from the weight of historical knowledge is an artistically oriented culture, especially one conceived as the creative expression of a community's life-affirming attitudes and beliefs.

Variations on this theme—in forms not as extreme as that presented by Nietzsche—are found in the Latin American wave of postpositivist philosophy taking place at the end of the nineteenth and the beginning of the twentieth century. During this period, as the interest in metaphysics, aesthetics, and theory of value rises, so do the more creative perspectives on cultural identity in Latin American philosophy, and also among some thinkers who are not strictly philosophers. The Argentine Alejandro Korn (1860–1936), the Uruguayan Carlos Vaz Ferreira (1872–1958), the Cuban José Martí (1853–1898), the Peruvian José Carlos Mariátegui (1894–1930), and the Mexicans Antonio Caso

(1883–1946) and José Vasconcelos (1882–1959) are some of the thinkers who begin to shape the context of Latin American thought and philosophy from a perspective sensitive to aesthetic concerns, moral theory, and/or theory of values. Through their effort and that of like-minded others, a historically undeveloped region begins to produce a developed form of *pensamiento*. The Latin American mind—or *conciencia*, as the Mexican Philosopher Leopoldo Zea would describe it—begins to acquire some characteristics of its own. But for this to take place, a break needs to occur between the Latin American thinker and the belief that theory and science, particularly in their historically determined European and North American forms, will be able to solve all of Latin America's problems. This suspension of belief in Western canonical knowledge as the miracle saver for all of Latin America's problems is manifest in Antonio Caso's conclusion to his *La existencia como economía,como desinterés y como caridad* (1916, 1943). Caso states:

> Reader: What is said here is only philosophy, and philosophy is an interest in knowledge. Love is action. Go and act in love. Then, in addition to being wise, you will be holy. Philosophy is impossible without love, but love is perfectly possible without philosophy because the first is an idea, a thought, but the second is an experience, an act. Your century is egoistic and perverse. Nevertheless, love the men of your century that appear not to know how to love, who act only out of hunger and covetousness. He who does not live in this way will never know love. All of the philosophies of the men of science are worth nothing in the face of the disinterested action of one good man. (52)

To place this in the framework of cultural identity theory we might say, expanding upon Caso, that science is what Europe (and later the United States) are privileged to bring to Latin America, but love does not have to come from a fancy laboratory or research center. It flows free from the heart. The humblest peasant in rural Latin America, the woman laboring in necessary but unrecognized tasks—these are some of the people whose cultural life philosophy we should be defending. They form the base of Latin America societies and they deserve a dignified life. Philosophy needs to extend its concerns to their needs and hopes, as many thinkers of the region have argued and have come to realize.

If we think through this problem from a metaphysical perspective, bearing in mind the issue highlighted by Nietzsche regarding the weight of the past upon present existence and the impossibility of history to rewrite itself once the past solidifies itself as past, the question arises as to the burden placed on the conscience of Latin Americans by the historic conquest of America taking place approximately half a millennium ago. The Latin American person may well regret that "time does not run backward" (139; a phrase borrowed from Nietzsche's *Zarathustra,*). In particular, she or he may regret that the split caused by the Conquest over what José Carlos Mariátegui called the "spontaneous" development of indigenous cultures could not be made whole again (Mariátegui, 3). The superimposition of European cultures—British, French, Spanish, Portuguese, Dutch—upon native American cultures, and the later importation of Africans as slaves to this continent causes a series of irretrievable losses in the history of our continent.

On the historical occasion of the quincentenary I think it is appropriate to mention not only the high points of Latin American history but also our sense of loss for unrealized possibilities. For the indigenous people of the continent, this irretrievable loss involves the capacity denied them to develop their own lifestyles without foreign intervention and foreign-induced genocide. For the descendants of Africans, the loss involves the failure of Hispanic-American culture to address racism in time to prevent the enormous and unnecessary discrimination practiced against black people for several centuries. For women, the loss involves the extraordinary delay in securing rights of equality and/or equal opportunity in their respective societies and religious communities. For the Hispanic-American mestizo, the split in the European genealogical tree that created him as its Latin American specimen has signified his apparently never-ending confinement to an economy of deficit, from which he has suffered many ailments, including the symptoms diagnosed by Samuel Ramos of a recurring feeling of inferiority vis-à-vis European man. It has been argued by thinkers such as Ramos and Leopoldo Zea that the mestizo's historic condition involves an unfairly determined "race" to catch up with his European or North American counterpart, against whose successes he constantly measures himself.

In general, the characteristics inscribing the region's irretrievable losses include the destruction and/or marginalization of some cultural formations for the sake of the economic, scientific, and technological advancement of others. A series of gaps or rifts appear in the historic, chronological development of Latin American cultures that not even the most skillful and articulate rationalization on behalf of the Conquest can cover up. The only way to deal with this rift, if Nietzsche's analysis of culture is right, is to attempt to bridge it through the mediation of human creativity and the production of art. This is because an artistic culture serves to liberate history from its "spirit of gravity," from the lost opportunities that time, in its constantly forward movement, is incapable of bringing back. Where such an artistic mediation is lacking between "what was" and "what could have been," human beings become the dwarfs of history, with their creative abilities amputated or reduced considerably.

This view of the relationship between a community, history, and time implies that history cannot give back to a people what it takes away from it, in terms of identities lost through the passing of time and failed opportunities of actualization. Nevertheless, art and myth can sustain the cultural identity of peoples through centuries and millennia, replenishing their creative energies, to the point of transforming them into creators of new historical values. This means that the disclosure of cultural identity has boundless, imaginative dimensions whose concrete temporal expression is found in artistic and literary production. This boundless, imaginative dimension of cultural identity, seldom acknowledged from the standpoint of chronological time, complements and energizes the historical component of cultural identity. The letter binds the individual irretrievably to events determined by his past, which are thought to be unalterable. The former, insofar as it appears to transcend time, impels the person onward toward future creation.

To summarize the main points thus far, then, I would note that the collective memory of a community or a people, which serves as the living "medium" of their cultural identity, contains a historical as well as imaginative component. Stated otherwise, one could say that such a collective memory does not refer only to a historical type of recollection, with a focus on verifiable facts such as dates of treaties, texts of constitutions, and the territorial divisions created by wars. It is (also) a collective memory of a people's desires, their pains, their sense of overcoming of their historical limitations, and so on, as expressed in their hopes for the future, and in their literature, music, and art.

II

If we were to untap these two dimensions—aesthetic and historical—of our collective memory as Latin Americans, how would a discourse on cultural identity position itself, roughly five hundred years after the Conquest? Would it simply be the discourse of the facts that apply to our culture, or one that speaks, at best, of its values? Or would it also be, perhaps, a discourse of hope, feeling, and desire based on the lived experiences—past and present—of the Latin American and Caribbean people? Alongside the latter option, at the site of intersection of poetry and history with respect to the question of the meaning of a Latin American cultural identity, I would like to place the vision of "Nuestra América" elaborated by the nineteenth-century Cuban poet and political leader José Martí (1835–1895). By way of contrast, I would suggest that we locate, at the disjunction between poetry and history, the vision of the Latin American nation-state held by the Argentine educator and president, Domingo F. Sarmiento (1811–88).

These two visions, which stand as each other's antitheses, are also located at dissimilar points of the political spectrum. The political debate between the positions, representing the views of Sarmiento and Martí on the issue of what constitutes a Latin American cultural identity, covers at least three points: (1) whether it is more important for Latin Americans to follow events and ideas developed in Europe or North America than those developed in our own region; (2) whether the contributions of indigenous people and those of African descent should be included within the scope of Latin American culture; and (3) whether Latin Americans should promote the notion of a regional Latin American and Caribbean identity uniting all the region's republics or settle (separately from one another) for a national identity whose primary extranational ties will be with European an Anglo-American interests. On each of these issues, Martí took the pro-Latin Americanist position, which he understood as inclusive of the various ethnic and racial heritages, while Sarmiento backed the well-known dualism between "civilization" and "barbarism." Sarmiento held that the only reasonable route for a Latin American nation to follow was to import the greatest amount of learning and social organization from the developed countries of Western Europe and, by extension, the United States, even if the ultimate result of this type of importation were the extermination of the indigenous population of the region.[2]

Let us call Martí's position the continentally integrated, racially inclusive "grassroots" notion of Latin American cultural identity, in contrast to Sarmiento's other-directed, foreign-dependent, anti-indigenous, nation-specific notion of identity. In terms of what was noted earlier about the imaginative component of cultural identity, I am interested in following some manifestations of the *desire* for an integrated Latin American identity, as evident in the grassroots notion, in contrast to the desire to disassociate oneself from other Latin Americans insofar as they are not heavily dependent on Europe or some other foreign power capable of scientific and technological dominance. The individual adopting the first position wants to affirm who he is as a member of an all-inclusive Hispanic-American community; the individual adopting the second position wants to be what he is not, and to stop being what he is. Incapable of being European and not willing to be merely a Latin American, he calls himself an "enlightened American" (*un americano ilustrado*). The adjective serves to exclude others, for example, other "latinos," from admission to the same category. It is an identity based on privilege, whose concept of freedom and self-determination for the Latin American nation in question will also entail a national order where freedom exists precisely for the sake of the privileged, at the expense of those who are marginalized.

Martí's classic defense of a grassroots approach to Latin American cultural identity can be found in his well-known essay "Nuestra América."[3] He coins the term *our America* to refer to the union of all Hispanic-Americans in the affirmation of their own tradition and culture:

> The people [of our America] stand up and greet each other. "What are we like" (*¿Cómo somos?*) they ask themselves; and they start telling each other what they are like. When a problem arises in Cojímar, they don't go searching for the solution in Danzig . . . [Latin] America begins to have its own thought. Its young people roll up their sleeves, bury their hands in the dough, and raise it with the leavening of their sweat. They understand that too much is imitated and that salvation lies in creating. To create is the password for this generation. We'll make wine from the plaintain, and if it is sour, [well then] it is our wine! (42)

With this idea—it is our wine, let us be proud of it—Martí hopes to defeat the arguments of Sarmiento, whose position represents the classical antigrassroots approach to the concept of cultural identity.

Sarmiento had complained that there is no point for Argentines to acquire any knowledge of what went on in other parts of Latin America, or to hope for any important relations with other Latin American countries, except insofar as European-based concerns served to unite them. For example, he states:

It should not be surprising that we show such indifference toward what happens, say, in Mexico or on the other side of the Andes. Where is there an enlightened American who doesn't have to confess that he follows with much more eagerness those events taking place today in Ireland, than those occurring at the shores of the Plata River? Where is there an enlightened American who hasn't taken sides between Mr. Guizot or Thiers, or between O'Connell and Sir Robert Peel? And, meanwhile, how many men would be able to name, without hesitation, the presidents of the [Latin] American republics? . . . Each [Latin] American state exists within its own limits (*vive en sus propios límites*), and what goes out from it, with few exceptions, is a useless scattering of its strength, not an expansion; it is a loss, not a gain . . . ; the only real interests, deserving of [being formalized in] treaties in [Latin] America as the European [interests] scattered throughout all the [Latin] American ports that are connected among themselves. (*Cuestiones*; cited in Biagini, 73)

By "European" Sarmiento primarily means British, French, or other non-Hispanic interests in South America. As Hugo Biagini has argued in a recent study, Sarmiento also suffered from an acute case of "Hispanophobia" (62). Not even the literary and artistic achievements of Spanish culture are able to please him. About Spanish poetry, he writes: "In the millions of verses and versifications Spain produces" one cannot find "a Byron, or a Goethe, or a Lamartine, or any single name that makes it outside the Peninsula." Of Spanish painting, he states: Modern Spain has neither a sacred nor a profane [type of] painting" (*Viajes*; cited in Biagini, 64). About Spanish contributions to history and philosophy he writes: "Historians, philosophers, these are words that ought to be withdrawn from the Spanish language" (*Obras* vol. 4, 40; cited in Biagini, 64). And he also complains that the so-called discovery of America was not a product of scientific reasoning: "Columbus did not come in search of America, he only ran across it, without knowing it" (*Colón no vino en busca de la América, sino que tropezó con ella, sin saberlo durante sus días*) (*Obras* vol. 29, 320; cited in Biagini, 65).

From a grassroots perspective, however, Martí offers a superior argument. He is not forced to reject Hispanic-American culture when he affirms the Latin American region's cultural heritage. Neither is he forced to reject the idea of Latin American commonality or unity. Martí is able to couple the notion of self-criticism (hence, the notion of cultural development and change) with that of cultural integrity and unity. In this spirit he states:

> The people [of Latin America] must live while criticizing themselves, for criticism is health; but [they must] criticize themselves with one single heart and one single mind. (*Los pueblos han de vivir criticándose, porque la crítica es la salud; pero con un sólo pecho y una sola mente.*) (42)

Martí's vision of Latin American unity is made possible in large part because of his rejections of racism against blacks and indigenous Americans:

> There is no racial hatred because there are no races . . . [there is] the universal identity of the human being. The souls emanate, equal and eternal, from bodies diverse in form and color. (43–44)

Sarmiento, in contrast, stressed the differences between the races, blaming the more disadvantaged races for the major problems of a society in development:

> It is a fatal fact that children must follow the traditions of their parents, and that changes with respect to civilization, to instincts and ideas cannot take place except by changing [one race for another]. . . . Anyone who studies carefully the instincts, [and] the industrial and intellectual capacity of the masses in the Argentine republic, Chile, Venezuela, and other points, has the opportunity of feeling the effects of that inevitable but harmful amalgamation of races incapable of and unsuited for civilization . . . it is our duty to fill the deficit of fitness (*suficiencia*) left to us by Spain in the dubious border dividing civilized from barbarian peoples. (Educación; cited in Biagini, 79)

Here Sarmiento seems to have associated *suficiencia*, fitness, with *inteligencia*, intelligence. Superior fitness, he reasoned, should therefore equal superior intelligence. What he forgot, in his rush to reach this conclusion, was to realize that one must measure fitness of sufficiency by more than a narrow standard. He proved incapable of appreciating the diversity of achievements offered by various cultures, including much of his own Hispanic-American heritage. Martí, in contrast, had known how to savor his heritage well. "The European university," he noted, "must give way to the American university. The history of America, from the Incas up to now, must be taught up to our fingertips, even if that of the archons in Greece remain untaught. We need it more. Our Greece is preferable to the Greece that is not ours" (40).

III

The contrasts in perspective between Martí and Sarmiento show more than a difference in political orientation between the two men. They show a tension between the poetic imagination of Martí and Sarmiento's compulsion to imitate a positivist European notion of science and progress.[4] Sarmiento is part of a group of thinkers, including the Argentine Juan Bautista Alberdi (1810–1884) and the Chilean José Victorino Lastarria (1817–1888), who susbcribed to a positivist model of development based on European conceptions of science and technology.[5] Scientific knowledge as such, however, is not a solid ground upon which to base a community's cultural identity, since such knowledge attempts precisely to follow its own laws in abstraction from the fears, desires, and hopes of the actual population. Even when science is at the very vanguard of human knowledge, it needs to take into account other expressions of the human spirit, such as art or an ethics critical of actions coupling the notion of "progress" with practices of cruelty.[6]

Today, as the world witnesses a change in international politics to a new world order that still finds itself advancing new versions of the old dichotomy between civilization and barbarism, we do well to reflect on the virtues of Martí's position and the limitations of Sarmiento's. Such reflection is needed, especially, since the new world order advocated by the United States and other Western developed countries takes for granted the superiority of a model of scientific-technical development based on the sophisticated manipulation of human natural resources. In this world order, the future of peoples and cultures of nondominant countries is contingent on the role they are willing to play in promoting the ruling countries' technological (and therefore financial) advancement. If there is global success at this sort of manipulation of the less equipped by the better equipped technologically, I think it is not a cause for rejoicing insofar as such large-scale forms of manipulation seem to represent the reversal of a grassroots, person-to-person, community-to-community type of human interaction. In terms of social justice, we are witnessing an accelerated process of the gap between center and periphery, the developed and the underdeveloped, so as to fit the ever-expanding interests of the developed sectors. The latter's technological equipment, ironically, is supposed to make human life more comfortable and pleasing (but in the end only for the winners in this game of development).

The proposed new order is, in some respects, an extension of the negative side of the Conquest, that is, the side of Western civilization that has previously created the split between Indian and Spaniard, non-Western cultures, imagination and reason. It believes its image of culture is superior in comparison to cultural traditions practiced by others whose material and technical development may not be as advanced. It then feels justified in reducing the scope of other cultures and in marginalizing the people represented by such cultures from a central role in the development of world history.

The split sustaining the new world order between the privileged and the nonprivileged, between those having and those lacking access to lives of dignity and self-determination, represents a wound in the evolution of the human conscience. At the moral level, as Martí and Caso advised, this wound can ultimately be healed only by love, and, at the aesthetic level, as Nietzsche warned, it can only be healed by a "myth" powerful enough to give us a different perspective on history. It is a wound that cannot be healed by science, technology, or philosophical theory as such. Of course, science and philosophy should attempt to reach some lucidity about these problems and do whatever they can to resolve them. But as long as science and philosophy are used as instruments of privilege, they cannot heal wounds caused by privilege. What is needed, as a priority, is a better sense of balance in the thinking and action of individuals and communities, particularly when it comes to assessing the demands of self (or the internal needs of a community) in relation to the demands of others. Stated in global-political terms, the priorities of the mainstream North American sentiment about world politics are askew, since it is assumed that what is good for North America is not only good in itself, but by extension, good for the rest of the world. This attitude, in turn, reproduces a state of affairs where there is little tolerance and respect for the cultural integrity of others who are differentially positioned with respect to the interests of the ruler of the world.

Where does Latin America stand today, in this tension between a technologically invasive world order and the desire[7] held by many people to support their cultural traditions in the face of rapid changes in

world history? Latin Americans are at a relative advantage (in comparison with the North American mainstream) to resist the dwarfing process of a technological age that makes all knowledge unrelated to its own
advancement obsolete and discardable. This is because our imaginative
capacities to relate to and value our own cultural traditions, in many
respects, are thriving. For example, Latin American literature is recognized all over the world, and other artistic expressions such as Spanish
art and Afro-Latin music are well received and established. And,
although there is a need to keep fighting against all forms of prejudice,
discrimination, and racism, as recent indigenous protests in the south
of Mexico and other parts of our America make evident, it seems that
the several centuries that have put to the test the Hispanic-Latin American continuum have also succeeded in making our cultural heritages
stronger. We have lived with very large ethnic and racial differences
among ourselves. Where we have learned to practice internal criticism,
as Martí advised, we have grown the richer for it. Another unifying
aspect of our culture includes a strong orientation toward family life
that very often is able to pull together families across generations
regardless of internal differences among its members as to the choice of
lifestyles or place of residence.[8]

Today the ties between Latin America and Spain may be observed
to be on the increase, in part because a consensus seems to have been
reached by parties on both sides of the Atlantic regarding the acceptance of diversity within an extended Hispanic culture. In terms of the
challenges raised by the advent of the twenty-first century there is less
likelihood of cultural fragmentation or isolation for a people united by
language, regional concerns, and mutual solidarity and tolerance. The
most important task ahead, now that our collective memories appear
to stand on relatively secure ground, is not to let the notion of Latin
American identity turn into something superficial. As long as the aes-
thetic-imaginative dimension of cultural identity is kept alive and well
nourished, impelling our sense of historical agency forward in solidarity with the grassroots concerns of our peoples, it is reasonable to think
that Latin Americans and Hispanics will continue to have a very strong
sense of group identity as members of an extended community and
culture. This bridging of the Atlantic, however, depends on acknowledging the ethnic, racial, and linguistic differences within such
extended cultures and on supporting those important elements of
diversity, as well as commonality, which mark Hispanic America's
large-scale, often hybrid, cultural formations. From this standpoint,

America is not to be regarded as the site for the actualization of European projects but as the site of cultures that have achieved a distinction in their own right, in the light of their own complex evolution and multiple sociocultural heritages.

Notes

1. Friedrich Nietzsche *On the Advantage and Disadvantage of History for Life*. Trans. Peter Preuss. Indianapolis: Hackett, 1980. This work is the second of Nietzsche's four "untimely meditations" (*Unzeitgemässe Betrachtungen* 1873–1876).

2. See Hugo Biagini *Filosofía e identidad: El conflictivo caso argentino* (Buenos Aires: Eudeba, 1989), pp. 61–82.

3. José Martí, "Nuestra América". *Política de Nuestra América* (México: Siglo XXI, 1979), pp. 37–44. First published in México and New York in 1891.

4. On Sarmiento's acceptance of positivism, see also Leopoldo Zea, *The Latin American Mind*.

5. Jorge J. E. Gracia and Iván Jaksic, eds., *Filosofía e identidad cultural en América Latina* (Caracas: Monte Avila Editores, C.A., 1983), pp. 28–30. See also Iván Jaksic, *Academic Rebels in Chile: The Role of Philosophy in Higher Education and Politics* (Albany: State University of New York Press, 1989), pp. 41–66; Leopoldo Zea, *The Latin American Mind*. Trans. James H. Abbott and Lowell Duham (Norman: University of Oklahoma Press, 1967); Ofelia Schutte, *Cultural Identity and Social Liberation in Latin American Thought* (Albany: State University of New York Press, 1993), pp. 120–24.

6. See the discussion of Francisco Miró Quesada's work in Schutte, pp. 131–36.

7. This also means that the notion of "family" can include many different arrangements: from the traditional extended family and the nuclear family (both parents and children) to couples without children, single mothers and their children, and so on.

Works Cited

Biagini, Hugo. *Filosofía e identidad: El conflictivo caso argentino*. Buenos Aires: Eudeba, 1989.

Caso, Antonio. "Existence as Economy, Disinterest, and Charity." In Jorge E. Gracia *Latin American Philosophy in the Twentieth Century*. Buffalo: Prometheus Books, 1986.

Mariátegui, José Carlos. *Seven Interpretative Essays on Peruvian Reality.* Trans. Marjorie Urquidi. Austin: Universtity of Texas Press, 1971.

Martí, José. "Nuestra América". *Política de Nuestra América.* México: Siglo XXI, 1979.

Nietzsche, Friedrich. *On the Advantage and Disadvantage of History for Life.* Trans. Peter Preuss. Indianapolis: Hackett, 1980.

———. *Thus Spoke Zarathustra.* Trans. Walter Kaufmann. New York: Viking Press, 1966.

Sarmiento, F. Domingo. *Civilización i barbarie: vida de Juan Facundo Quiroga.* Santiago de Chile: 1845. (Buenos Aires: Ediciones Estrada, 1940).

Zea, Leopoldo. *The Latin American Mind.* Trans. J. H. Abbott and L. Dunham. Norman: University of Oklahoma Press, 1963.

CONTRIBUTORS

JAIME CONCHA is Professor of Spanish at the University of California–San Diego.

SANTIAGO DAYDÍ-TOLSON is Professor of Spanish at the University Wisconsin–Milwaukee.

JEANE DELANEY is Associate Professor of History at Carleton College.

MARÍA ESCUDERO is Assistant Professor of History at Royal Holloway College, London University.

JAMES D. FERNÁNDEZ is Associate Professor of Spanish at New York University.

VIRGINIA GIBBS is Assistant Professor of Spanish at Luther College.

WILLIAM KATRA is Associate Professor of Spanish at the University of Wisconsin–Eau Claire.

MARINA PÉREZ DE MENDIOLA is Associate Professor of Spanish at the University of Wisconsin–Milwaukee.

OFELIA SCHUTTE is Professor of Philosophy at the University of Florida–Gainsville.

ANTHONY STEVENS-ARROYO is Professor of Puerto-Rican Studies at Brooklyn College of the City University of New York and Director of the Program for the Analysis of Religion Among Latinos at the Graduate School of CUNY in New York City.

CARLOS STOETZER is Professor Emeritus of History at Fordham University.

JOHN TOLAN is Assistant Professor of History at the University of North Carolina at Greensboro.

INDEX

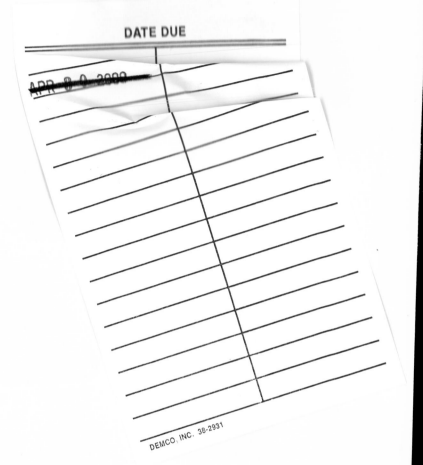

DATE DUE

APR 0 0 2000